The Reynard
Story

As part of our ongoing market research, we are always pleased to receive comments about our books, suggestions for new titles, or requests for catalogues. Please write to: The Editorial Director, Patrick Stephens Limited, Sparkford, Nr Yeovil, Somerset BA22 7JJ.

The Reynard Story

From Formula Ford to Indycar Champions

Mike Lawrence

Patrick Stephens Limited

First published 1997

British Library cataloguing-in-publication data:
A catalogue record for this book is
available from the British Library.

ISBN: 1 85260 576 6

Library of Congress catalog card no. 96 78552

Patrick Stephens Limited is an imprint of
Haynes Publishing, Sparkford, Nr Yeovil, Somerset BA22 7JJ

Designed and typeset by
G&M, Raunds, Northamptonshire
Printed and bound in Great Britain by
Butler & Tanner Ltd, London and Frome

Contents

Acknowledgements

Grateful thanks are due to Adrian Reynard, Rick Gorne, John Thompson, Bill Stone and DAMS for supplying many of the photographs which illustrate this book. With especial thanks to Anita Smith who guided this project through to completion.

Introduction

This is not a book about motor racing. It is about a philosophy, an attitude, a way of life which happens to find its expression through motor racing. The public stars of the sport, the ones who get besieged by autograph hunters, are the bit-part players in this story, while its heroes could walk through the crowds at a Grand Prix and not be recognised.

Because I write about motor racing, people sometimes assume that I attend a lot of races, and they imagine that this week it's Brazil and next week it's Italy. The fact is that I only attend races as a spectator, for my own pleasure and not as part of my professional life, because I do not write about motor races – I write about motor racing.

The last place in the world in which to get sense out of someone involved in motor racing is at a race track. At a race track they have too many things on their mind. Besides, it's only after the car which has retired has been taken back to the factory, and has been stripped down, that you discover why it retired. 'Gearbox problems' may satisfy the punters, but it is no explanation for the people who make the gearbox or for the people who build the car in which the gearbox is fitted.

If I do not get to many of the glamour spots, at least I have an extensive knowledge of industrial estates within a 60-mile radius of Heathrow airport, because that is where the world centre of the motor racing industry is based. It is in such nondescript places, among carpet warehouses and factories making widgets, that designers, engineers and craftsmen create the machinery by which drivers grab the headlines.

It is a far cry from the razzmatazz of a Grand Prix or of the Indianapolis 500, yet it is in such places that the engines, transmissions, chassis and the host of smaller, but vital, parts are made to the highest standards.

Some of those engineers will be seen at circuits for racing and testing, but they will not be watching what the spectators come to see, because they are in a different competition. Their rivals are men like themselves who are not gripping steering wheels, but who are looking at computer read-outs and working out ways by which they can give their drivers an extra edge.

They may never have even sat in a racing car, but they are racers at heart. Back at the factory there are men and women making the machinery, and they are racers too. It is not in the sense that they go motor racing or are even motor racing enthusiasts. You may make washing machines for a living but that doesn't mean to say that you hang around launderettes at weekends – *Look at that Bendix go!*

They are racers in the sense that they have the racer's mentality. The guy welding wishbones is not a racing driver, he's a welder, a craftsman, but when needs be he'll work all hours to get jobs finished. If a racing car factory is to be successful, there will be many occasions when the clock on the wall becomes the enemy, not the signal that it's time to go home to the family or go down the pub for a few beers with your mates.

The British motor racing industry is by such a long way the best in the world, there is no point in discussing which is number two. Benetton is an Italian team, officially, but it is based at Enstone in Oxfordshire, which is a long way from Naples. Ferraris are designed near Guildford. Mercedes-Benz Formula One and Indycar engines are designed and built in Brixworth, Northamptonshire, and the Yamaha Formula One engine comes from Rugby. Close scrutiny will reveal the fact that many components, from engines and chassis down, which are apparently the work of major manufacturers overseas are actually designed and made on industrial estates in England.

When one says 'British' racing car industry, one has to spread the net a little wide because Australians and New Zealanders are an integral part. A racing car designer told me: 'One conclusion I have drawn over the years is that the Americans, Japanese and Germans all operate to the same rules, that is why they will never be any good at designing racing cars.

'Motor racing is total warfare, and England is the most belligerent nation on earth. We pretend not to be, and invent myths about "cricket" and "playing the game", but we've been to war with more nations than any other country under the sun. That's why one small country built the biggest Empire in history and why the world speaks English even though, Heaven knows, it's an illogical language. Most of the world's major sports were codified in England but then, to paraphrase George Orwell, sport is only warfare without the guns.'

Reynard showed its first customer car, for Formula Ford 2000, at the 1975 Racing Car Show in London. It was one of 14 manufacturers showing FF2000 cars and not one of them was incompetent. In fact all, bar one, had known periods of success and the only one which had not was Reynard because, at the time, it had just one win and two fourth places to its credit. Yet, of those 14 makers, 10 no longer exist and two have never progressed beyond the minor formulae. Of the remaining two, one was Lola which, in 1975, was already the oldest maker of production racing cars in the world and the other was Reynard.

This is the story of how Reynard progressed from a stand at a Racing Car Show to the company becoming the world's Number One.

We are talking, of course, about production racing cars, not Formula One, but almost every driver on a Grand Prix grid in 1996 has driven a Reynard at some point in his career and, usually, it has been at a significant point. Johnny Herbert, for example, won the British Formula Three Championship in a Reynard, and won with a Reynard on the company's debut in Formula 3000. Michael Schumacher used a Reynard to win the German Formula Three title, while Jacques Villeneuve became Indycar Champion in one.

In fact, the only leading competitor in Formula One in 1996 not to have raced a Reynard was Gerhard Berger, but when he made his step into grands prix Reynard was still only in Formula Ford. The only driver in Formula One whose career was not advanced by driving a Reynard was Martin Brundle who had the misfortune to buy a Formula Ford 2000 car in 1980, which was one of only two uncompetitive cars the company has made in its history.

Reynard has not yet made it to Formula One, as so many of its customers have, and there is a very wide gap to bridge. McLaren International, for example, employs more than twice the 150 people at Reynard, and that is simply to get two cars on the grid for 16 races each year, whereas Reynard makes cars by the dozen. The focus of an operation such as McLaren is awesome.

Reynard, of course, does not have to operate a transport division, because it sells cars, it does not run them. It does not have to have a sponsorship division, it does not have to employ race mechanics and a separate test team, and it does not have to entertain hundreds of sponsors' guests – it reserves its parties for its workforce. While McLaren basically sells a marketing opportunity within a global television network, Reynard sells a product. Of course, customers can sell on their use of that product to their sponsors, but that is up to them.

Makers of production racing cars approach the market in a different way from a Formula One team. They are judged by success on the tracks. They have to win races because that is the way that they attract customers, whereas Formula One teams can survive for years, and consider the odd World Championship point to be a success. Of the 11 teams in the 1996 World Championship, five have never won a Grand Prix. Arrows has made over 500 starts without a win and Tyrrell has not won a race since 1982.

Try selling a production racing car when you have gone 14 years without winning a race. Every driver is a future World Champion in his own eyes, at least until the time comes when he has the idea knocked from him. You cannot sell him a car on the grounds that it could win and that it is enough to be taking part – he has to be convinced that it *will* win.

Winning races is the ultimate consumer test. If you read the consumer magazines, you know which is the very best microwave oven, but most of us make compromises. We do not go for very best; we go for the best we can afford provided that it does a reasonable job. We are not likely to sell our children into slavery just so that we can get a better microwave, but when it comes to a driver getting a better racing car, don't be so sure.

If the survival of Formula One teams depended on the number of people who bought their cars, how many would last a year? The reason why Reynard has survived and prospered is that it makes cars which win races – it's as simple as that, and it's as complex as that.

Every one of those 14 manufacturers at the 1975 Racing Car Show dreamt of success, and if you were then asked to nominate the company which, 20 years on, would join Lola as a winner of the Indianapolis 500, it is unlikely that you would have put serious money on Reynard which, then, had made only one car for a customer. Yet that is what happened.

This book attempts to tell why and how it happened. It is not a book about motor racing so much as a book about people engaged in a highly competitive industry where the survival rate is poor.

It has been written from an English perspective, from the point of view of the men who make the cars on an unglamorous industrial estate in Oxfordshire. Reynard is a world player, and in every country where motor racing takes place people's perception of Reynard will be different.

In Hungary, Reynard is best known as the supplier of Formula Ford cars for a national series. In Japanese Formula 3000 it is viewed as the young rival to Lola, whereas in European Formula 3000 it was the dominant force for many years, sometimes creating a one-make formula by virtue of elbowing out all opposition. American team owners have another perspective, since Reynard was known only as a supplier to junior formulae until it burst into the Indycar scene – Americans did not have the experience of seeing Reynard first-hand at an intermediate stage as European and Japanese teams did in Formula 3000. In America, Reynard is the successor to March as the English rival to Lola, which won its first Indianapolis 500 as long ago as 1966.

I have been a fan of Reynard for a long time, but ultimately I am a more devoted fan of the British racing car industry. Writing about Reynard has given me even greater respect for its rivals such as Lola, Van Diemen and Ralt, all of whom have helped me with this book.

The business of selling production racing cars is quite unlike any other. In no other business can you lose your entire market in a matter of weeks, yet that is what happened to Reynard in Formula Three in 1993, as it happened to Ralt over the winter of 1992/93. Reynard has put other firms out of business and has constantly faced the threat of having the same done to itself.

The fact that Reynard has survived and prospered is remarkable given the nature of the market and the strength of the competition. You can make the twentieth best washing machine in the world, and somebody is doing very nicely by doing just that, but you cannot hope to sell a racing car which is not viewed as being potentially the very best.

I can only hope that this book sheds a little light on the business of building racing cars, and that the reader will end up with not only greater respect for the achievements of the men at the Reynard Centre, Bicester, but for the achievements of every maker of production racing cars, even those no longer with us, who have made a mark in the most difficult and fickle market in the world.

The fact that so many thoroughly competent outfits have failed puts Reynard into perspective.

Mike Lawrence
Chichester

Chapter One

Prologue

28 October 1993: I am called to the Reynard Centre in Bicester for a meeting between Adrian Reynard and four of his lieutenants: Jim Blenkinsop (Operations), Paul Brown (Reynard Composites), John Thompson (F3000) and Malcolm Oastler (Indycar).

The only item on the agenda is the progress of four trainees. Each is a graduate who has come to Reynard Racing Cars for a year, and only one seems to be short of the quality which is mentioned time and again – attitude. He has complained that he has not been given interesting work, but he has not yet grasped the fact that it is the point of the training scheme to do dull, even menial, work as part of gaining an overall view of the job of building racing cars.

Since everyone recognises that the trainee still possesses the qualities which got him taken on in the first place, the shortfall in attitude is not seen as an obstacle, more of a 'glitch' to be overcome. He has had a privileged upbringing and is not used to the discipline of 'Boot Camp', so his programme is adjusted – he will still have his share of menial work, but it will be spread in a different way.

Another trainee, who is otherwise doing well, is perceived to have a problem with an aspect of personal presentation. Paul Brown is nominated to advise him, and Adrian says: 'Tell him he is doing this right, tell him we're all pleased with him, and then remind him he is part of the team here.'

I cannot rule out the strong suspicion that the tone of the meeting has been stage-managed for my benefit, but I recall a conversation with Adrian some years before when he said: 'I put my trainees through the mill to see what they're made of, and most of them come through.' The atmosphere of this meeting is not one of bullet-headed sergeant majors making and breaking rookies by taking 'em to hell and back, it is more like a group of dons discussing which of their undergraduates are likely to become research students.

Two of the four trainees receive no pay for putting in a 12-hour day, seven days a week when necessary. The other two are assisted by tiny grants – just £50 a week. It is not much reward for going through the education treadmill, getting the A-levels, fighting for a place on a university course and then spending three years working for a degree. A cynic could call it exploitation, but the four have been selected from the 600 who apply each year. The traineeships are not advertised, but Adrian visits campuses to spread the word; he replies to each applicant personally and interviews about 100 candidates each year before inviting 20 for a second interview.

A young Australian will shortly join the scheme, and he is unusual because only Adrian has met him. Adrian says: 'He wrote to me several times and I wrote back, but I gave him no encouragement. He phoned me several times and I was still discouraging. One day he phoned me and I was brutally frank: it was a long way to England, he'd never get a work permit, and so on. Then it turned out that he was phoning me from downstairs!' *There* is someone who showed the right attitude, and Adrian is tickled pink at the man's audacity.

The progress of each of the four trainees is discussed along with the overall shape of his programme. One is clearly destined for the design office, another has shown a particular aptitude for organisation and Jim Blenkinsop has his eye on him for his department. In each case their strengths are given their head, but they still have to go through the mill.

John Thompson, in charge of the Formula 3000 programme, recalls how he was a racing enthusiast who had even won a minor race in a friend's Reynard when, in 1984, he was accepted as the first trainee. 'I came to join a racing car maker with stars in my eyes, and the first job they gave me was painting the factory floor. I was devastated, but I soon realised that making racing cars actually does mean having painted floors and a clean workshop, and that somebody has to do it.'

David Brown, from 1995 Mika Salo's engineer at Tyrrell, recalls: 'I had to build a staircase. They had this space in the roof they wanted to use and they told me to get on with it. It's there to this day.

'Accepting the traineeship was quite a difficult decision. I had a firm offer from Austin-Rover, but all my applications to racing car companies had met with a blank except for Reynard and March. I had an initial interview with March, and was invited back, but Adrian offered me a place on the spot so that was it.

'I arrived with all my projects from university, but he was more interested in the fact that I had been racing a Mini I'd prepared myself. He never did ask to see all the academic stuff I'd brought with me, it was the practical side that appealed to him.

'I'd been through school and university and I was offered £186 per month, which is not much for all those years of effort. Adrian, though, had a couple of houses in Bicester where the trainees could live, so that was food and pocket money – and he gave me a chance when nobody else was prepared to. He was straight down the line and said, "If you're good, you'll persevere, and we do give people opportunities at an early stage of their careers." He was as good as his word. Within six months of my finishing my traineeship, I was designing the Reynard Formula Three car.'

Jim Blenkinsop says: 'Their time spent in the buying department makes them realise that Reynard does not exist to make racing cars, it exists to make money. If you're not making money, before long you're not making racing cars. The bottom line is sound business practice, and that is true of every company. Having said that, you have to acknowledge that the motor racing industry is different from most others because building cars is a seasonal business – everyone understands that, and there is also a great deal of enthusiasm and a willingness to work long hours when necessary, although I was brought in three months ago to create systems which will spread the load.'

Paul Brown, who has a design portfolio which includes Formula One, Formula Two and Group C cars says: 'I have never before come across a company which has such an atmosphere of co-operation. I once worked alongside X, who was a brilliant designer, but was totally paranoid. He'd sit hunched at his drawing board afraid that anyone might see what he was doing, like the kid at school who shielded his answers in the spelling test. Here, people are open with each other, and that comes partly from the fact that they understand the whole process, the trainees go through all the departments and as a result everyone works together.'

There are a few other telling details from the meeting, which could not have lasted more than 20 minutes. A Reynard had just won the Kent-engined section of the Formula Ford Festival, and it was a design which Malcolm Oastler had essayed over the winter of 1987/88. Adrian pointed out the success, but without crowing. He merely said: 'It seems there has been little advance in Formula Ford 1600 over the past seven years.'

Malcolm had come to the meeting from helping to assemble the first Reynard Indycar – one of the senior officers working alongside the men – attaching brackets and fasteners to the tub. In fact, earlier, although I had been looking for him, I'd walked past him in the workshop. I can think of designers at a much lower level who would not be seen on the workshop floor without standing to one side and clutching a clip-board – a combination of status symbol and comfort blanket.

Adrian is fond of a quotation from James Watt, inventor of the steam engine: 'Simplicity is supreme excellence.' He says: 'That sums up my philosophy. In the production racing car business you have to take account of what the market can afford. If we found that solid gold wishbones were guaranteed to win races, we'd be silly to use them because the races would be won by those few teams able to afford them and everyone else would give up. We would destroy our market.'

I have been to more racing car factories than most people, and have found that each has a distinct ambiance. Some of them overwhelm the visitor. For example, the headquarters of McLaren International are intimidating, but they deserve to be since McLaren has earned the right to present itself as the Mount Everest of the sport. What is less acceptable is when lesser outfits imitate the grandeur without the achievement to back it.

I have visited successful firms, yet when they have talked about moving up a level I have not been convinced because the feel of the place tells me that it's unlikely to happen. It is tiny details such as the managing director not knowing everyone's first name, the doors to his, and the chief designer's office being kept shut and the fact that the MD has not told his designer that someone is coming to write a piece about the company. In such factories you are likely to see jokey signs (such as 'You don't have to be mad to work here, but it helps') and pin-up pictures, all of which are poor substitutes for genuine good humour and morale.

I have been to firms where, without anything being wrong on the surface, I have smelled impending failure. March was like that in the late 1980s. I can think of another firm which was heavy on PR and which had just had a big cash-injection and a first-rate designer, but nothing was quite right. I could not put my finger on why that was, because everyone was brimming with confidence and it had just appointed a smooth PR man. Perhaps that was why I did not feel comfortable. Whatever the reason, the place had the smell of doom, and six weeks later it was in liquidation.

Reynard is the last successful racing car manufacturer to have been founded by someone who built a special for his own use and found himself being pestered to sell it. Reynard is also the only one of the dozens of firms which began in Formula Ford, each with stars in its eyes, which has made a successful transition to higher formulae. Plenty of outfits have tried to make the leap, but all others have foundered.

Rick Gorne, Adrian Reynard's partner, is in no doubt why Reynard has succeeded. 'There are two reasons: the way we design cars and the way we sell them. We've assembled a team of designers and engineers who are not only united in a single aim, which is to win, but they are united in their philosophy of how things should be done. As for selling, some people have taken the view . . . "Here's the car, buy it if you want" . . . whereas we take the view that the customer needs to be looked after. It's a people business. The reason why we've been so successful in opening new markets is that we've always responded quickly to enquiries.

'It is this approach which made us farm out our Formula Ford business a few years ago, because if you do things properly it takes as much time to sell a Formula Ford car as it takes to sell a Formula 3000 car which has a vastly larger profit margin. But the point is that you cannot sell the Formula Ford customer short. He has the right to expect the same standard of service as the guy spending ten times as much, because, at his level, he's still making a big investment.

'We were stretched to satisfy everyone, so to look after our Formula Ford customers, we came to an arrangement with Fulmar Competition Services, who were geared up to give them proper service. We supplied about 40 per cent of the components, FCS made the rest to Reynard designs, and everyone was happy. We made money, FCS made money and the customers got a good car and excellent back-up.'

At Reynard some of the office workers are interested that I'm there to write a book. 'Oh, the stories we could tell you,' they say, 'you wouldn't believe them.' Actually I would believe them because I've already heard them from Adrian – in detail. Besides, everyone in every office can tell stories which each believes to be unique to their own company. In my experience, however, it is only people who have pride in their business who take that line with outsiders, and when I mention the Indycar, receptionist Karen Moss says: 'We won first time in Formula Three, we won first time in Formula 3000 – we're keeping our fingers crossed.'

Their pride in the company is almost tangible, and I never do hear the startling revelations they could make if they wanted to. The point is that everyone feels part of the team. A few months later almost the entire workforce gathered at the factory to watch Reynard's debut in Indycar on satellite television. Of course they did, from the receptionist to the chief designer, everyone wants Reynard to win.

I had expected nothing less. I'd known Adrian for a long time and liked him the first time I met him. He is one of those rare individuals who has a gift for friendship. I had been to the factory many times over the years and it has not always been the vibrant place it is today. In fact, there were times when I would have said that it was brash and pleased with itself. It strove to make an impression (I can remember the plans to market Reynard leisurewear when the company was not even in Formula Three), but those days are long gone. It now exudes an atmosphere of quiet confidence, and you get a distinct impression of strength in depth.

To go back a few weeks before that management meeting. It is 23 September 1993 and I arrive at the Reynard Centre expecting the usual hassle when parking on an industrial estate. Pleasant surprise, a space marked 'Visitor' is free. It is only later that it clicks that the only designated parking spaces are for visitors. It is the management who have to fight for space. This is management for the 1990s, and the secret of Reynard's success is, above all, good management. It is above design, innovation and quality control because good management creates a pervading atmosphere in which these elements are able to develop.

Despite my past familiarity with the Reynard Centre, I notice subtle, almost imperceptible, differences and, as the day goes on, I realise there is a uniting synergy. I have a few minutes to wait so I flip through my copy of *Autosport* and two items catch my eye; one is that Reynard expects to sell 15 Indycars for the start of the 1994 season – an unprecedented number for a manufacturer making its debut in the category – and the other is that Adrian Reynard has been awarded an honorary doctorate in engineering from the Oxford Brookes University.

I am at the Reynard Centre to discuss this book. I'd always hoped that one day I'd write the Reynard story, but had thought it would not be for a while yet. Then there had been a phone call from Adrian asking me to discuss the project with him. The reason he asked me was that I had written the history of March, which reviewers were kind enough to say was probably the most accurate 'warts and all' portrait of a racing car maker ever published. My chief qualification, therefore, is that I won't give him an easy time, and I do require access to information and documentation, while accepting that some information has to remain confidential because of contractual obligations.

After the opening pleasantries Adrian says: 'We've been in this game for 20 years and I like to think that we've learned something. We've reached the stage where we think in terms of a philosophy for the way in which we operate, if that doesn't sound too pretentious, and how we can fulfil that philosophy. We've been working in this direction for some time and it has started to come together.

'The fact that I've been given a doctorate by my old college is part of that. I left without gaining a degree, but I was recently asked to present graduates with their degrees.

'We began in a little workshop in Bicester with virtually nothing, and now we employ 88 people, which means that there are 88 families which depend on us, and we are in a seasonal business – nobody buys racing cars in summer. I can remember when, come the end of May, March (which used to be just down the road) would lay people off and they'd all be down at the local Job Centre. We have been through some rough patches, there have been periods when the factory's been on short-time, and there was more than one occasion when I had to guarantee the monthly salary bill by pledging my house to the bank, but we have avoided seasonal redundancies.

'You know the sure signs that a company is about to go down the tubes? It wins a Queen's Award – we won one in 1990 and we nearly went bust in 1991. It gets the company helicopter – we had one. The directors get flash cars – we used to have them, but now there are no company cars. You parked your car in the space reserved for visitors. I abolished all the other designated spaces because I wanted to create a new atmosphere.'

All the little signs add up to a synergy. Later I hear on all sides that Adrian has succeeded in imbuing his company with a philosophy or, at least, a coherent attitude. It is some time since he has actually designed a car. His role is now that of a guide to the company. He likes to call himself a Performance Engineer but, as anyone there will tell you, he is sufficiently expert in all aspects of the motor racing trade to know whether something will work.

'I see myself as an environmentalist, planting the seeds, keeping the soil fertile and ensuring that the garden is cared for and watered. We've made mistakes, and I'm happy to tell you about them for the book – I certainly don't want a whitewash. But I like to think that we've learned from our mistakes and we have something to pass on.'

July 1996, and nearly three years have passed since that initial meeting. Adrian was out of the country for a year campaigning the 1995 Indy season whilst cultivating new contacts in the United States motor industry, and there have been a number of changes. The Reynard Centre has expanded and there is now a smart new office block with enough room in the reception area to display a number of successful Reynard cars, together with the sprint motor cycle with which Adrian took international records while still a student.

There is a new receptionist because Karen Moss has been promoted to being Adrian's Personal Assistant. There are not many firms where that can happen. Karen has been given her opportunity and she has blossomed. It may seem odd to highlight a receptionist and not an engineer, but Karen is the embodiment of the Reynard philosophy. Everyone at Reynard has a chance to develop.

Reynard *did* win first time out in Indycar, and its continuing success in the category means that the workforce has expanded from 88 to 150. There is also a new division – Reynard Special Vehicle Projects. Jim Blenkinsop has moved on and has been replaced by Peter Morgan, who once raced against Adrian in Formula Ford 2000.

Apart from Jim, everyone else is still on board, which is unusual in the motor racing industry where successful people are ruthlessly head-hunted. Malcolm Oastler, for example, is now a superstar designer and he has been wooed with offers from Formula One teams which would make most people's eyes water, but he stays put because he is happy where he is.

There is now a second Queen's Award for Industry and there is also again a company helicopter. 'It's a work tool,' says Adrian, 'which costs not much more than an S-class Mercedes-Benz to run, and which saves a great deal of time. I flew three people to a meeting yesterday and I reckon that it saved about 16 man-hours and that is a very valuable saving. We still do not have company cars.'

If there has been a noticeable change in the intervening years it is that the place emanates even more of a buzz, and that is remarkable given that the workforce has almost doubled in a very short time. When that happens a company can lose its spirit because it can easily be diluted by an influx of newcomers. What is clear is that the spirit has not been diluted, that the 'new bugs' have adapted to the culture that Adrian began to create around 1985–6.

I was invited, along with my partner, to the 1995 Reynard Christmas party, and I asked her to look around the room and tell me who she thought were the major players at Reynard. She could not pick them out. There was none of the usual subtle signals given out by the rich and famous. Nobody walked to the bar in a particular way, nobody held forth in a corner surrounded by toadies and – this is the clincher – nobody looked uncomfortable. That is because Adrian has been successful in creating the culture of which he speaks and which has been able to grow without him. In fact, for most of 1995, he was absent from the factory and based in America.

There have been other changes which are all part of the Reynard philosophy. The trainee scheme has been expanded so that it can include engineering undergraduates serving their year in industry, and the company now offers work experience for school pupils. Peter Morgan, who is in overall charge of these schemes says that the ambition is that, one day, a school pupil will come to Reynard on work experience, return as an undergraduate, then become a trainee and, finally, join the staff.

In place, too, is a share ownership scheme for key personnel, and a profit-sharing scheme for all Reynard workers of 10 per cent of the company's profits. In 1995 £400,000 was given to the workforce (the size of each bonus was in a ratio to the individual's normal salary) and, thoughtful touch, it was paid just before Christmas.

Adrian says: 'Since we introduced the bonus scheme, we've noticed little changes. You no longer see the odd bolt lying on the floor in the workshop, someone will always pick it up and and put it in the right box. That bolt is part of our profit and everyone has a share in it.'

One of the prizes for winning the Indianapolis 500 is a ring. Because a Reynard won the 1995 race every male member of the staff received a replica ring, engraved with his name, and every female member of the staff received an equivalent pendant. Here we speak not of gimcrack jewellery. My partner, a Deputy Headmistress and not accustomed to such things from the Education Authority, was also astounded to see an employer actually saying 'thank you' to every member of his staff, over and above the cash bonus, the Christmas party and the party to celebrate winning the 1995 PPG Indycar title.

Reynard has come a long way from one worker and some second-hand equipment operating in premises which were so humble that Adrian discouraged visitors on the grounds that if they they saw the place they might not take Reynard seriously.

I admit it, I have been an unashamed fan of Adrian Reynard for a long time. He has that effect on people. You will see, as the story unfolds, that at every key point in his career he has been able to convince the right people to share in his dream and, so far as I have been able to ascertain, while sometimes people have gone against logic to support his dream, nobody has regretted their decision.

Sometimes the delivery date has been a moveable feast but, ultimately, Adrian delivers what he promises.

I said at the start that this is not a book about motor racing. Every time there is a motor race, someone wins it – Man in Car Wins Race – Man in Another Car Comes Second. This is the story of an industry typified by a student who wanted to be a Formula One World Champion. He built a car to go motor racing, because he was too strapped for cash to buy one. Someone else looked at his car and found it good, so the student sold it and became a constructor.

The fact that it was a racing car that the student built is almost incidental.

Chapter Two

Adrian Reynard

Although Reynard Racing Cars is the epitome of the modern race car maker – high-tech, thrusting and ambitious – Adrian Reynard is the last of an old British tradition. He is an enthusiast who wanted to go motor racing and who could not afford to buy a competitive car, so he made one for himself and, because it was good, he was asked to make cars for other drivers. Colin Chapman of Lotus started like that, so did Eric Broadley of Lola, Derek Bennett of Chevron – also John Cooper, John Crosslé, Jack Turner, John Tojeiro, Arthur Mallock and a host of others.

Times change and it is unlikely that there will ever again be a special builder who develops into a major racing car maker. The more usual way for a new marque to be founded today is for an entrepreneur to assemble a team of experienced people and for an individual intent on a career as a designer to join a manufacturer fresh from university. Eric Broadley is on record as saying that if his younger self applied to him now for a job, he would not employ him because he is not an engineering graduate and he could not take the risk.

It is almost possible to become a Formula One designer without ever having touched a spanner. On the other hand, Reynard and Lola are both influenced by the fact that their founders rolled up their sleeves and made their first cars from scratch.

Adrian's grandfather, Frank Reynard, owned a bicycle shop in Easingwold, Yorkshire which became a garage and then expanded into a bus company. Frank was a great influence on Adrian's early life and is pictured second from the left, with Adrian's great uncle George fourth from the left.

Above left Frank Reynard is pictured during a TT race in 1924. He was a successful motorcycle racer, and his victory trophies are now displayed at Adrian's house in Oxford.

Above right George Reynard, Adrian's great uncle, was also a highly successful motorcycle racer. He is pictured competing in 1928. It was George who gave Adrian his first moped at nine years old, furthering his interest in anything mechanical.

It is not surprising that Adrian came through the old route since his family has a strong tradition of engineering and competition. His great grandfather ran a bicycle shop in Yorkshire, which became a pioneer garage and then expanded into a fair-sized bus company through the enterprise of his grandfather, Frank Reynard. Frank was a successful motorcycle racer who rode in the TT races when they were the pinnacle of the sport. The cups he won in other events are displayed in a cabinet in Adrian's home along with TT trophies won by his great uncle George, who was even more successful, and was the man who gave the young Adrian his first moped when he was nine. 'We had a very small back garden and I rode it round and round, wearing a track in it.'

Gordon Reynard, Adrian's father, was a fuel systems engineer with de Havilland, the aircraft maker, and Adrian's mother, Daphne, trained at the de Havilland Technical School as a draughtswoman. Gordon always had a car, and in the 1940s and 1950s this was the exception rather than the rule, so that was another strand in Adrian's upbringing. Then Gordon left de Havilland to work for the Anglo-Iranian Oil Company (now BP), first on aviation fuels and then on the automotive side, which meant that he became involved with BP's motor racing programme and there were always free tickets to meetings.

He was also allowed the use of high performance cars which BP used in the development of oils and fuels, and Adrian was often taken out in them. 'I'll never forget the time he brought home an Alfa Romeo,' Adrian says, 'and we clocked 112 mph along the new M1. It was my first experience of the ton.'

Born on 23 March 1951, Adrian grew up fascinated by mechanical things and, from an early age, he decided that he was going to be a racing driver. His father remembers making a 'racing car' from sand on a beach when Adrian was one year old and Adrian 'drove' it while making brmm, brmm noises.

'My father took me to Silverstone and Goodwood as a matter of course. I remember seeing Stirling Moss at the end of the 1958 British GP and his face was black with the

Left Adrian as a schoolboy. Adrian's father worked for the Anglo-Iranian Oil Company, or BP as it is now more commonly known, hence the logo on Adrian's school jumper.

Right The first time Adrian met Jim Hall, one of Reynard's first Indycar customers in 1994, was at the United States Grand Prix at Watkins Glen in 1963. Adrian was just 12 years old as he watched Jim competing in his BRP-BRM. Jim's Indycar team worked closely with Reynard until his retirement in 1996. 'I think that it's been good for both of us. With Malcolm, we had an understanding of what they were trying to do, and I think they had a better understanding of what the car needed to do. It's been a good relationship. I think they're real go-getters, a good company, young guys, chargers. It's been fun to work with them.'

Far right When Adrian's father was posted to America on a two-year contract, Adrian bought his first kart for $175 with his own money earned mowing lawns at a dollar an hour.

dust from his Vanwall's brake pads. I went home and blackened my face, leaving white bits for the goggle marks. That taught me that boot polish doesn't come off skin very easily!

'When I was about nine I went to a village fête and had a ride on a go-kart at a shilling a lap. Karts had only just arrived in England, so it was a big deal. Soon afterwards my father bought an American Get-kart with a Power Products motor, which was the last word in karts, and I was just about able to reach the pedals. The early days of karting were a bit ad-hoc and often people would turn up at a car park or disused airfield, lay out a track with a few straw bales, and go racing. I was too young to race at official meetings, but I raced in these events and it confirmed my ambition. I was going to be a racing driver, and that was that.'

Adrian passed his 11-plus exam to grammar school – Alleyne's in Stevenage, which was founded in the reign of Elizabeth I. 'It was considered to be a very good school, but I didn't particularly like it – in fact I found it pretty uninspiring. I was not interested in games or any of the other activities, so I tended to make my life away from it. Besides, I knew what I was going to do in life, even if I wasn't quite sure how I was going to become World Champion.

'At the time many drivers who were short of money designed and built their own cars, and that seemed like the best possible option for me. The only trouble was that I was always better at subjects such as Geography and English than those which might be useful for a designer – a grasp of the annual rainfall in the Amazon Basin does not have a direct bearing on motor racing.

'In 1963 my father was posted to Stamford, Connecticut, and the family went with him, which sowed the seeds of my affection for America. When the Grand Prix circus came to the North American races my father had to organise fuel for the teams contracted to BP, so we were involved fairly closely. In late 1993 Jim Hall came to stay

with us for three days. He's since run Reynards in Indycar, and I dug out a photograph of his BRP-BRM at the United States Grand Prix at Watkins Glen in 1963. Standing by the car was a small boy – me. You can imagine that, 30 years later, having Jim Hall arrive as a customer, and stay as a guest in my home, was pretty special for me.

'We saw quite a lot of America, including the Indianapolis Motor Speedway which I went round – on a bus – never dreaming that one day I'd return to watch my own cars race, and win, there. My father bought a clapped-out Mini for $80 and he stripped it down to the last nut and bolt, then showed me how to reassemble it. He'd put the crankshaft in, then take it out, and I would then put it in again. We had quite a lot of land attached to the house, and once the Mini was back together I drove it around the backyard.

'While we were living in Stamford I decided that I had to buy my own kart, so I began mowing lawns at a dollar an hour. It was an early example of being an entrepreneur, which has been an important aspect of my life. When we returned to England, my father and I each brought back a kart and we went racing together, stuffing them into the back of a Chevy station wagon he'd bought in the States and which he still owns. I learned how to tune the engines, and won quite a few races.

'In the local junior Championship in 1965 I was runner-up to a chap called Pete Wilbraham and then, shock! horror! my father told me that I had to concentrate on my forthcoming O-level exams, and the karting days were over. There was, too, the fact that he had been paying for it all and it was getting expensive. Soon afterwards the karts were sold.

'So I had to concentrate on schoolwork, which bored me, but Pete Wilbraham showed me a cheap alternative to karting. He had some Villiers-engined motorcycles which he used to scramble round local gravel pits, and when I was 14 I bought a BSA Bantam for £4 and joined him. Before long I was trading in 'bikes, buying them cheap and doing them up, although they were only for use in our scramble races.

'The difference between that and karting was that I was on my own, without my father picking up the bills – and that gave me a sense of independence and worth. I did it by myself. The upshot was that all my money went on petrol and castor oil, which I used because it made the exhaust smell just like a proper racing 'bike.

'School continued to be uninspiring. I knew that I needed Maths for my future plans, but as soon as I got to the sixth form I encountered calculus which was a mystery to me – it still is. While mathematical theory was beyond me, in my spare time I developed a strong practical sense of engineering which was ultimately of more use.'

Although Adrian was not brilliant in the formal sciences, his ability in technical drawing and design was apparent from an early age, and he won his school's Sixth Form Technology Prize two years in a row. For his prizes he chose a drawing board and drawing equipment and, later, the first Reynard was drawn using it.

'Opposite the school was a motorcycle shop run by George Brown, who had been a top road racer until he had a serious accident. He had then become even more famous for sprinting and record runs with his Vincent-engined special, 'Nero'. I latched on to George who allowed me to work in his shop on Saturdays. George did not pay me, but I picked up a lot just by being with him and seeing how he and his brother Cliff worked, and he took me to sprint meetings where I'd act as his mechanic. It was fantastic because I was in motor sport, on the inside, and that was what I lived for.

'George and Cliff took me to world record attempts at Elvington airfield in Yorkshire. It was almost mystical to get up before dawn and unload the 'bikes, fill them with methanol, wait for dawn when there was minimal wind and then see George blast down the runway at over 200 mph.

'They did everything on the 'bikes themselves – it was pure practical engineering, and that influenced me greatly. They also gave me my first lessons in welding, and I bought my first welding bottles when I was about 16. Most 16-year-olds spend their money on

clothes, girls and records, but I was interested in making things and I thought that owning a welding kit was a possible way to earn money. Before long I was making garden stands and selling them in a local ironmongers. My welding was not that good, but it was a start. I don't think I made any profit from the enterprise, but I felt that I was doing something. I was making things, I was selling them, I was active.'

When Adrian left school he set off on a tour of Europe with a friend. While crossing the Pyrenees the gearbox in their car broke. They managed to get a tow to take them to the very top of the range and then they freewheeled all the way down and into Andorra where they camped. They then phoned someone in England who they knew was coming out, and three days later he arrived with a replacement gearbox which they then fitted – with a bicycle spanner.

'In 1969, when I was 18, George allowed me to buy one of his old motorcycle frames and one of a batch of special two-stroke Royal Enfield engines he owned. He sold me the pair for £100 and, in the 1970 record runs at Elvington, I was there as a competitor, not as a mechanic or spectator. My grandfather, Frank, came along to watch – he was pleased to see the family tradition continuing.

'I had fitted my 'bike with a sidecar, which I had designed and made myself, and which was weighed down with 135 lb of ballast to simulate a passenger. Royal Enfield had made the engines for record breaking, but had lost interest, which is why George finished up with them. They were good units, but not up to the 3-cylinder Kawasakis, and it was for that reason I chose the sidecar records, rather than the solo classes.

'I broke some records and established some others – by the end of the runs I held six British National and five World records. This was another big step for me since it was something I'd done completely by myself. My father had been posted to New Zealand, my sister and I were staying with relatives, so I'd done everything on my own. I'd funded the 'bike myself and I'd also designed and built the sidecar. It was a major landmark in my growing up.'

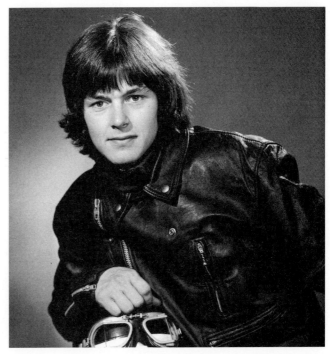

Left An early influence on Adrian was working as a mechanic for George and Cliff Brown during George's world land speed record attempts. The picture shows an attempt at Elvington airfield in Yorkshire in 1968.

Right Adrian in 1970 prior to breaking the first set of world land speed records at Elvington airfield. He was supported by his grandfather, Frank, who was pleased to see the family tradition continuing.

'Before the record attempts I had competed in quarter-mile sprints, and in my class I had two main competitors. We used to share the results, depending who had the best run on the day. It was not the motor sport of my ultimate ambition – driving a Formula One car to the World Championship – but it was what I could afford, and it was power, engineering, competition and speed. Further, it gave me a focus to my life, it kept me off drugs and booze and kept me out of trouble. I only hope that I can persuade my own kids to do something as consuming. It doesn't matter what it is, but I think that it is very important for youngsters to have a focus.

'I'd hoped to go to university, but while I got an A grade in my A-Level Engineering Drawing, and passed in Physics, I flunked Maths. On the advice of my father I applied to several car firms for an apprenticeship with a college course attached. Ford turned me down, which is slightly ironic when one considers the subsequent relationship I've had with Ford. However, I had other offers and accepted one from British Leyland which involved a sandwich course at the Oxford Polytechnic.

'It proved to be a good choice; I loved the apprenticeship and I loved the college. The social life was terrific and I was learning things which were useful. Looking back, not going to university was the best thing which could have happened to me because I finished up among people of my own level rather than being swamped by the brightest of my generation. In that context I could achieve things which perhaps I could not have done had I gone to Oxford University rather than to the Polytechnic.

'One of the things I did was to start a car club, and soon I was organising auto tests, rallies, social events, auto-discos, days spent blasting around Silverstone in our road cars, and so on. It was very difficult to organise anything which was not a success, and that gave me a lot of confidence. For the first time in my life I began to think of myself as a leader.

'I had a great social life, worked hard at my studies, sprinted my 'bike at weekends and, as an apprentice, I had a wage rather than a student grant. Ten pounds a week was good at the time for someone in my position, but it wasn't enough to get by on, bearing in mind my sprinting. Still, I had my welding bottles, so I earned money by doing chassis welding in the car park at the Poly. Most of the students' cars were rusty, so I was always in work and I was able to charge £1 an hour. It was very good money since it was cash in my pocket.

'Of course, it sometimes had its downside: there was the time when I set fire to a car, and the time when I welded new sills on to someone's pride and joy and he found that the doors wouldn't close! On those occasions I did not think it was right to offer a bill.'

One of the events which Adrian organised for the car club was a visit to March Engineering in nearby Bicester – 18 years later Adrian would come within 24 hours of buying it. At the time, however, the visit to March was a big deal for him because March represented real motor racing, the sort he wanted to be involved in, and it was considered to be one of the most exciting outfits around.

March had been set up in 1969 in a fanfare of hype but, against all expectations, it had delivered what it promised and in a very short time had established itself as the world's most successful maker of production racing cars. The company's first employee was a New Zealander, Bill Stone, who had come to England to race, but he had hung up his helmet when he realised that he was being beaten by drivers young enough to be his sons. By 1971 he'd become the Production Manager at March and had switched to motorcycle trials. Riding trials bikes over the moonscape left by the builders as they completed the Murdoch Road Industrial Estate was a feature of the lunch break at March. Setting fire to drums of magnesium swarf was another.

When Adrian arrived in Bicester with his party of fellow-students he had no idea that one day he'd own his own factory less than a mile away and that the visit to March would set him on that course. As Production Manager, Bill Stone was the man to show the party round, and he recalls that Adrian saw a frame that he was building for a new trials 'bike. That, in turn, sparked off an animated conversation about motorcycle design and would lead to a lifelong friendship. 'We hit it off from the word "go",' says Bill, 'he was a very likeable young man with a lot of enthusiasm, and he was obviously very bright.'

Adrian's face still lights up with pleasure when he remembers that day: 'Bill was really friendly and informative and we got on like a house on fire. I revered Bill because he was an insider in motor racing, he was making cars and they were winning races. He was at the centre of things.

'Several months later when I'd completed a new sprint motorcycle, with a frame I had designed and built myself, I took it over to the March works to show him. Bill thought it was great and he gave me a lot of encouragement. Bill was a key member of March. He was an insider, yet he took an interest in what I was doing. I can't tell you how important that was to me at the time.

'My new machine was perhaps the lowest motorcycle in the world. I'd learned a lot about geometry, drag and all the rest, and while it still used the Royal Enfield engine, it was a lot quicker than my first 'bike. In late 1971 I returned to Elvington with my new combination and broke all my existing records.

Adrian sprinting during the 1971 season. This was the first complete bike that he designed and built himself.

'It was not a straightforward day, however, because most of the time I had a misfire due to fuel starvation. In fact, I had not had a clean run when it began to get dark and some of the timekeepers wanted to go home. Keeping the times, however, was Denis Jenkinson who had been Eric Oliver's passenger when he won the first motorcycle/sidecar World Championship and who had navigated Stirling Moss to victory in the 1955 Mille Miglia. Jenks was the best race reporter in the world and, like everyone else, I used to read his pieces in *Motor Sport* every month. Like George Brown, he was one of the "gods", someone who was on the inside of a world to which I wanted to belong, a world which seemed so inaccessible to an outsider.

'Finally, I fitted a larger fuel pipe and, although everyone else was packing up to go home, Jenks let me have another go. I can never thank him enough for that, because it meant I took my records and, with those under my belt, I decided that it was time I opened a new chapter in my life.' The 'bike is now on the wall in the reception area of the Reynard Centre.

Jenks remembers it well: 'I took to Adrian immediately because he was a rare occasion. He never completed a run, but he kept coming back. I liked his determination and his general attitude. Towards the end of the day some of the timekeepers were looking at their watches and getting a bit uptight as they thought about knocking off – they were muttering things like: "Who is this kid?" I took the view that the track was open until five, and so long as people wanted to keep trying, they had the right to do so. The day was for them.

'Eventually Adrian did his runs, set his records and then he walked all the way to the timing box and thanked us for our forbearance. That took us by surprise, nobody had ever thanked us before. I'd already admired his determination and attitude, and now I thought: "What a thoroughly nice young man," and next time we were at the same meeting I went out of my way to look him up. His subsequent success has not surprised me.'

Adrian during a record breaking attempt at Elvington in October 1971. Thanks to Denis Jenkinson's patience, Adrian continued until 5 o'clock and broke the records he set the previous year.

Adrian's final sprints at Uden, Holland in 1972 where he represented Great Britain as part of the British Sprint Team. Adrian achieved fastest time of the day.

Adrian continues: 'Even after I'd begun my apprenticeship I was still working in George Brown's shop every Saturday, and although my wage had risen from zero to £1, you can hardly say I was being mercenary. The trouble was that working in the shop was eating a lot of time and the £1 I received barely paid for my petrol to get there. Having set records with a machine I had made myself, I decided to stop motorcycle sprinting and move on to four wheels. With a mixture of sadness and excitement I stopped going into George's shop, where I had learned so much, and I planned my next move.'

Chapter Three _____

The First Cars

'For many years my ambition was to have saved £1,000 by the time I was 21 and, by selling my first sprint 'bike, I just about achieved that, which meant I could go motor racing. I toyed with the idea of building a car for one of the 750 MC's club formulae and, since Bill Stone was the one person I knew in real motor racing, I went to him. Bill steered me away from special-building and towards Formula Ford and he volunteered to come with me to look at some second-hand cars.

Motor racing historian, Ed McDonough, recalls: 'I think that I can claim some of the credit for Adrian's later success. I had a Lotus 51 and was thinking of selling it. Adrian came to see it, but I changed my mind and he went and bought a Ginetta. Had he bought my Lotus he would not have learned nearly as much about engineering a car.'

Adrian continues: 'We finally chose a Ginetta G18B which I picked up for £600, including the trailer. It was not a bad car: the space-frame was good, but the wishbones were rubber-mounted and it had no Rose joints, although at the time that meant

Adrian's first ever car was a Ginetta G18B, bought in 1971 for £600 including the engine, gearbox and trailer. He thought that the handling of the car, and his subsequent slides, were typical of any Formula Ford car, but was later to discover it was because of suspension compliance.

nothing to me. When I drove it I got into some lurid slides, which I thought was par for the course for Formula Ford, but what was actually happening was that the softly-mounted suspension was inducing deflection steering.

'Bump-steer, castor angles and so on were mysteries to me. I do not think that I was the only one because, some years later, I sold Formula Ford 2000 cars to someone running a so-called professional team – I'll spare his blushes because he's now quite well-known. Not only did he know nothing about the basic dynamics of a car, but I believe that while his cars were polished between races they did not have a spanner laid on them. The image of some racing teams does not always square with the reality.

'I became a "real" racing driver in 1972 when I was still a student and still doing my chassis welding in the car park. I'd just finished my HND and then I faced a dilemma: should I stay on for a fourth year and do a course which would raise my qualifications to a level comparable with a degree and allow me to become a chartered engineer? I felt that I should, because I was capable of doing it, but there was still the lure of motor racing.

'British Leyland was then paying me £20 a week, which was a lot of money for a student, and was willing to fund my fourth year at college. Since Formula Ford was much more expensive than sprinting it meant I had to do a lot more welding to pay for it.

'Then, in a race at Brands Hatch I crashed at Clearways and wrecked the Ginetta. It was nearly a complete write-off, but I rebuilt it using two sections of railway line as a chassis jig (do not enquire closely where they came from!), and by the time it was finished it was better than new. I got some results with it – places not wins – and while

Below left Adrian at a drawing board at British Leyland in early 1973. His final year College project was to make a lateral strain gauge accelerometer, but Adrian decided instead to design and build a car, and he completed part of the design at British Leyland.

Below right Adrian welding a wishbone at British Leyland for the first Formula Ford 1600 chassis.

my knowledge of the car had been pretty thin when I started, by the end of the year I'd picked up most of the basic skills of setting it up.

'By the end of 1972 I had run out of money and things were desperate. As part of my fourth year course I had to do a practical project, and my tutor nominated me to make a lateral strain-gauge accelerometer, which I thought was an extremely dull way of spending my time. In any case I knew that I would fail my exams and so, with nothing to lose, I decided to switch projects and design and build a Formula Ford car. My tutor and I became strangers as I forgot about the lateral strain-gauge accelerometer and set about designing a car.

'I sold the Ginetta and built my own engine using a new block and second-hand bits bought from scrapyards. The chassis was built in the apprentice school at British Leyland where I was careful to call it a Formula Three car. I thought it would be undiplomatic to let on I was making a Formula Ford, although I doubt if anyone was fooled. I welded up the chassis, got people at BL to make and machine some parts, scoured the scrapyards and even sent the chassis frame down the BL paint line.

'Had I had a rich father, or a sponsor, I wouldn't have bothered making my own car. I'd have gone out and bought one. As it was I either had to make my own or modify my ambitions.

'Once I'd got on with the job of designing the car, however, I began to get a lot of satisfaction from it. I began to incorporate some ideas of my own into what was otherwise a conventional design, and these included incorporating cross-braced tubes from the roll-over bar to the top of the chassis frame. Later that became standard in Formula Ford 1600, but I believe that I did it first and it made a huge difference to the torsional rigidity of the chassis. I used a torsion rig at BL, which showed where the frame's weaknesses were, and we finished up with a very rigid frame, probably the

stiffest Formula Ford 1600 at the time – it was just over 2000 ft/lb per degree, which was the magic figure at the time.'

Meanwhile, Bill Stone had decided that he wanted to go into business on his own account and that Adrian would be an ideal partner. 'He had so much drive,' Bill remembers, 'I can remember times when he'd knock on our door with a drawing in his hand and he'd been working 36 hours solid on solving a problem. My wife, Maura, would feed him and then we'd pack him off to bed.

'In some ways he was undisciplined, and I like to think that Maura and I knocked a few of the rough edges off him. Being 12 years older I could play the Dutch uncle and put him right on a few details like not signing cheques for new components unless you have the funds to meet them, but he took it all in good part and he learned. The essential thing was that he always had an air of excitement around him.'

Adrian continues: 'I kept in touch with Bill, and when he learned that I was building my own car he said: 'That's interesting, why don't we go into business together?' I was 22-years old and I couldn't understand why Bill wanted to go into partnership with me. Still, in February 1973, we set up Sabre Automotive. I contributed my welding bottles and a lathe to the new company, we bought a second-hand drilling machine at an auction, and Bill put in £30 cash. We were on our way.'

'Sabre' was formed from their initials – Stone, Adrian, Bill, Reynard – and the 'E' stood for 'Engineering'. Sabre Automotive set up business in a shed in St John Street, Bicester, and the motoring press recorded the fact that Bill Stone, the well-known racing driver, had left March to set up his own business and, tagging along on his coat tails, was an ex-British Leyland apprentice who had raced in Formula Ford. It was Bill's reputation which got Sabre snippets in the press, Adrian was merely a 'graduate in mechanical engineering' and that was stretching the truth . . . Adrian was still a student.

Left The manufacture of the first Reynard chassis – a Formula Ford – took place at British Leyland's apprentice school in September 1972. Adrian felt that, for diplomacy's sake, the chassis should be described as a Formula Three car.

Right Torsion testing the Formula Ford chassis at British Leyland in 1972. High torsional stiffness became an essential feature of all subsequent Reynard chassis.

Above The first Sabre Automotive workshop was at 20–22 St John Street in Bicester and was little more than a lock-up. Adrian is pictured making the trailer he used to tow his Formula Ford 2000 car behind his Pontiac.

Left Inside the Sabre workshop when it was acquired in 1973. It was previously used by a maker of coffins for the local undertaker.

It was also Bill's contacts and reputation which brought in business and, before long, Sabre was doing fabrication work for, among others, March, Chevron and Mallock. Many years later, Reynard would steal March's main market, Bill would marry Susanne Mallock, and Paul Owens, then a mainstay of Chevron, would become a director of Reynard.

Adrian says: 'Throughout 1973 I built my car and engine on the quiet and I became adept at covering my tracks at work and at college. I finished the car off in our shed in

St John Street and went to Hewland to buy a gearbox. Jim Buss of Hewland kindly let me have 10 per cent trade discount – I don't know what he thought of this kid turning up saying that he was a racing car constructor.

'When the car was finished I proudly wheeled it down the workshop and discovered that when I steered to the right, the car turned left! Jack Knight helped me to fix that (Jack Knight Developments still provides all our steering racks). At the end of my fourth year, in the summer of 1973, when I was expected to present my lateral strain-gauge accelerometer for my final college assessment, I presented the first Reynard racing car.'

Regardless of its ingenuity, Reynard 73F-001 could not be mistaken for a lateral strain-gauge accelerometer, and Adrian's tutor was not amused. He recommended that Reynard, A. be failed – and he was. It was a correct decision which is not altered by the fact that, 20 years later, when the Polytechnic had become the Oxford Brookes University, Adrian was the first recipient of an honorary doctorate, and he presented degrees to students who had fulfilled the obligations of their course.

There is an irony here, but Adrian is relaxed about it. 'I had got from the course everything that I had wanted to get from it. At the end of the year I drove the Reynard 73F at Silverstone and won my first race with it. It was not a championship event, but the car was a huge improvement on the Ginetta: its chassis was stiff, its engine was crisp, we were on the weight limit and it was pretty good aerodynamically. Then I took it to the Formula Ford Festival, but there was to be no dream debut in the big time since I spun off during the heats.'

During the whole history of Formula Ford in Britain, the number of races won by people driving a home-built special can be counted on the fingers of one hand. Regardless of the fact Adrian's first win was in a clubbie at Silverstone at the fag end of the season, the first time a Reynard raced, it won. The first time a Reynard Formula Three car raced, it won. The first time a Reynard Formula 3000 car raced, it won. The first time a Reynard sports car raced, it won. The first time a Reynard Indycar raced, it

Inside the workshop about six months later. An early Formula Ford chassis is in the foreground, surrounded by rudimentary machinery, including Adrian's first welding bottles.

The Formula Ford was finished at Sabre in 1973. It took Adrian one year to complete the design and build of the car.

Adrian's first car was debuted in the autumn of 1973 at Silverstone, where he won his first race. The truck cost a total of £60. Pictured is Duncan Reed, a fellow apprentice and Oxford Polytechnic student, who helped as a mechanic for Adrian.

won – and there were also first time wins in Toyota Atlantic and for a Reynard-designed Touring Car.

Adrian takes up the story: 'By the end of 1973 I'd had to leave BL because there was no suitable job for me at Cowley. Considering that they had given me an expensive training for four years, that says something about the company. British Leyland did not operate a policy of cross-fertilisation: Cowley was the old Morris works and had become an assembly plant, whereas all the designing took place at Longbridge in the old Austin works.

'As a Cowley trainee I was in the Morris camp and I could not automatically make the transition to the Austin camp although the two companies had then been part of the same group for over 20 years.

'Sabre Automotive was not making enough money to employ me. I was making my contribution through ideas and we were growing steadily, but we were still very young. I therefore looked around for a job, preferably one in motor racing. I applied to be a mechanic on the Shadow Formula One team and they turned me down, thank Heavens. Had Shadow taken me on I might have spent the rest of my life as a racing mechanic.

'There was no other way you could get experience inside motor racing unless you were lucky enough to land one of the junior designer posts, and they only came once in a blue moon – teams and manufacturers did not then have large design staffs. As late as 1980, John Barnard designed the revolutionary McLaren MP4/1 with one part-time assistant.

'Years later it was the knowledge of how I had so nearly taken a wrong turn in my career that led to my establishing the traineeships we offer. Our trainees are often not paid, but they do get priceless experience. They get the chance to discover what they can do, and they either get a job with us or, because of their training, with another company.

'Since there were no openings for me in motor racing, I phoned the guy who ran the engineering department at Longbridge and identified the area that I wanted to go into, which was Prototype Build and Development. Soon afterwards I trailed my Formula Ford car to Longbridge and slotted into the parking space of Ron Nicholls who was the head of that department. When he arrived he was furious because he could not park, but by then I was standing outside his office ready to persuade him to take a look at my car.

'Ron recovered from his outrage and could see the funny side of the situation. He agreed to look over my car and was intrigued by what I'd done. A few weeks later he invited me to join his department as a very junior member working on the Mini, Allegro and Princess ranges.'

Adrian's cheek paid off on that occasion, as on many others – although he may be the only person in the world who will admit to having worked on the Austin Allegro.

His father, Gordon, recalls another instance of his son's cheek. That Christmas Adrian went to stay at the family home which is on a private estate in Sussex. 'He'd entered the Boxing Day meeting at Brands Hatch with his Formula Ford and, on Christmas Day, he announced that he needed to run it up and down the road to test it. You can imagine my reaction. We live on a quiet private estate, and while he could go back to the Midlands after the holiday, Daphne and I had to face the neighbours.

'Adrian was very persistent, so finally I said, "OK, dead on three o'clock. Everyone will be around the television watching the Queen's speech. I'll go to the end of the road to help push you round and then it's straight back and into the garage before people have time to twig what's going on." And that's precisely what we did.'

Adrian continues: 'I spent exactly a year at Longbridge where I learned a lot and, in

On completing his apprenticeship towards the end of 1973 Adrian was unable to gain employment with British Leyland at Longbridge as there were no job vacancies in the prototype development department. He clamped his Formula Ford in Ron Nicholls's parking space at Longbridge so that he would be forced to see him for an interview, and this resulted in him being offered an apprentice position. This is the prototype car prior to completion, with fibreglass plug bodywork on the top section.

particular, I got involved with the problems of vehicle dynamics. I then decided to enrol for an MSc in vehicle dynamics at the Cranfield Institute so I could put my learning on a more formal basis. In the meantime I carried on racing and met Jeremy Rossiter, who was the next person to play a key part in my career.'

Jeremy recalls: 'At the time I was Sales Manager for Spax shock absorbers, (he later became the owner of the company which is now part of a larger engineering group) and Adrian had written to me enquiring about dampers. Early in 1974, at Brands Hatch, I went looking for him. I located his ex-Post Office Escort van and was told by a tall blonde that Adrian was around the paddock looking for Jeremy Rossiter.

'We actually met as he was carrying back part of his bodywork after a multiple shunt at Clearways. I'd been part of the screaming pack of Formula Fords when it happened, but I can't remember much about it because I'd had my eyes shut at the time. It was a case of everyone leaving their brains behind on the grid and getting stuck in, and Adrian was well involved in the fracas. Next day, one of the national papers had a picture of Rupert Keegan maintaining level flight about eight feet above the wreckage with British Air Ferries writ large on the side of his car – you can imagine the caption.

'The British Oxygen Company was sponsoring the race and a senior executive of BOC was present to hand over the prizes. He was not at all impressed by what he had seen, and when the commentator gave him the mike to say a few words, he announced to the whole circuit that he had no idea that his company was sponsoring a bunch of hooligans. Soon afterwards BOC withdrew its backing.

'We were young, we were wild, and we were having fun. Before long Adrian and I became good friends. I was impressed by the way he went motor racing and by the company he kept – the tall blonde was just one of a string of like persons who accompanied him. Over the season it also became clear that Adrian's car was much

During one of Adrian's early races, at the Race of Champions meeting in 1974, Rupert Keegan flew through the air, and Adrian, amongst others, was involved in the fracas. The accident wrecked Adrian's car, and he is pictured walking back to the pits with pieces of bodywork, where he was to encounter Jeremy Rossiter for the first time.

better than the Dulon I was driving and I was able to negotiate a swap.

'I first drove the Reynard at Silverstone and it was immediately obvious that it was better and more responsive than my Dulon in every department. It did everything so much more easily and I finished fourth to take my first championship points of the season. I took fourth in the Silverstone Finals meeting as well. Just over a second covered the top seven cars and all the stars of the formula – drivers such as Geoff Lees – were present.'

In fact, the secret of the superiority of the 73FF was the stiffness of the space-frame. Adrian had used a torsion rig at Cowley to measure its stiffness and had been able to compensate any shortcomings. This is not a trivial point: very few makers then tested their space-frames for stiffness, yet it is one of the most important parameters of a design. The Dulon space-frame was certainly not stiff so, presumably, it had not been tested. The fact that Adrian began by doing things properly helps explain why Reynard is still with us and Dulon is a footnote in history, yet in 1974 it was a respected manufacturer.

Adrian takes up the story: 'After about 12 races I was broke again but, because Jeremy's Dulon was a known quantity, I was able to sell it for £3,000. I doubt that I'd have got that much for my special. It meant that I was out of racing once more, but it also meant that I had the funds to lay down a modest production line at Sabre Automotive, making replicas of my car in kit form.'

Bill Stone says: 'Adrian sometimes plays down his input to Sabre Automotive in the early days, because he wasn't a full-time employee, but he made a huge contribution.

Adrian inside the Sabre workshop preparing a car.

Above all, he contributed his Formula Ford design, which was of fundamental importance to the company. But from the beginning, even when working at Cowley and Longbridge, he was always around the place bringing exciting ideas. Although not all of them were realised, they were always a boost and they kept us focused.'

At the Racing Car Show in 1975 Reynard shared a stand with Spax for the first public display of a Reynard Racing Car – the Formula Ford 2000. Adrian paid £100 towards the cost of the stand.

Back to Adrian: 'We were interested in Formula Ford 2000 which John Webb at Brands Hatch had introduced in 1974. At the 1975 Racing Car Show, Sabre Automotive shared a stand with Spax Dampers and displayed the first Reynard Formula Ford 2000 car. It was based on the initial design except that it had a "shovel" nose and side-mounted radiators.

'By then I had left Longbridge and had started my MSc at Cranfield, so I was on a student grant once more and that made paying for my share of the stand a little difficult.'

At the Racing Car Show Reynard faced some stiff competition because there were no fewer than 14 manufacturers making cars for Formula Ford 2000, and some of them were very experienced and successful: Crosslé, Elden, MRE (later Tiga), Palliser, Dulon, Van Diemen, Hawke, Royale, Starfire (later Delta), Merlyn, Lola, Nike and Ray, but Adrian was able to tell the *Autosport* reporter that Reynard was the only Formula Ford 2000 manufacturer there which had actually sold a car. That was a perfectly true statement, the car was the one which Jeremy Rossiter had bought.

For anyone who was not on the scene at the time, perhaps a few comments might be helpful to put Reynard into context. Crosslé (from Belfast) and Lola are two of the three longest-established motor racing manufacturers in the world. The other is Mallock, and all three sold their first production cars during the winter of 1958/59. At the time Crosslé was one of the leading constructors in Formula Ford.

Lola was using its considerable expertise to make Formula Ford cars to take up any slack in the production year, to form relationships with drivers at an early stage in their careers and also to bring on young designers. Van Diemen was then a relative newcomer but would, long-term, become the most successful of all makers supplying cars for junior formulae. It would also become Reynard's main rival in the Ford Formulae in the 1980s.

Royale was then top of the heap in Formula Ford, and had future Benetton – and Reynard – designer, Rory Byrne, on the staff. All the other makers had known their share of success and it had been with a Merlyn that Jody Scheckter had made his reputation in Europe.

Reynard, by contrast, had two fourth places plus a win in a minor club event, to its credit.

It does not sound promising until you stop and realise that, at the age of only 24 Adrian had not only become a racing car constructor, but had negotiated sponsorship for a works team. Further, he had earned every penny which had gone into his racing and had become a constructor while still a student.

Five Reynards would be made in 1975 – one for Formula Ford 1600 and four for Formula Ford 2000 with Adrian and Jeremy taking two of them and running them as a team sponsored by Spax. Adrian was paid a retainer of £500 for being a works driver, and Spax paid his entry fees plus £50 per race provided that he competed in at least 10 races. It is unlikely that anyone else in Formula Ford 2000 in 1975 had such a good deal – but then Jeremy Rossiter had been caught up in Adrian's dream. He would be the first of many.

Adrian's net outlay for the 1975 Formula Ford 2000 season, off-setting expenses with prize money and selling his car at the end of the year, was £2,860. Jeremy says: 'You'd best assure readers that you've not missed off a few noughts. Racing was not cheap, but the budget then was much closer to the national average wage than it is today. My total outgoings were £7,040, which included a complete car at £3,200, and that was mine to sell at the end of the year.

'At the Racing Car Show Adrian had a single pole mounting for the rear wing, which

Adrian is pictured (left) driving a Reynard 75SF in close proximity to Damien Magee during his first Formula Ford 2000 season in 1975.

I think was a first. Everyone looked at it and said it would never work, but he was confident. We tested at Snetterton and I had a series of almighty spins at the Esses. When I arrived back at the pits Adrian observed that the rear wing, and its pole, was no longer part of the car. We never did find it.

'One thing which impressed me is that Adrian produced a comprehensive advice sheet on how to set up a car which was given to every customer. It covered everything from the torque to be used when tightening the nuts, to ride height and trimming a car's handling. It gave every Reynard customer a distinct advantage because nobody else was doing it and, bearing in mind the average level of technical competence in Formula Ford, it would have been a God-send to anyone who got hold of a copy.'

Of the two Reynard works drivers, Jeremy was the more successful, with a win, four seconds, a third and five lap records. Adrian's best result was a third place, but he set two lap records and never finished out of the top six – when he finished. By his own admission he was more than a little wild behind a steering wheel, but it was a respectable season for a low-budget team in a very competitive formula.

It is widely believed that Reynard made its Formula Three debut in 1985, but it was actually at the British Grand Prix meeting in 1975 with Jeremy driving. 'The year before, Tony Brise, who I knew well, had put a Formula Three engine in the back of his Atlantic car and had blown everyone off. I thought we'd do the same if we put an F3 engine in the back of the Reynard. Adrian was far from convinced, but I borrowed a Ford Pinto engine and we ran the chassis in FF2000 spec – I reckoned that what I lost through smaller brakes, tyres and wings I'd gain in reduced drag.

'At the start of qualifying, which was damp, I put in some good times because the car was so controllable. Then the track dried and I slipped down the order. I guess I started to try a bit too hard because I finished up in the catch-fencing at Woodcote.

'Since Adrian did subcontract work for March, and knew Robin Herd and Max Mosley, we were able to take my bent car to the Formula One pit lane and weld it up in the March pit. Can you imagine that happening today? I doubt whether Formula One teams even carry welding equipment any more.

Adrian driving a Reynard 75SF during the 1975 season.

'Anyway, we missed the cut, although I was first reserve. Unfortunately, that little experiment broke the rhythm of the season and we spent the rest of the year trying to get back to where we had been before.'

Although the performances of 1975 were promising, customers were not crushed in a stampede to buy Reynards. Six more cars were made in 1976, with four of them going to the States, thanks to a tie-up with Hawke which acted as Reynard's agent in North

At a Formula Ford 2000 race meeting at Snetterton in 1975. Adrian and others are working on the sump to stop an oil leak. Gordon Reynard is on the left in shorts.

America because, during 1975, Adrian had gone to work for Hawke.

Adrian recalls: 'As Jeremy has said, in one of the first races with my new car I met Rupert Keegan, because we were in the same accident. We became friends and we still are. I'd been at Cranfield two terms when Rupert phoned me and said: "Come and build us a Formula One car."'

Rupert's father, Mike Keegan, was a colourful character, and the approach was typical of his style. Demobbed from the RAF after the war, he had bought an ex-military Dakota and had started his own airline when Heathrow was two biplanes and a windsock. There must be a book in Mike's career. There has certainly been a television series, called *Airline*, which told how some ex-RAF pals bought a Dakota and went into business and survived by sailing close to the wind. When a newspaper suggested that the series was based on Freddie Laker, Mike was quick to lay claim to it – hinting that, lurid though the television version sometimes was, it had been toned down to make it believable.

Mike built up British Air Ferries, and after Rupert began racing he bought into Hawke because he had been astonished by the size of the bills he was expected to foot as a result of Rupert's accidents with his Hawke DL11. Eventually Mike owned Hawke outright and, being the man he was, decided that he had to take it to Formula One with Rupert as the driver. Was Adrian interested in designing the car?

'Was I ever? The starting salary was £4,000 a year, which was more than I'd ever earned, and it would rise to £6,000 in the second year. It put me in another dilemma because I was doing my MSc at Cranfield. My tutor, however, took the view that the purpose of the degree was to get a job and if I'd received a good job offer then I should take it.

'There was nothing tricky about the design I laid out, it was a standard British Formula One kit car with a Cosworth engine and Hewland 'box. But where I hoped to gain an advantage was in the aerodynamics, so I began by building a third-scale wind tunnel model and embarking on a test programme. One of my ideas was to create a low-pressure area under the car, but looking at the model today I don't think I'd have achieved much. It was the design of a 24-year-old who had a lot to learn, but I think the one piece of good thinking was that I'd identified aerodynamics as the key area – this was before the ground effect days – and that thinking has stayed with me ever since.'

Mid-way through 1975, as Adrian was designing his Formula One car, Rupert Keegan entered Formula Three. Still aged only 20, he was quick but was chiefly noted for a succession of accidents. That put the idea of Formula One a little further away, and Mike decided that perhaps they should proceed at a slightly slower rate. 'He said that they'd decided to put Formula One on the back burner and would I design a Formula Three car for Rupert, and do it quickly?

'It did not worry me too much. I thought it was only a postponement and, besides, a Formula Three car would be good experience. In fact, I think my Formula One car would not have been that special and Mike probably did me a favour by putting the idea on ice.'

The Hawke was Adrian's first monocoque car, and when it was announced it was widely admired both for its looks and for the fact that it had probably the strongest roll cage in Formula Three. Most striking, however, was the neat engine cover and the delta-shaped rear wing.

Adrian recalls: 'Since Mike Keegan owned BAF, the Press was invited for a flight over to France in a Carvair, but the intention was to unveil the car, mid-air, over the English Channel. It was in the front of the plane and Mike invited all the journalists forward to inspect it. They gathered round in the cargo hold and suddenly there were frantic

Adrian drawing the suspension of the 1976 Hawke Formula Three car at his drawing board in the front room of his home in Oxford, which he converted into a study.

messages from the captain asking everyone to go back to their seats because, with the shift of weight, the plane was in an uncontrollable dive! I think you can safely say that everyone was happy to oblige.'

It was while working for Keegan that Adrian met Gill Harris, a tall striking brunette who was a ground hostess with BAF. The relationship had its challenging spells in the early years, but Gill is now Mrs Reynard and they have four children on whom Adrian dotes.

'One of my ideas on the Formula Three car was to use a rubber oil tank mounted in the monocoque, and while this de-aerated the oil pretty well, I think it probably also restricted oil flow. The subcontractor delivered the monocoque late, which put us behind schedule. Early in the car's test programme we had an engine blow up, possibly as a result of the rubber oil tank, and after that the impetus went out of the project.

'Then some of the bushes in the monocoque began to work loose, which robbed it of torsional stiffness, and that was my fault because I had not closely supervised the subcontractor who had made some alterations to the design based on his own ideas. In my naïvety I thought one just delivered the drawings and everything would be done as specified. It was an eye-opener to me and the experience still forms the culture at Reynard – designers work closely with the production staff to co-ordinate design and build.

'Brian Henton, who was then one of the best of the rising generation of British drivers, drove the car and liked it – he lapped within two tenths of the lap records at Silverstone and Snetterton. Things looked promising, but in the meantime Rupert had begun the 1976 Formula Three season with a 1974 March and he was a transformed driver. He'd been quick in his F3 outings the previous year, but had frequently crashed. Now he was a winner – in fact he won the first four races of the British Championship, beating Bruno Giacomelli in the works 1976 March.

'That put a different complexion on things, and the Hawke, being untried and undeveloped, was seen as too much of a risk when Rupert was on a roll. When Giacomelli began to win races, often with Rupert in second place, Mike decided it was best to play safe, so he bought a Chevron B34 which helped Rupert to clinch the Championship.'

The Hawke Formula Three car was taken over by Jan Lammers and re-engineered by Pat Symonds. Pat had been on the same course as Adrian at Cranfield and they had become friends – it was on Adrian's recommendation that he took over the design. Later Adrian would recommend him to Royale where he cost Reynard wins and sales. He would become Rory Byrne's right-hand man at Toleman and Benetton, and for a while at Reynard when Adrian attempted to enter Formula One in 1991.

Adrian resumes the story: 'I'd been brought into Hawke to advance the Keegans' ambitions – there's no problem about that, but since there were no plans to develop and sell the Formula Three car, and no indication that the Formula One project would be revived, I was left in a quandary.

'That was resolved when Rupert secured a Formula One drive with Hesketh for 1977, and when that happened Mike lost interest in Hawke, and key personnel began to leave. I was among the first, and at the end of 1976 I loaded all my worldly possessions into my Pontiac Tempest (I've always liked American cars) and headed back to Bicester to become an employee of Sabre Automotive.'

Chapter Four

Bill Stone

New Zealand has influenced motor racing out of all proportion to its size – there are three million people and seventy million sheep in a country larger than Great Britain. The thin population and the country's size means that cars are not just desirable, they are essential and, while driving licences are granted at 15, many Kiwis are accomplished drivers long before then. A good many are also excellent mechanics since all spares have to be imported and it can be a long way from the nearest dealer. That is why, if you throw a rock in a motor racing paddock, you are likely to hit a Kiwi.

Bill Stone is typical of the breed, a quietly spoken man with a wealth of practical engineering expertise and, despite a lack of diplomas on his wall, a sharp intelligence. It is little wonder that he and Adrian gelled so easily.

Born in 1939 in Ngaruawahia, North Island, Bill grew up on his parents' farm. When his father went to fight in the war, his mother ran the farm and Bill learned to drive tractors at a very early age which, in turn, led to an interest in driving cars. 'I didn't have much of a formal education. I went to a secondary school in Pukekohe where I was good at rugby, like most New Zealanders, and I was very good at metalwork and technical drawing, the hands-on things. But I didn't like school very much and I left as soon as I could, with no qualifications, and did farm work.

'When I was 18 I got a job driving earth moving machines, and when I was 21 I moved to Australia. By that time I was interested in motor racing. I bought lots of books on the subject and went to watch as often as I could. Before long I had bought a second-hand Jaguar XK120 with which I did a little competition work, a few sprints and a hill climb. Hill climbing is very popular in New Zealand, and over the next few years I would compete with whatever car I owned at the time, mainly saloons, but I had my eye on single-seaters.

'The first single-seater I bought was a special with a Triumph 100 motorcycle engine and VW Beetle suspension – a very interesting combination on gravel hills. The bug had really bitten me by then and I began to harbour thoughts about becoming a professional driver. After a season with the special I traded it for a Cooper Mk 9 Formula Three car, fitted with a 500 cc Norton 'double-knocker' engine, which I used on the hills, circuits and grass tracks.

'It was an improvement on the special, but it was an obsolete machine. Still, I kept it for a second season, but fitted an 1100 cc V-twin JAP engine. It was lethal. It was very fast, but had hardly any brakes and impossibly skinny tyres – two-and-a-half inches at the front. Along the straights it was as quick as the latest Formula Junior cars, but whereas they'd be braking 200 yards from a corner, I'd be braking from 400 yards. I began to have some fairly heavy shunts, luckily without much personal damage. Of necessity I learned how to rebuild chassis, wishbones and so on, all of which stood me in good stead later.

'Racing was just a hobby which I supported by driving trucks. Then, in December

1964, I bought an early Formula Junior Cooper, one Denny Hulme had raced, which was fitted with a 1500 cc cross-flow Ford engine. Formula One was then for 1500 cc cars, and in January 1965 I entered the New Zealand Grand Prix since my car was eligible. I didn't win, but I got to race against, and socialise with, the likes of Clark, Hill and Surtees. In all, I raced in four New Zealand Grands Prix. The record books say that I was a Grand Prix driver!

'All my money went into racing: marriage, a home and a family were on the back burner, but while I had decided to be a racing driver, leaving New Zealand was not then on the agenda. That was an idea which grew gradually as I raced against the real stars who'd come for the Tasman series. I was never a great natural driver, but I was learning and improving, and the diversity of racing at home helped because I went from gravel hill climb, to tarmac circuit, to grass track, and so on. At the same time I was building my own engines, gearboxes and chassis spares, which gave me a sound basis for the future.

'By 1967 I had a Brabham with a Ford Twin-Cam engine, so I was moving up the ladder, and I ran in the New Zealand national championship. I'd drive earth moving machines, or whatever, for half the year, save my money and then, come the season, I'd quit what I was doing to race professionally. I think I was the only driver who did that and I could just about survive. The trouble was, I was not getting any younger and, after meeting Frank Williams at the end of 1967, I decided I had to come to England.

'Frank was wheeling and dealing in cars as well as racing himself, and he said he'd

Bill Stone at the New Zealand Grand Prix in 1966. Two years later he came to England with his crash helmet and spanners.

help to set me up. So I sold up and, in May 1968, I arrived on Frank's doorstep with a mechanic called Jim Stone (no relation), to take him up on his word. Frank got me a crashed Brabham BT21 Formula Three chassis and I set about building it up in his workshop.

'I took the chassis along to Arch Motors, who had made it, and they quoted me three weeks to fix it. I didn't have that much time so they allowed me to straighten it out there. They liked what they saw and offered me a job during the winter build season.

'Together with Jim Stone I led the gipsy life, racing in Europe, trailing the Brabham behind a Ford Thames van in which we camped. We'd do three or four races on the Continent and then come back to do one in England, so we could stock up with spares. I could usually finish in the top eight, and in those days they paid good starting money and prize money, so Jim and I could just about get by.

'At the end of the season I went to work for Arch Motors while Jim got a job with McLaren, where he stayed for some time. For the 1969 season I bought a McLaren M4A, which seemed a good move, but it proved to be my undoing. After I'd rebuilt the car, I found I hadn't enough money to go racing, but then I had a call from Robin Herd, who'd designed the McLaren, asking me to build the first March Formula Three car. The people at Arch Motors had mentioned my name, and so I became March's first employee, building the 693, a fairly simple space-frame car which Ronnie Peterson drove. It's still in existence and stamped on the chassis is S1/69, the 'S' is for Stone. As soon as that was built, I went racing my McLaren with no great success, and at the end of the season I went to work for March.

'Just before I did so, I ran in a "European Championship" meeting at Karlskoga, Sweden. Howden Ganley, Bert Hawthorne and I formed the New Zealand team and we finished third overall. Then we were disqualified because we were affiliated to the RAC, not the FIA, but Howden was the guy who had introduced Robin Herd to Bruce McLaren, so got him started, and later Sabre Automotive would make his space-frames when he was running Tiga. There are so many connections in motor racing.'

As Bill said, he was the first employee of March Engineering – which would become the most successful production racing car maker in the world – just as, later, he became the first paid employee of Reynard. Over the years the stories of March and Reynard would sometimes cross over and link, which is hardly surprising since they were both based in Bicester.

In fact, Bill and Ray Wardell, March's second employee, had never heard of Bicester when March took over a new factory unit there in October 1969. When the company moved in it consisted of Bill and Ray, a Ford Transit van containing all March's tools and spares, and the 693 on a trailer. Bill had his old Thames van, which held all his worldly goods, and his McLaren. 'They showed Ray and me where Bicester was on the map, gave us the keys, and we drove up in convoy.'

While they set up the unit they lived in the Transit. They'd get up in the morning, cook breakfast on a camping stove, and then get on with the job. They soon tired of this and moved their sleeping bags to the flat roof of one of the offices in the unit, sheer luxury.

The first March Formula One and Formula Ford cars ran in public just four months later, which gives some idea of the commitment of Bill and his team. When he and Adrian established Sabre Automotive, it was Bill who set it on its feet.

'After I joined March I raced for a bit longer in Formula Ford, and I had some input into the March Formula Ford 1600 design, but I knew I wouldn't make it when I began being beaten by drivers almost young enough to be my sons. At the factory we had Bill Wright who was a first-class motorcycle trials rider. I switched to trials 'bikes and Bill and I used to practice in our lunch breaks on the rough ground around the factory as the industrial estate was being finished.

By 1972 I was in charge of sales at March, so when a group of students came along from the Oxford Poly, led by Adrian, it was my job to show them around. Adrian saw a motorcycle frame I was building, a copy of the Spanish Bultaco, and that led to us talking about motorcycles, and he struck me as an exceptionally bright and interesting character.

Bill Stone as Team Manager in 1980 with the New Zealand built Atlantic Cuda.

'That chance meeting led to a friendship which has lasted ever since. By that time I was keen to leave March to set up my own business, but I realised that my limitation was in design and I saw in Adrian the potential to be a designer.

'Eventually we decided we'd set up a company, Sabre Automotive, and Adrian contributed his welding equipment, it was that basic. We bought some equipment second-hand at auction, and we were on our way. Adrian had nothing to do with the day-to-day running of the company, which could not afford to pay him a wage, but that does not mean he was a sleeping partner. In fact, he made a large contribution because he had a head full of ideas and he was an absolute powerhouse. We'd discuss ideas and then he'd go off to draw them. He was regularly working extremely long hours; very determined and persistent.

'He was incredible. Once he'd got an idea he'd stick at it until it was finished. There were always little design jobs coming up, and we'd simply phone Adrian and he'd come in, sum up the problem, and then go away and do the work.

'Around 1976/77, my wife and I decided that we wanted to return to New Zealand. After Adrian came back to us from working for Hawke we talked about the move, but it took us about 18 months to make the transition. I ran the business; my wife, Maura, worked almost as hard as I did by keeping the books and so on; while Adrian was the intellectual force.

'It would be fair to say that sometimes Maura and I had to keep him in check. He often had very big ideas and needed to be brought down to earth.' Adrian's parents speak warmly of Bill's influence on their son. 'It obviously was not a simple matter to hand over the business, and Adrian bought out my share by foregoing his share of the profits over a period of time.'

Bill and Maura returned to New Zealand where he carved out a successful business career. He and Adrian kept in touch, however, and Bill Stone by no means disappears from the Reynard story.

Chapter Five

Dreams and Drawing Paper are Cheap

Adrian takes up the story again: 'Sabre Automotive had not made me any money, but we had reinvested our profits in some tools and, as 1977 dawned, we had four employees fabricating parts for March, Tiga, Chevron and Mallock. I decided to upgrade my '76 design, which was still broadly based on the original car and, because we did not have extensive premises, we sold it as a kit. That was partly because we did not have the resources to make up the cars and partly because our workshop was so humble that we did not want to encourage visitors in case the premises undermined the impression we were trying to create.

'Sabre Automotive made 16 kits, we had not then set up a separate company to manufacture and sell the cars. Jeremy and I each had one and the remaining 14 were all sold in Britain. Formula Ford 2000 was very strong that year, with up to 40 entries at a meeting and some good drivers and teams involved.'

During 1976 the New Zealand racing driver and bass guitarist, Rob Wilson, had been Tiga's works driver in Formula Ford 1600, and one of Tiga's co-founders was Howden Ganley who had raced under the NZ banner with Bill Stone in 1969. Rob supported himself with his music and was a member of Edison Lighthouse which had a hit with 'Love Grows Where My Rosemary Goes'.

Part of Rob's job (Oh, the glamour of being a works driver!) was to drive the Tiga van to Bicester to pick up space-frames which Sabre made for the company. Rob became interested in the Reynard Formula Ford 2000 car – it helped that it was Kiwi talking to Kiwi – and decided to buy one for 1977. It caused a rift with Tiga but, at Mallory Park, Rob became the first private customer to win in a Reynard.

There were two main championships in 1977 and Jeremy Rossiter finished second in both, each time beaten by the personable South African, Rad Dougall, in a Royale entered by Ted Toleman. Ted's team would graduate to Formula Two, then to Formula One when its main sponsor took it over. The Benetton Formula One team has its origins in Formula Ford 2000.

While Jeremy established Reynard as a serious contender, *Autosport* recorded that Adrian 'had a torrid time between flashes of inspiration.'

Although Rad took both titles, the Royale RP25 was probably not as good a basic design as the Reynard, since it suffered from chronic understeer, but between them Rad, Rory Byrne and Toleman made it into a winner. Rad was the outstanding driver of the year (he would later be a winner in Formula Two) and Toleman had a large budget so could throw tyres at the car until some worked.

So far as the Reynard story is concerned, it brought Adrian into regular contact with Alex Hawkridge, Toleman's Joint Managing Director and a man who would have a long and continuing influence on him as a friend and advisor, and also with Rory Byrne who would head the abortive 1991 Reynard Formula One project.

Jeremy recalls: 'I'd made the mistake of doing Formula Atlantic in 1976, which had started with a lot of promises from the organisers, but which had fizzled out. After that experience I was glad to be back alongside Adrian who'd become a very close friend. He's godfather to my eldest son James and he was partly instrumental in our relocating Spax from London to Bicester within sight of the Reynard Centre. In Formula Ford 2000 I had a great season and won six races.

'One thing that I discovered was that Adrian and I set our cars up completely differently and neither of us could drive the other's. Adrian's car was set up to be quick on the perfect line, mine could be taken by the scruff of the neck and abused. That we could set them up so differently speaks volumes for the design and I'm sure it came down to it having a very stiff chassis which meant you could make major adjustments to the settings. I think, too, that because the chassis was so stiff that the engine worked better because there were no forces being directed into the block.

'Reynards were also immensely strong, as Adrian and I proved a few times. During practice at Brands Hatch in 1978 my brakes failed going into Clearways and I rammed the railway sleepers there with such force that the guy behind drove straight into the pits because he was convinced I had been killed. I have Adrian's design to thank for the fact that I survived, let alone the fact that I was driving again before the end of the season.

'Adrian knew, too, precisely how much his cars weighed and he would bring them in under the weight limit having previously calculated where he would place his ballast for optimum weight distribution. I remember once at Silverstone scattering parts of the bodywork around the circuit and then being disqualified for being 2 lb underweight. I'd discarded more than that in fibreglass, but it shows how very fine were the limits to which he operated. The sponsor of the series later presented me with a 2 lb weight!'

The success of the cars on the circuit boosted Sabre Automotive and gave Adrian a focus after his disappointing association with Hawke. 'For the first time I was pulling my weight in the company. I went to work each day to weld, or order parts, and at weekends I raced and used that as an opportunity to sell cars. We expanded our business and began to introduce lines such as oil tanks which we sold to some of our rivals like Royale and Van Diemen.

'It was during 1977 that I met Rick Gorne, who is now Managing Director of Reynard Racing Cars. We were at Thruxton and I was one of the quicker drivers on the day, so I was feeling pretty self-important. I was in the groove during practice and heading for a quick time when I came across Rick who had spun his Elden at the chicane and was facing the wrong way. That spoiled one good lap, and the next, and then I caught him up again on the circuit and he got in my way – which spoiled another lap.

'For some reason, possibly one of us had pitted, I came across him yet again and this time he was so anxiously looking in his mirrors to see where I was that he got on the wrong line and spun on the straight, which ruined yet another lap. I felt that I should give this youngster a little friendly advice, a few tips and pointers.

'After practice,' says Rick, 'this long-haired hippy came up and demanded to know who the **** I thought I was?'

Adrian says: 'That was my first meeting with Rick and I must have been insufferable. Rick appeared to be sheepish at my outburst, but I got the impression that he wasn't taking me very seriously. We didn't start our friendship there and then, but I used to take my girlfriend, Gill, to the meetings and she got to know him before I did. This was no surprise because Rick was a flamboyant young man, good looking, a little flash and very likeable. He was then being run by Richard Dutton who was interested in my cars. Dutton bought three and Rick drove one of them. It was then that our friendship began to flourish.'

A Formula Ford 2000 race in 1977 at Zandvoort. Pictured, left to right, are Richard Dutton, Rick Gorne, Rob Wilson, Steve Farthing, and Gill, Adrian's future wife.

'Back at the shop, Bill Stone was getting a bit restless and he began to think of a return to New Zealand. He'd come over here to go motor racing and had ended up simply working, and he could do that equally well at home. I bought him out by relinquishing my share of the profits for two years and he went home.

'It meant that I was running Sabre all by myself, but I felt confident that I could do it, although I was sad to lose a friend. Bill had taught me a lot of things, including business ethics and how to do things correctly. He was the first person I knew in motor racing and he is fundamental to the Reynard story. Without him we would not be where we are today.'

Bill says: 'I think that had I stayed, the company's history would have been entirely different. My guess is that I would have continued to run Sabre while Adrian would have taken on more consultancy work, as he did for Hawke and later for March, and we would have operated more or less separately. Had I still been in place, Rick Gorne might never have been involved and Reynard would not be as successful as it is.'

Adrian continues: 'The core business, fabrication, was one thing, the building of racing cars was another, and it was with some trepidation that I faced 1978 with a new version of the car. This time we started to manufacture more in-house components and placed less emphasis on the kits.' Twenty-three cars were sold in 1978 and Jeremy led the Formula Ford 2000 Championship until that heavy accident at Brands Hatch. In future years he switched to Sports 2000 and was Lola's works driver.

Jeremy's car was rebuilt and Adrian borrowed it in June to take a maiden FF2000 win at Silverstone, and he followed that up with wins at Snetterton and Thruxton. Adrian's performances can be summed up by the fact he set pole position (five times) more often than he won, but apart from his three wins he took three seconds and three thirds.

It was a fine performance in a year which was exceptionally competitive in Formula Ford 2000, and it looked for a time as though he might be the first manufacturer since Colin Chapman to be capable of becoming a top-line driver. 'I was racing against my

Adrian was asked to drive the Ehrlich Formula Three car at the Monza Lotteria in 1977 for Dr Ehrlich. His engineer (far right) is Paul Crosby, who went on to engineer Reynard drivers in the Formula 3000 era, including Jean Alesi, David Coulthard and Gil de Ferran.

While recovering from a heavy accident at Brands Hatch, Jeremy Rossiter was unable to compete in a Formula Ford 2000 race at Silverstone in June 1978, and asked Adrian to race his car. This was Adrian's first Championship victory. Sharing the moment is Peter Scott Russell, then Silverstone's commentator.

customers, but that was OK: when business was slack you could always nerf one into the Armco!'

Meanwhile, Rick Gorne, having become a Reynard driver, had emerged as another front-runner in Formula Ford 2000. On four occasions he took pole position, and finished the year with four championship wins, three seconds and four thirds, and other wins in non-championship races. It might have been an even more successful year had he made a better choice of engine.

For Adrian, one of the highlights of the season was the many scraps he had with Mike Blanchet's Lola. 'Mike was a terrific driver and was always fair on the track. In fact, he was much fairer than I was, some of my manoeuvres were pretty desperate at times. Mike was joint Managing Director of Lola Cars and it's ironic that in later years, after we've both retired from driving, we should have been competing first in Formula 3000 and now in Indycar. We've always had a good relationship, however. He was a gentleman on the track and he has remained a gentleman in business.'

Mike Blanchet remembers well: 'I remember once at Snetterton, I'd been involved in something on the first lap which dropped me to the back of the field. I caught up and passed Adrian who was leading. I'd raced against him enough to know what he'd do and he did it. He tried to overtake me with all four wheels on the grass. I'd anticipated that and left him with nowhere to go. I believe Adrian finished second.'

Peter Morgan, now Reynard's Production Director, recalls the only time he raced against Adrian. 'It was at Oulton Park, and he and me in my Lola were battling for the lead. He was all over me, and there were times when our wheels interlocked.

'I won, but I had never before encountered such a wild man on the track. I was furious and afterwards I was going to give him a piece of my mind. Suddenly he bounded up, his faced wreathed in smiles. "That was terrific," he said, "of course, it was just as well I backed off when our wheels interlocked, it could have been a nasty

Mike Blanchet and Geoff Wyatt, Adrian's mechanic, with Adrian at Snetterton in 1978.

Snetterton, 1978. Adrian's truck was a converted furniture lorry that he bought for £800. Harry Jones and Geoff Wyatt are working on the car while Adrian holds the tracking gauges. He took two cars to meetings, with numbers 69 and 96, but was later banned as he had twice as much practice as any other driver. Jonathan Palmer is walking past in the background.

accident." I could think of nothing to say, it was sheer cheek, but you just could not help liking him.'

On a different occasion Rob Wilson told, almost word for word, the same story – another day, another race. Who knows how many other people out there have the same tale to tell?

Rick Gorne says: 'Adrian was very quick and could usually get a good grid position. We were all pretty wild in Formula Ford 2000 – we had as many restarts as starts. I soon got used to seeing this yellow car parked on the grass as I was on my second lap.

'We went into the last race at Snetterton with Adrian just ahead of me in the Championship. He was quicker than me that day, and for some reason I started well down the grid. On the last lap he had an 'off' and although he recovered, I had momentum and by taking a deep breath in the last corner I was able to just take him on the line. We were only fighting for fourth place, but it put me one place ahead of him in the series and made me the year's most successful Reynard driver.

'He was so angry with himself that he did not drive to the scrutineer's bay, but got into his car and, still wearing his overalls and helmet, drove straight out of the circuit. Winning meant a lot to him.'

Adrian resumes the story: 'By the end of the season I was running a Brazilian, Placido Iglesias, in a spare car, which was good for business. One of the things about my cars was that they were easy to make, so there was a reasonable profit margin in them and, on the back of a successful year I was able to buy a bigger house and look around for new premises. They were building factories in Telford Road, Bicester, and I found a helpful bank manager. One advantage of the new factory was that it was large enough for us to assemble cars there, and I decided to run a two-car works team and to race in the European Formula Ford 2000 Championship.'

A Reynard Formula Three car was drawn for possible production in 1979, but it was not made because the money was not available. In fact, Rob Wilson was very keen on the idea and negotiations were entered into, but finally his sponsor decided he had to have a Ralt RT3 – and Rob became the first driver to win in one, as he'd been the first private customer to win in a Reynard.

'Dreams and drawing paper are cheap' says Adrian, a man who has encountered the problem more than once. Had the car been made and had it proved successful, it is possible that Adrian might have progressed as a driver to Formula Three. As it was, 1979 was to.be his last season as a driver.

'Our works team consisted of David Leslie and Mike O'Brien – David won 15 of his 31 starts and took both British championships. Mike had a pretty good season as well, also winning races, but he had to be content with third place in both series because the second places tended to fall to Simon Kirby, also in a Reynard. We had a very good year and it's no bad thing for a private owner to be able to split the works team.'

David Leslie remembers the season with a great deal of pleasure. It was the first time that all he'd had to do was to turn up and drive the car. Mike O'Brien, by contrast, was not considered by everyone to have been a team player. At Mallory Park, his mechanics eyed the lake, and eyed their much-loved driver, and decided to combine the two.

Fourteen manufacturers had displayed Formula Ford 2000 cars at the 1975 Racing Car Show. By 1979 the category was essentially between Reynard, Lola, Van Diemen, Royale, Delta and a newcomer, CTG. Nine of the 14 had gone, some had failed in Formula Ford 2000 and had switched to other formulae, but Palliser, Dulon, Hawke and Merlyn had gone for good. In terms of FF 2000, Reynard was playing with the big

In 1979 the Reynard works team consisted of David Leslie and Mike O'Brien. Adrian is on the grid at Snetterton talking to David Leslie. Geoff Wyatt is again looking after the car.

boys – nobody had more experience than Lola, CTG had former Formula One designer Len Terry on board, Royale had Pat Symonds, Van Diemen had former Lotus designer Dave Baldwin (and still does) while Delta had a car which had been designed by Patrick Head.

In terms of design talent, Formula Ford 2000 was a remarkable arena in 1979, and among the opposition was future Formula One driver Roberto Moreno in a Royale. Junior formula it may have been, but the talent that year was far from ordinary, and yet Reynards dominated the British field as no manufacturer had done previously. It was the year in which Reynard really joined the establishment, and it is just as well it did so, because in the very near future it was to need the goodwill which that season generated.

When you have dominated a season, you gain respect. Hard times were just around the corner for Reynard, but there was a sufficient residue of respect for it to continue to be taken seriously. Had Reynard merely been a good competitor, as Delta was, it is unlikely to have survived the sudden downturn in its fortunes. It was also the year in which Adrian had his greatest success as a driver.

'During the summer I went off to race in the European Championship and won my first race at Zandvoort, which surprised a few people, and then I went on to win again at Jyllandsring and Nivelles to clinch the EFDA series.' That was almost the end of Adrian's career as a driver, but before he finally hung up his helmet, he spent the winter in New Zealand contesting the Formula Pacific Championship.

After Bill Stone returned to New Zealand in 1978 he became Works Manager for a large truck-trailer company. Meanwhile, Jim Stone had also returned home and he enjoyed some success with his Cuda formula cars, which he built with his brother. 'Adrian wanted to visit New Zealand and a Cuda had won the previous year's Formula

During 1979 Geoff Wyatt and Adrian went to Jyllandsring in Denmark to contest the Formula Ford 2000 Euroseries. Adrian won the race and subsequently the Championship. He rented a van to transport the car around Europe.

Pacific Championship,' says Bill. 'Since Adrian had just won the EFDA Formula Ford 2000 Championship, I was able to put together a sponsorship deal to run him in the Formula Pacific series.

'The Cuda was a good car, but ground effect had arrived and so too had a number of Ralts, which changed the balance of power. Adrian designed a ground effect conversion for the Cuda and I built it up. We communicated by phone, letter and fax. In my view the Cuda was no more than a mid-field runner that year and Adrian drove brilliantly to finish fifth in the series.'

Adrian continues: 'In winning the European Championship I achieved everything I wanted to achieve as a racing driver. I realised I could not carry on dividing my time between driving, running a race team, designing, running a factory and selling cars. I'd also had a fairly hectic social life involving a French actress, Françoise Pascal, who was in a hit television show at the time. Françoise came to all the races with me and all-in-all the relationship, while very enjoyable, was time-consuming, although it did show me that there was life outside of work.

'Something had to go. I was committed to driving my own cars, and Formula Three would have been the next step, but I realised it would be at least two years before I had a Formula Three car up and running (in fact it was five years) by which time I'd be 30 and too old to make the grade. And that was it. I've never since had a desire to step into a car.

'I've toyed with the idea of having a run in one of my Formula 3000 machines, but the fact that I've been making them for years and haven't got round to organising a session says it all. The same goes for Rick, although we've done the odd celebrity saloon car race when it's been for a good cause.'

Adrian secured sponsorship from Canadian Club whisky, for a total of £500. Adrian gave them superb coverage when he celebrated winning the 1979 European Formula Ford 2000 Championship at the final round at Nivelles, Belgium.

One of the last pictures of Adrian as a racing driver, taken in 1979 at Zandvoort after winning the Formula Ford 2000 Euroseries race. This was effectively the end of Adrian's driving career.

During 1979 Rick had moved up from Formula Ford 2000 to Formula Atlantic, but had a serious accident which broke both his legs and he was forced to retire from driving. He took a job as Competitions Director for the BARC, which kept him in the swim, and his friendship with Adrian developed.

'1979 had been a terrific year for us,' says Adrian, 'we sold a lot of cars and had a great deal of success on the circuits, but I was spreading myself too thinly and I decided to cut back. I retired from driving and decided to have a proper life. That was a mistake because 1980 was a disaster.'

Chapter Six

Whelk Pots and Formula One

'For 1980 the basic chassis remained much the same, but I designed a ground-effect body while keeping the full-width nose, which is a fairly basic error. Of course, nobody in Formula Ford did wind tunnel testing – there was not even as much wind tunnel work in Formula One as most people at the time believed – and we basically designed by eye. My eye must have been out, since our 1980 car was a dog; it was a brick down the straights, it understeered badly and we fell out of favour.

'We sold only 11 cars that year, although that was partly due to economic recession. One of our customers was Martin Brundle, but despite that he still managed to get into Formula One. If a driver of Martin's talent couldn't win with the car, there was not much hope for our average customer.

'Another reason we slipped behind was that the 1980 Royale was very good; it had been designed by Pat Symonds, who had followed me at Hawke, and I'd recommended him to Royale. He showed his gratitude by nearly putting me out of business. The only bright spot was Dave Greenwood winning the British Super-Vee Championship in an 80SF, it at least showed that the car could handle an extra 50 bhp.'

Reynard ran a two-car works team for Frank Bradley, whose main business is jellied eels, but who more recently owned the European arm of Swift Cars for some years, and Graham Duxbury, a South African who was highly rated. Frank says: 'In those days I was a good driver and I thought 1980 was going to be my year, works driver and all that. Graham and I each had a works mechanic, and mine was better than his – mine knew the front end of the car from the back.

'The car was a dog. Adrian did not intend it to be one, but it was, and at the end of the year I switched to a Van Diemen. Poor Graham was totally demoralised by the experience and went back to South Africa with his tail between his legs, a great shame.' It was the end of Graham's attempt to break into European racing, but not the end of his career, and subsequent successes included a win in the Daytona 24 Hours.

'Adrian eventually admitted that the car was no good, and since I felt I had been sold a bum steer we reached an agreement. I was selling whelks at the time and he made me 1,500 whelk pots – you throw the pots into the sea and the whelks crawl in . . . I paid Adrian £3.15 a pot, but it cost him £3 each to make them. It did us both a favour since it kept his cash-flow going and I've still got a few Reynard whelk pots.'

'I've had a great deal of fun with my motor racing, and Adrian is part of that. We've had some wild times together and, despite that 1980 season, we're still great mates.'

Adrian continues: 'Things were desperate and I needed any work I could get. I'd had to put the staff on a two-day week and I sold many of my personal possessions to stay in business. When car production had taken off I had let the subcontract side of the business stagnate and that was a mistake, although such work was harder to come by because every racing car maker was hit by the recession, and Chevron, one of our customers, had folded.

'We were still doing work for March Engineering, but they were also having a hard time and couldn't pay their bills. It got to such a state that a lot of our revenue came from using the back of the factory to store unsold March Formula Three and Super-Vee cars along with jigsaw puzzles for another company.

'Meanwhile, Rupert Keegan was driving an ex-works Williams FW07 entered by John Macdonald's RAM team. John was running these cars with great success in the Aurora (British) Formula One Championship, and the team scored a 1–2 in the series. When they entered World Championship events, however, it was another matter and Rupert was not qualifying. Eventually he told John that he wanted an engineer he could relate to, someone like me.

'John agreed and we went testing at Snetterton, and there was an improvement, although whether it was because of the adjustments I made, or whether it was because of the confidence Rupert got from my just being there, is something we'll never know. Whatever, Rupert went better and John took me on board for a few races and he gave me a free hand. In the last race of the year, at Watkins Glen, I did a good engineering job on Rupert's brain and he qualified 16th, ahead of Villeneuve and Scheckter in the Ferraris.'

As Adrian was getting his first taste of Formula One, John Macdonald and Robin Herd, who was then the sole owner of March, were talking about forming a new team. It seemed an unlikely alliance, since Robin is an Oxford double-first and John is an ex-North London car dealer and a bit of a rough diamond, but they were united by the fact that each is a racer at heart.

Robin owned a subsidiary company, March Engines, which was based at Cowley away from March Engineering, and March Engines was set to work not to design a new car, but to copy a Williams FW07 which John owned. The prototype was fine, but March cut corners in subsequent cars, which caused major problems. For example, March squared off the slight curvature at the rear of the ground effect tunnels which the Williams had – and lost half the downforce.

While March Grand Prix was trying to build a Williams, and the elements for a major row were falling into place, Adrian was feeling disappointed that he had not been asked to become part of the new team after his work with Rupert Keegan. 'Looking back, I don't know how we survived in 1981. We reverted to an update of the 79SF and discarded the ground effect bodywork, but we sold only six of them. It was a bleak year with virtually no business.'

It was during 1981 that Alex Hawkridge suggested to Adrian that since he had been in Formula One as an engineer, and had proven that he was not out of place there, he should consider designing the 'Ultimate Formula Ford car'. Adrian says: 'I had not had much experience of Formula One when I started to design the car but, for the first time in my career, I had worked with another team and had seen how they did things. It helped open up my mind and, although I've always believed in simplicity, I realised that we had to move beyond the fairly basic designs I had been building.'

Adrian's new car retained the virtues of his previous design, good aerodynamics and a stiff chassis which was down to the minimum weight limit. The new frame was made even stiffer by the use of aluminium skinning, bolted at six-inch centres with high-tensile Allen bolts. Some cried foul!, but Adrian had read the rule book. 'I gained a massive amount of torsional stiffness by doing this, which was perfectly in line with the rules which stated that panels bolted on at six-inch centres were unstressed.

'I gained even more rigidity by using a back-to-back roll hoop, which also improved driver safety and upper torso protection and became an identity feature of all Reynard Formula Ford cars. We were up to 2,250 ft/lb per degree stiffness which was an

Adrian worked for Rupert Keegan's father's company, British Air Ferries, designing the Hawke 1976 Formula 3 car and still-born Formula One car. Adrian was Rupert's engineer during his Formula One career, and his first experience of engineering an F1 car was the Williams FW07 at Imola. John Macdonald, the team owner, and Andy Miller, current Director of Paul Stewart Racing and team manager of PSR Formula Three team, are also pictured on the right.

Adrian and Rupert Keegan at Watkins Glen in 1980. Adrian was engineering Rupert's Williams FW07.

improvement of about 15 per cent on where we had been before.' It is unlikely that many other Formula Ford makers could have told you the torsional rigidity of their frame.

'Suspension was inboard all round with rocker arms at the front and, possibly for the first time in Formula Ford 1600, the fully-enclosed bodywork extended behind the rear axle line. Built into the body panels was a shaped section which reduced rear-end lift. This was an imaginative interpretation of the rules, which forbade aerofoils, but it was some time before it was rumbled.

'There was not a lot of science applied to Formula Ford cars at the time and I am sure that ours was the first to see the inside of a wind tunnel. By the time we came to build the car I had some wind tunnel experience with March Grand Prix which was useful, and we took the prototype to the full-scale tunnel at MIRA – it was not until 1985/6 that I started wind tunnel testing with models. Testing without a moving road has its limitations, but we were able to develop a very effective airbox for the car at MIRA.'

He might also have said that his car was very pretty, the double roll-hoop adding to its aesthetic appeal. With its pencil-slim nose and tiny side radiators, it looked like a miniature Grand Prix car, and such things matter to drivers making perhaps the biggest decision of their entire careers. The wishbones were also plated, in Formula One style, which added to the appeal.

While Adrian tried to save his company by drawing his first all-new design since 1973, all was not well at March Grand Prix. In Brazil, both Marches failed to qualify. It wasn't just that the cars were slow, they were badly made, and on one car a wishbone broke away from the tub. Other teams chuckled as March Grand Prix tried to beef up the monocoques by reskinning them, right there in the pit lane. It was a first in motor racing. John Macdonald said to anyone who would listen: 'The car is a pile of shit, and that's official!' Robin was in Brazil, and the relationship, which was already shaky, was irreparably damaged. Robin flew home.

The upshot was that the very experienced Gordon Coppuck was loaned from March Engineering for a few races, and he made some improvements. Gordon's involvement, however, was temporary and before mid-season Adrian received a call from Macdonald asking him to rejoin March Grand Prix, and that call probably saved Reynard. Business was still poor, but Adrian's consultancy fee was paid into Sabre Automotive to pay the wages and to keep the factory going.

'I had only one meeting with Robin Herd while I was with March Grand Prix. He sat in on one of the debriefs I did after a test, and he said: "Fine, fine, sounds great," smiled, and disappeared, and that's all I ever had to do with him. Our only other connection was in the 1982 team brochure where his picture is alongside mine and I am billed as Chief Engineer and he is Chief Engineering Executive.'

Adrian's presence had an immediate effect, and Derek Daly, who by then was the sole driver, managed to qualify for the first time in the season at the next race, the Spanish Grand Prix at Jarama. True, it was only in the 22nd slot and Daly finished 16th and last classified runner, but it was progress.

Things were even better at the French Grand Prix where Daly qualified 20th and so received starting money. Part of the subtext of the season, however, was a tyre war – Michelin was the only supplier at the beginning of the year and then Goodyear returned and Avon appeared. In France, March Grand Prix switched from Michelin radials to Avon crossplies, and the car worked better on them.

Real progress came at the British Grand Prix where Daly had a new chassis which was shorter and 58 lb lighter. In the race Derek had to pit after two laps with a loose gear linkage and he rejoined a lap down, but he brought it home seventh. Had it not been for that lost lap it might have been third, which would have put the team on Broadway. From then on, Daly normally occupied 19th or 20th place on the grid, which was a creditable performance considering that he didn't have a turbo engine, or one of the special Cosworths which some teams had commissioned from engine builders, and nor did he have trick qualifying tyres.

Adrian's contribution was acknowledged, and he was taken on by March Grand Prix for 1982. He spent the winter refining the car and, more to the point, Sabre Automotive became busy once more as the general economic climate improved. It helped, of course, that Adrian was in Formula One.

The stories of March Engineering (as distinct from March Grand Prix) and Reynard are linked from the 1970s, when Adrian first met Bill Stone at March, to the 1990s. In 1982, for example, March sold 20 Indycars and won five races with cars derived from Adrian's work on March's copy of the Williams. March made a packet while Adrian struggled to meet the wages of his workforce which was then on short-time. Before the end of the decade Reynard would wipe March out of the Formula 3000 market and would come within 24 hours of buying March Engineering.

By late 1981, two of the new Reynard 82FF Formula Ford 1600 cars had been built, with Wally Warwick taking the first customer car. 'James Weaver drove the prototype in the Formula Ford Festival at Brands Hatch, and it created a very favourable impression. We had built it on a shoestring and it was far from well-sorted, but it had some inherently good features, such as the fact that it was extremely forgiving.'

James put it on the front row of the grid for the final and brought it home third. It was a sensational debut and *Autosport* referred to the car as 'undoubtedly the most revolutionary Formula Ford 1600 to be seen this side of the Atlantic and probably anywhere in the world.' Perhaps it was a little too revolutionary for some people

The revolutionary 82FF Formula Ford car was inspired by Alex Hawkridge, when he suggested to Adrian that he should design a state-of-the-art Formula Ford car. It debuted in the Brands Hatch Formula Ford Festival in 1982 in the hands of James Weaver, who came 3rd in the final.

because, although it brought increased sales, it did not pull Reynard out of the mire. Some rival manufacturers began to spread rumours that the car was illegal, which did Reynard no favours, but the rumour-mongers are no longer in business.

Then again, Reynard was trying to break into a new market which was dominated by Lola, Van Diemen and Royale, all of which had consistently produced race-winning cars, while it had been three years since a Reynard had last been in the winner's circle. Most young drivers were not prepared to take a risk on a newcomer to Formula Ford 1600. One who did, however, was Andrew Gilbert-Scott who led the Townsend Toresen Formula Ford 1600 Championship until his budget ran out.

Then, out of the blue, Adrian received a phone call from an officer in the United Arab Emirates Airforce who was staying at a hotel in London. 'The pilots liked their toys and had been through karts, hovercraft and dune buggies. Someone obviously thought that Formula Ford would be a fun way to spend off-duty hours, and this guy rang all of the main makers. They responded by promising to send brochures and to arrange a meeting sometime. My response was to load a car onto a trailer and park it outside the pilot's hotel in London's West End that same evening. He was about my age, which helped, and we clicked. I didn't leave until I had the order.

'That phone call saved Reynard because we were still finding it tough to shift cars in Britain, and the odd thing is that the cars were never used. I can only think that, by the time we delivered the last one, the pilots had found a new way of having fun. Several years later I found the cars gathering dust in a hangar, only one had ever been run, and Rick Gorne brokered the deal by which they were sold on to America.'

On top of the cars which went to the United Arab Emirates, 19 other Reynards were sold abroad, but representation was thin in Britain. 'During 1982 we tried to make an impression in Britain, but it was hard work. Van Diemen had a stranglehold on Formula Ford 1600, helped in no small way by the fact that every year Ralph Firman found a

Adrian sold about a dozen cars to the United Arab Emirates Airforce for the pilots' amusement. The UAE Airforce officer was talking to all the racing car manufacturers, so Adrian drove to London and parked a car outside the officer's West End hotel. The sales pitch worked.

brilliant Brazilian to drive his cars (it had been Ayrton Senna in 1981) and, to be frank, our car was still not that great.

'In the States, however, Jackson Yonge did us a lot of good by setting a new lap record at Palm Beach, while Dave Knapp and Gord Cullen each won regional championships. It seemed pretty remote at the time, but it was important because 1983 would see the start of Formula Ford 2000 in the States, and we needed all the help we could get.'

While Sabre Automotive enjoyed a revival, even if Reynards were not winning much in Britain, Adrian continued to work for March Grand Prix which was based two minutes walk from his own factory. Since he was spreading himself between two jobs, and not finding it easy, he kept the pressure on Rick Gorne to join him. Meanwhile, people were beginning to take note of the man who had become, at 30, the youngest Chief Designer in Formula One.

'We were getting a good press and people were saying that March Grand Prix was a team which should make progress. Over the winter I re-engineered the car, made it stiffer, and managed to shed another 50 lb. We didn't have too many reliability problems, the car looked good and it was a lot quicker straight out of the box.'

Since Adrian had applied fundamental engineering to the problem, and had not come up with anything tricky, he had put the car into the state it should have been in at the start of 1981. The times recorded by the new driving team of Jochen Mass and Raul Boesel in the early races in '82 would have put them on the front row of most grids in '81, and Mass and Boesel were nobody's idea of star drivers.

Unfortunately for March Grand Prix, everyone else had made equal progress. Adrian did well to bring the weight down from the 630 kg of the first car to 580 kg, the legal limit, but others had their cars down to 550 kg and were making up the difference by disposable water ballast. Sorry, it was 30 kg of perfectly legitimate brake coolant which

Left In 1982 Adrian was Chief Engineer at March Grand Prix. The team drivers were Raul Boesel, currently a Reynard Indycar driver, and Jochen Mass. Adrian is pictured with Jochen Mass at the French Grand Prix at Paul Ricard.

Right March ran in Rothmans livery during 1982. Pictured at the launch are, from left to right, drivers Raul Boesel and Jochen Mass, David Richards (now Chairman of Prodrive), Adrian and John Macdonald.

was dumped on the warm-up lap, if it was ever added at all, and replaced before the final weigh-in. Further, there were more turbo cars in the field and Goodyear and Michelin had made large strides, while March Grand Prix was contracted to Pirelli which was struggling to catch up.

When March Grand Prix appeared at the second race of 1982, the cars were in a new livery – Rothmans. To land such a sponsor was a spectacular coup and outsiders expected March to climb up the grid, but throughout the season it remained resolutely static. From the moment the sponsorship arrived, to the end of the season, only twice did a March qualify in the top 20. The problem was a little like a man close to death by starvation being shown a table groaning with food. The natural inclination is to gorge, but that can kill. When John Macdonald was shown the groaning table, he gorged and he is the first to admit that perhaps the money was not spent as judiciously as it might have been.

Adrian: 'Everything looked good. I was in charge, John seemed to have faith in me, we had Rothmans money and I thought: "At last I've got a chance to do a good job." I was happy just to be in Formula One as the Chief Engineer of a team which seemed to be on the up, and I instigated a wind tunnel programme and chose some more machinery. The place was buzzing, the factory was tiled and everyone had company cars.

'I was just about to action my wind tunnel programme and suddenly it was axed. The machines I had ordered weren't coming and I was restricted on this, that, and the other. We had been using Pirelli tyres, which had been free, but at Monaco we suddenly switched to Avon crossplies which had to be paid for. I couldn't understand what was going on.'

John Macdonald: 'Adrian was new to Formula One and had no idea how the money was spent or what everything cost. He also did not know that early in the season we

were told that Rothmans had decided not to stay with us, and I was trying to make them change their minds.'

The Rothmans deal had supposed to have been for three years and John had been in the process of setting up a three-year programme, but he had failed to educate his sponsors in the realities of racing; that it would take time to use the money effectively – improvements this year, a new car next year and so on. Rothmans had been sold a 'Give us the money and we'll be winners' sort of deal, and when the results didn't immediately appear they wanted reasons.

Then again, there were those in racing who were jealous of the fact that John had landed so big a sponsor. They whispered in the right ears, 'Macdonald's a plonker, now if you came with us we could do a really super job for you.' John knew what was going on and the switch to Avon from Pirelli was symptomatic of his panic. It was a desperate move because it meant offending a major supplier and giving up free tyres, but a test session had shown the car worked better on Avons. Then, a week or so before the Monaco Grand Prix in May, Avon announced its withdrawal from Formula One and John, caught in a cleft stick, bought all its remaining stock.

Unfortunately, the Avons did not improve by being stored in John's factory, while Pirelli was improving race by race. Monaco was the last chance of hanging on to Rothmans sponsorship but, since neither car qualified, that chance disappeared and the three-year programme John had instigated, and which Adrian was to implement, was axed.

Away from the power politics Adrian says: 'I felt as though I had lost engineering control and that John had lost confidence in me. As a result I was working even harder to try to catch up and I wasn't doing myself any good. I was working a 15-hour day, going in early, working late, and trying to run my own business in between. I realised I wasn't enjoying it. I wasn't in control of my own destiny. I felt John had lost faith in me and so the relationship disintegrated.'

John said in 1989: 'I never lost confidence in Adrian but, as I've said, he was new in Formula One, it's still his only period in Formula One, and he did not understand all the financial problems and politics. In fact, I can prove I still have a lot of confidence in Adrian since I now buy Formula 3000 cars from him.'

Just as working for John Macdonald had given Adrian new insights when it came to designing the Reynard 82F, so the experience of 1982 helped to shape his later philosophy. 'I think that John did not give his designers sufficient responsibility and it is a lesson I took to heart. Today, if one of my engineers campaigns for a development programme or an item of expenditure, we will discuss it and I will evaluate it. If he is still passionate about it, more often than not I will let it go ahead even if I'm not totally convinced. I take the view that I can't be right about everything and that he may have seen something I haven't understood.

'I think I had something that John didn't understand, and he did not allow me to develop it. John was essentially conservative: if something hadn't appeared on, say, a Williams then it couldn't be any good because if it was good Williams would have thought of it. There was always this dampener, which meant that we were doomed always to be a copier.'

Adrian's work with March Grand Prix was noticed by the discerning and, before the end of the year, he had received the ultimate accolade. Colin Chapman asked him to work for Lotus. Being in Formula One had been important to Adrian, even if it had been with a team in crisis, and Chapman's offer was very tempting.

There was a condition, however, which was that he would have to give up Sabre Automotive. Adrian says: 'I was summoned to Ketteringham Hall, the stately home in

Norfolk which was Team Lotus' headquarters. I was seated at this huge table and, as I left, I noticed that I'd been so nervous that I'd left sticky palm prints all over it. Chapman was the sort of man who demanded 110 per cent from everybody. I try to give nothing less, but I could not give it all to him while I retained Sabre Automotive and I felt that I could not give it up.'

There are a number of ironical points. Had Sabre been more successful, Adrian could have employed someone to run it. Had Bill Stone still been in place, Adrian could have gone to Lotus and pursued a separate career, in which case it is likely that Reynard would have stuck to the lower formulae. Then, as fate would have it, Chapman died that December. Much of the attraction of working for Lotus was to come under the influence of arguably the greatest racing car designer in history, it would have been cruel had Adrian given up Sabre Automotive to move to Norfolk and then be denied the main reason for the move.

Adrian refused the offer from Chapman, and he must be one of the few who have. He had his loyalties and he had his own agenda, but it must have been in the back of his mind because otherwise he would not have turned up at Ketteringham Hall for the interview.

Shortly after he turned down Lotus, Rick Gorne threw in his lot with Reynard and the future was set. Rick recalls: 'For the Formula Ford Festival we put together a three-car team with backing from BP. It was a Big Buck deal – they paid us all of £400. The event was an unmitigated disaster – a plug lead came off in the heats on one of our cars and the other two did not get beyond the quarter finals. We went home feeling very despondent and decided to concentrate instead on Formula Ford 2000; it was what we both knew and liked.'

Chapter Seven

Rick Gorne

There have been many post-war racing car manufacturers. Indeed, there have been over 500 in Formula Three and its close relation, Formula Junior, alone. Most are now obscure footnotes in the history of the sport, a handful have enjoyed spells of success, but only a tiny number have been consistently successful. Look at those who have survived and you will invariably find that they have had a guiding designer who has been backed by someone who understands business.

In 1982 Reynard was just a face in the crowd. Adrian had designed the 'ultimate' Formula Ford car, but not many people were buying it and it wasn't winning many races. If you look back to the Formula Ford scene of 1982, you would be a brave person had you picked Reynard from the throng as the company which would succeed. That it did so is, in no small measure, to the credit of Rick Gorne, who brought to the company a profound knowledge of motor racing and a clear vision. He is a man who is able to see the whole picture and at the same time is fastidious in his attention to detail. It is a rare combination.

Rick was born in July 1954 in Scunthorpe, Lincolnshire. His father is a Pole who served in the Polish Resistance during the war and, afterwards, went into business trading in surplus military hardware. 'For a child it was magic, you never knew what was going to be in the yard: it could be trucks, or it could be the cockpit of a jet aircraft. My father did very well in this line of business, and then he bought a stock of fire-salvage carpets and set up in the carpet business. Before long he had three stores in Lincolnshire.

'I was the oldest of four children. We were a very close-knit family and I grew up surrounded by a lot of warmth. When I was 10 I went to a boarding school in Henley-on-Thames which I hated at first because it was a long way from home, but I finished up loving it for the independence it gave me. I was not one of the cleverest kids – in fact I was pretty lazy – but I seemed to be a natural leader. My teachers recognised this and made me a prefect with responsibility for a junior class, which gave me an insight into how to handle authority and other people at an early age.

'Like Adrian, I was good on the arts side and useless at the sciences, which is ironic considering the business I'm in – I'm the least technical person in this organisation. I was also pretty good at athletics and soccer, which is always useful in a boarding school.' You have to prod Rick to remind him that he was also a member of the British Junior Water-Ski team, and water-skiing remains his favourite relaxation.

'When I left school I did a Business Studies course at a college in Lincolnshire, and then went to work for my father, selling carpets in one of his stores – and I loved it. I loved the business of selling, of clinching a deal and making someone feel good about their purchase. It gave me a buzz then, and clinching a deal still gives me a buzz.

'In 1973 I went to my first motor race, the International Trophy at Silverstone which was won by Jackie Stewart. That got me hooked on the sport, and I happened to mention this to Jackie recently. He looked at me and said, "Please Rick, don't lay the fact that you are involved in motor racing at my door." Jackie has since become one of our customers through Paul Stewart Racing.

'Soon after seeing my first motor race I started karting with a 250cc Zip-Bultaco, mainly driving on airfield circuits in Lincolnshire, and that led to Formula Ford in 1976. I bought a second-hand Alexis which turned out to be uncompetitive. Since I was paying for myself I did only about 10 races, but I was eager to move up, and the following year I struck a deal with Richard Dutton to race a two-year-old Elden in Formula Ford 2000. This time I had some sponsorship from a local design studio, and before long was finishing in the points. By the end of the season I was pretty competitive.

'I met Adrian during the season, at Thruxton when he came over to discuss my driving – he's already told the story. Despite that unpromising introduction we became friends, and at the end of the year the Dutton team decided to buy his cars. I had sponsorship from Barratt Homes – at the time I was managing one of my father's stores and we got the contract to carpet some Barratt show houses. I sold the idea of sponsorship to the manager I was dealing with and he, in turn, sold it to the board.

'With backing to do the job properly I had a very good year, winning nine races, although some of those were non-championship events. Much to Adrian's chagrin, I was the most successful Reynard driver of 1978, since I pipped him in the last race of the season. We were spending a lot of time together, making up a foursome with our girl friends and going water-skiing, but on the track there was always needle.

'At a two-race "super round" at Mallory Park I was on pole and I sailed off into the lead. Unfortunately, I had a problem with one of my front tyres – we later discovered that Dunlop had supplied me with an uncut 'wet' – and Adrian began to catch me. Naturally I made it difficult for him to overtake and he was getting ever more ragged

Rick Gorne (No. 2) and David Leslie battling in Formula Ford 2000 in 1978. It was during this season that Adrian and Rick became firm friends.

Adrian leading the pack at Oulton Park in 1978. David Leslie is taking the inside line and Rick is in sixth place. Adrian was shortly to spin off, while Rick finished in third place.

and frustrated. Eventually he ran into the back of me, but at least he had the good grace to bounce off and destroy his car against a barrier.

'Still, his act of wanton hooliganism dropped me way down the field, and every time I passed him, standing above his wreck on the barrier, I gestured my opinion of his driving. There is a limit to what you can convey with gestures from a cockpit, but I believe that I explored the outer perimeters of that limit.

Rick with Brian Clough and Mike Blanchet in 1978 at Mallory Park after a British Championship race. Tim Parnell is standing behind them.

'Afterwards he made himself scarce, but I went to find him to give him a piece of my mind, and when I did, all he could do was smile. I couldn't help myself, I smiled back. He has that effect on people – even angry racing drivers. I won the second race though. Come to think of it, it was Mike Blanchet of Lola who won the first event – the race I should have won. There we were, future World Champions, and now we're competing as salesmen.

'Barratt continued with me in 1979 when I entered Formula Atlantic with an Argo JM1A, an ex-Arie Luyendyk car. Then the company sponsored a meeting at Inglestone in Scotland, so naturally I had to be there, especially since it was the first race that the boss, Laurie Barratt, attended. So far as I was concerned it was a big deal because Barratt packed the place with corporate guests to see their man drive to glory. That probably added a bit of pressure on me because I was lying second to Jim Crawford, and normally I would have been happy with that, but I tried a bit too hard and went off and, of all things, hit an oak tree.

'An oak tree just happened to be the Barratt logo and I had oak trees painted all over my car. The next day, *The Scottish Herald* splashed the story on the front page: "Barratt race driver crashes into Barratt oak tree." That left a bad taste in everyone's mouth and Barratt withdrew its sponsorship.

'I was pretty badly hurt. I broke both legs, but when I recovered there was worse waiting for me than just losing my sponsor. I was being managed/guided by a man who, shall we say, didn't treat me fairly. Following the accident a number of debts mounted up, my 'friend' made himself scarce and someone had to pay. My house was sold together with my road car and I was left high and dry.

'I was still managing one of my father's stores, so I did have an income, but my father took the not unreasonable view that I should either concentrate on the family business or do my own thing. Selling carpets has its good points, but I wanted to stay in motor racing. So I applied for the job as Competition Director of the British Automobile Racing Club. I figured that by being in the swim I could pick up a sponsor, but the job

Rick Gorne celebrating after his first Reynard win at Donington Park in 1978. He was driving for Richard Dutton Racing.

was so time-consuming that I never did find a sponsor. In fact, if I had returned to racing I would have had to resign my job.

'As I've said, the job was time-consuming, we ran 50 race meetings a year, but it was not fulfilling. A lot of the real work was done by the girls in the office and I began to feel that I wasn't achieving much with my life. It was not all bleak, however, and I learned a great deal about business and dealing with people from Sidney Offord who ran the show – he was a great teacher and a lovely person – I learned practically everything I know about business from him. We needed sponsors for our races and he was wonderful with them, he brought a degree of professionalism to the job which opened my eyes.

'That was the good side, but I still needed a challenge and Adrian kept on asking me to join him. Finally I said I would, and on Monday 14 September 1982 I became Reynard employee number nine – at the time there was only Adrian, five guys in the workshop, a secretary and a bookkeeper.

Some years later Adrian would say: 'Rick was only in his twenties when he joined me, he taught me a lot and I taught him a lot, and he is now so much better at running the business than I ever was. He has endless patience with customers and the ability to deal with anyone from royalty to the Formula Ford 1600 customer who has just sold his house to finance his motor racing.'

'Rick has been fantastic for me, he motivates me and we bounce ideas off each other, but he knows he can make decisions without referring to me – 99 per cent of the time I know what he is thinking anyway. He's very good at pointing out my weaknesses in the nicest way and I've learned, through him, not to interfere but to delegate. I believe this has strengthened the business and it motivates people, if I'm not there looking over their shoulder all the time they get on with their job.'

Rick had a huge influence on the company from the moment he joined, and soon Sabre Automotive became the service element to a new company, Reynard Racing Cars. Before long there were overseas agents, and by the end of 1983 Reynard Racing Cars had landed its biggest-ever contract.

Rick in his new position at Reynard Racing Cars. He joined the company as Sales Manager in 1982 and was made a Director by Adrian Reynard within the first week.

Rick is a sort of salesman who could persuade you to buy your own left leg from him, but there is no shortage of persuasive people in motor racing. What has always set him above the rest is a combination of a global vision and attention to detail.

Ron Tauranac, who has designed more thoroughly competent production racing cars over a longer period of time than anyone else, has always taken the purist's view: 'This is the car I am making. If you want it then buy it.' It was a philosophy which worked for a time – actually a very long time. Ron never found the right partner, however, and in 1988 was forced to sell out to March Engineering. In 1989 he spoke of an unnamed rival who wined and dined customers, who offered discounts and deals, and he spoke those words as though they were stones in his mouth. Across one's mind fluttered an image of Rick showing an Eskimo how a refrigerator could enhance his igloo.

The manager of a team which was running Van Diemens in FF2000 in 1983 recalls: 'Rick was always on the phone, every week, telling me that I should dump our Van Diemens and buy Reynards. He started off with the idea that the Reynard was the better car, but as the weeks went on the offers got better and better. He finally came on to say that he had a buyer for our Van Diemens, for what we had paid for them, and he would let us have Reynards at cost.

'I didn't take him up on his offer. Our drivers were at a stage of their careers when they could have been driving supermarket trolleys; even with Reynards they weren't going to win races. Anyway, they were having accidents on a regular basis and I reckoned that the Van Diemen was stronger than the Reynard, and I was not at all happy about the cost of Reynard spares.

'None of us had encountered anything like it before. It upset some people, but I admired him for it. He made that company.'

The manager of a Formula Three team who was considering a move to Formula 3000 says: 'Even when we have not been running Reynards, Rick has been on the phone once

After the 1983 Formula Ford Festival at Brands Hatch, Adrian and Rick were celebrating Andrew Gilbert-Scott's victory. Penti Lauhtanen approached Adrian about buying a couple of cars, which Adrian said he would deal with the next day. Rick followed up the lead immediately and Penti took about 15 cars, and later became a Scandinavian agent. Jyrki Jarvilehto (better known as J.J. Lehto), Mika Hakkinen and Mika Salo were all to begin their careers racing Reynards in Scandinavian Championships.

After Reynard's first Indycar win with Michael Andretti in the opening round of the 1994 Championship at Surfers Paradise, Australia, Rick and Henri Riccitelli, an Indycar sponsor agent, recovered after a night of partying by swimming with some dolphins.

a month just touching base. When he found out that we were thinking of moving up to Formula 3000, he was on the phone proposing that we had lunch. He knew that we were almost certainly going to buy Reynards, but he also knows I like good food and wine.

'He opened the negotiations by offering Dom Perignon, and I countered with

Rick still maintains a close friendship with Reynard drivers Gil de Ferran and David Coulthard. They are pictured here at a charity event organised by Jackie Stewart at the Gleneagles Hotel in Scotland in November 1994.

Rick with David Coulthard, Gil de Ferran and ushers at Gil de Ferran's wedding to Angela Buckland in December 1993.

Bollinger. We probably spent more time discussing the restaurant than we did discussing the purchase of the car, but he makes you feel good about doing business with him.'

Rick says: 'I make it a rule to follow up every lead I get. When we first won the Formula Ford Festival we were celebrating with champagne in the team motor home. There was a knock on the door and a Scandinavian chap diffidently asked in broken English if he might buy a car or two. We were in party mood and Adrian politely said

Rick and 1996 Indycar Champion, Jimmy Vasser, celebrating in style after Jimmy's victory at Surfers Paradise in 1996.

Rick with Alessandro Zanardi, 1996 Indycar Rookie of the Year, at the Michigan 500. Rick was instrumental in securing the ex-Team Lotus Formula One star's Indycar drive in 1996 with Chip Ganassi Racing.

come back later or phone the office tomorrow, whereupon I leapt to my feet with a cry of "Hang on a minute!" and sat down with the guy in my car, and he gave us the deposits for two cars. He became one of our Scandinavian agents and took about 15 cars over the next two or three years. Many leads go nowhere, but if you follow every one you land the big deal. It was an incident from which Adrian and I both learned.'

While Adrian can point with pride to his designs and concepts, Rick's achievement is the growth of the company itself. When he joined Adrian in 1982 Reynard had a turnover of just £250,000 a year – by 1990 that had risen to £10 million (with more than 70 per cent of that in export orders) and Reynard was making more racing cars per year than any other manufacturer in history. Rick's proudest moment was the granting to Reynard that year of the Queen's Award for Export Achievement. He modestly dedicated the accolade to the whole of the British motor racing industry, but it was actually a personal triumph.

Any doubt about that is dispelled by looking at the motor racing industry in 1982 when Rick joined the company. Lola is still a major player, but what happened to March, Royale, Sark, Nike, Anson, CTG, Delta, Image, Pacer, Phantom, PRS, Quest, Aquila and Tiga? They were all serious contenders, and most had periods of success on the circuits, but none of them had the essential ingredient for long-term success which is a partnership between someone who knows how to make cars and someone who knows how to sell them and, moreover, can get the right people into the cars.

Selling 15 cars to an Arab air force is OK, it's keeping the workforce busy and it's cash in the bank. But it is also a cul-de-sac because nobody will give a toss if Flight Lieutenant X beats Squadron Leader Z round the perimeter track of a desert air strip. Make the deal, get your car with the right team and the right driver, and you need only sell the one at a special rate to be on Broadway, because soon you will have every serious contender forming a queue around the block. Actually, being racers, it won't be a queue, it will be a scrum, but all of them will be brandishing certified cheques.

In a nutshell, that is why Reynard alone of the many small firms who were around in 1982 has developed into a major force.

Chapter Eight

New Beginning

Early in 1983 we visited Sabre Automotive, and to call the atmosphere up-beat is to use understatement. Rick produced sheets showing sales and production forecasts for the next five years. It was something not encountered before in motor racing and his forecasts were uncannily accurate, which is remarkable given the nature of the business.

Rick had done his homework and could say that, on average, a racing car was involved in an accident once every eight starts, and that statistic was worked into his business plan, and the sale of spares became a large proportion of Reynard's turnover.

At the time, however, even the giants of production racing car makers (Lola and March, for example) had no coherent marketing or pricing strategy. March did not know how much cars cost to make, and the price was arrived at by some vague notion of what the market would stand, while Lola actually made a loss on its Formula Ford cars, but made them to take up the slack in the build season with the hope that it would make money on supplying spares later.

Adrian spoke of building a Formula Three car for 1984, in fact it appeared 12 months later. What was really surprising was his assertion that it would have a carbon-fibre monocoque, a world first for a production car maker. Carbon-fibre had only appeared in Formula One two years earlier and was still comparatively rare in Formula One in 1983.

Adrian also said that one day he would be in Formula One and, although it seemed a bit rich coming from a Formula Ford maker employing a handful of people (and it was then not even a particularly successful Formula Ford maker) he was believable. It actually defied rational thought. No Formula Ford maker had previously managed to even survive in Formula Three, but Adrian has the gift of making people believe in his dreams.

Just as Adrian had wooed Rick, so he began to woo Paul Owens whom he had decided would be the next vital component of the team because of his knowledge of composite materials.

Using their typical approach to a problem, Adrian and Rick pulled a stroke which any other maker could have done but didn't – they obtained a grant of £150,000 from the Department of Trade and Industry to research and develop carbon-composites. Part of their thinking was selling their expertise to other industries – at the time the word 'consultancy' was on the lips of every go-ahead constructor, but actually very little consultancy occurred. Building racing cars is seasonal and there are few consultancy contracts which can operate only during the relatively slack summer months.

Adrian takes up the story from the beginning of 1983: 'Having decided to concentrate on Formula Ford 2000, we updated the design and incorporated a more friendly back end with revised geometry, then we looked around for someone to run it. For some reason we struck lucky with Penistone Racing, which was a very good team run by Trevor Hegarty, with Tim Davies as the lead driver. Rick and I went to see them and persuaded them to use our car, which nobody in his right mind should have done given our recent results.

The all-new 83SF Formula Ford was shown to the world at the Racing Car Show in 1983. Adrian continued to share expenses with Spax Shock Absorbers, and they again combined stands to save money. In the background is Tim Davies's 83SF which dominated the season that year.

Adrian, Rick and Tim Davies at Brands Hatch in 1983 after one of Tim's many victories. The newly acquired leather jackets were standard Reynard team clothing for the two Directors.

Rick says: 'When you enter into a relationship, both parties have to want to do it, and I was phoning all the teams and potential customers. The only one who was showing any sympathy was Trevor Hegarty, so Adrian and I drove up to see him. Trevor believed in us, he believed he could make our car win, and a relationship grew.'

Adrian remembers the journey home: 'We were absolutely elated, we thought that we had cracked it at last – and, actually, we had. Come the first test session and Tim Davies was half a second under the lap record at Snetterton all the time – everything had come together, we had a good car, a good team and a very good driver.' Rick was back in Bicester getting excited phone calls from Adrian at the track every 30 minutes as the car went faster and faster.

When the season started, Tim Davies and his team-mate, Kenny Andrews, were right on the pace. Tim won his first race in his Reynard 83SF.

Penistone Racing was not the only customer. Other Reynard users included Mike Taylor, who would in 1988 take over production of Reynard Formula Ford cars; Julian Bailey, who would drive in F1 for Tyrrell; and Russell Spence, who would be a Reynard driver for most of his career. While Davies won 12 races and set pole position 13 times, this trio tended to fill the high points positions.

All was not entirely smooth, however, and the chassis life of the 83SF was short. Some teams were forced to replace the frame in mid-season, and were not too happy about it, but the problem was rectified for 1984 by strengthening the central section. The 83SF was not an unflawed car, and its chassis set-up was probably more critical than the Van Diemen, which was its main rival. This was not a major problem for a team as well-run as Penistone, or for a driver as talented as Davies, but it gave problems to less professional teams. Meanwhile, Mauricio Gugelmin in the works Van Diemen worked away at his car and made it extremely competitive.

Adrian says: 'Ralph Firman at Van Diemen did not take the challenge lying down, and he developed his cars so they were very close to ours by the end of the season. Ralph is a man I have a great deal of respect for because he produces competitive cars, year in, year out, and I know how difficult that is. Our approaches, however, are very different: I try to make advances by leaps in technology, while Ralph gets there through hard work and determination, and he has a great record of success. Ultimately, however, we're different men with different aims and objectives.'

Ralph Firman broadly agrees with that assessment. 'Adrian has taken a lot of risks, and they've paid off. You can't help but admire him for it.'

Adrian continues: 'Van Diemen was hot on our heels towards the end of the season, and since I was desperate to win the championship I went back to the rule book and discovered that the weight of the car was deemed to be its weight at the end of a race – it said nothing about the weight of a car during practice. So I built Tim Davies a car which was 70 lb underweight, a huge amount in Formula Ford 2000. He would practice underweight and would usually take pole position by about a second. That demoralised the opposition, and then we would ballast the car for the race. The rest of the field expected Tim to wipe the floor with them and so, provided he made a good start, he had the race in the bag before it began.

'Everyone suspected that something was going on, but nobody could quite work out what the story was. Howard Mason, the scrutineer, went into overdrive and he took our car apart several times, but he could find nothing wrong with it. He accused us of all sorts of tricks, and that way he gave us a lot of ideas, but it was simply the fact that we practised light and raced on the weight limit. Tim won the Championship, with Julian Bailey second in another Reynard.

'Before mid-season things were going sufficiently well to consider building a Formula

Tim Davies celebrating another race victory at Silverstone in 1983.

Ford 1600 car which is when I came into contact with Robert Synge. Robert had not long before established Madgwick Motorsport and was running a young Brazilian, Maurizio Sandro Sala, who was leading the Formula Ford 1600 Esso Championship in a Van Diemen.

'I still don't know why Robert wanted to change to a Reynard, especially since he was

Tim Davies and Kenny Andrews on the front row of the grid at Snetterton. Adrian discovered a loophole in the regulations, effectively allowing the cars to be run underweight in practice. Ballast was then added for the race. Mauricio Gugelmin is on the second row in a Van Diemen, and Gary Evans lines up alongside him.

Maurizio Sandro Sala was leading the 1983 Formula Ford 1600 Championship in a Madgwick-run Van Diemen. Having driven the Reynard, he changed chassis mid-season and went on to win the Championship. Sala couldn't believe how good the car was.

leading the series, but I guess it was because he had faith in us. It has often happened in our story: Jeremy Rossiter had faith, Rick had faith, Trevor Hegarty had faith, Robert had faith, and each time it really was faith because there was no tangible evidence to back us.'

Robert Synge confirms Adrian's theory: 'I knew that he could do it, I just knew it. The 1983 Van Diemen was not one of Ralph's better cars, and for once he did not seem willing to do much about it. In fact, Maurizio was the only Van Diemen driver who was leading a championship, the season was all about Lola and Royale. If Maurizio was going to win it, he had to change his car and I had more or less committed myself to buying a Lola when I went to see Adrian and he told me to wait a few more weeks. He promised that he would deliver the best car in the field.

'Those around me thought I was mad to take the chance. Lola was winning all the races, but I was getting free cars from Van Diemen and nobody has ever given up free Van Diemens. Maurizio was not convinced by the theory. He thought that he could have been winning in a Lola instead of waiting for a Reynard, but he turned around when he drove the 83FF in a test at Donington in July where Adrian engineered it.

'The Formula Ford 1600 lap record at Donington had stood for five years. It was one of those freak times that you sometimes get, and Maurizio hadn't got near it with the Van Diemen. But it was not long into the session before he was lapping a full second under the record.

'We were flabbergasted, but suspicious. In fact, Maurizio was so quick that we thought that Adrian had palmed us off with a bent car, a seriously bent car. We persuaded him to let us take it back to our workshop – he was not happy about it, but we insisted – and there we went over it with a fine-tooth comb. We had it weighed, had the fuel analysed and dismantled the gearbox to make sure it wasn't running with a limited slip differential. We went though it from top to bottom and found that it was completely kosher.

'We bought it. Adrian made a special deal and even supplied some sponsorship – Maurizio ran with Sabre Fabrications on the car. We raced it a few days later – Maurizio won the race, kept on winning and took the title.'

Rick remembers: 'Although a number of Formula Ford 1600 cars were sold abroad, and although Sandro Sala was winning races with the Madgwick car, we didn't make any more progress in Britain for what seemed a long time.' In fact, the Esso Championship was only one of many Formula Ford championships, and other cars were winning the races from which Sandro Sala was absent.

'Then, in the September, British Racing Prospects bought a car for Andy Wallace and he won races with it. In fact, he finished second to Sandro Sala in the Esso series and third in the RAC British Championship. Meanwhile, Wally Warwick was leading the Donington Championship and we were winning races overseas.

'The momentum was starting to grow, the Formula Ford Festival was approaching and while Wallace and Sandro Sala were clearly fancied, the guy doing most of the winning was Andrew Gilbert-Scott in a Lola.

'We built up a car and gave it to Andrew for nothing, just to see if he would drive it. He tested it, liked it and we did a deal to run it for him at the Festival. The rest is history, Gilbert-Scott won with Andy Wallace second. At one point Maurizio Sandro Sala was in third slot until he had a big accident with Ross Cheever.

'At the 1982 Festival we had entered a three-car team and it had been a disaster, probably our lowest point. One year on and we were on top of the world with a 1–2 in the Festival, and had it not been for Ross Cheever, who has since done great stuff for us in Japan, it might have been 1–2–3.'

By the end of 1983, 91 Reynards had been built, and in addition there was a batch of 40 kits for Ford of France – there had been just six cars in 1981 and the 45 of 1982 included the batch to the Middle East. The 1983 cars had delivered the goods as well. The Formula Ford 2000 car won a total of nine championships in Britain, Canada, Germany and Holland, and took the Benelux Championship, the European and the European Golden Lion series.

Even though the Formula Ford 1600 car arrived late in the season it clinched eight championships in Britain and North America and won both the British and Irish Formula Ford Festivals. It was a remarkable turnaround, and while it was great for Reynard, it hastened the end of some of its rivals such as Royale, and in essence the Ford Formulae settled down to a period of Reynard versus Van Diemen, with other outfits being bit-part players.

The company's new-found success allowed Adrian to buy a Volkswagen Golf GTi, the first new car he had ever owned. It was not the only departure in his life: his old girl friend, Gill, had left British Air Ferries and was running a flying school. Adrian had become interested in flying and he was to develop into an exceptionally competent pilot. He recognised that he had many common interests with what he describes as this 'bright and vivacious young lady' who also understood his career ambitions and drive. Later she became pregnant and Mr and Mrs Reynard now have four children.

The first big contract Reynard landed after Rick arrived on board came about when Ford decided to introduce Formula Ford to France in 1984. Rick says: 'Stuart Turner, then head of Ford Motorsport, spoke to the main Formula Ford constructors and chose us. It was a competition and we won. It was actually quite a complicated deal because

Andrew Gilbert-Scott and Andy Wallace drove Reynards in the Formula Ford Festival in 1983. Gilbert-Scott won the race and is pictured ahead of Maurizio Sandro Sala, Ross Cheever (subsequently a Reynard driver and winner in Japanese Formula 3000) and Andy Wallace.

initially the idea was to launch a one-make (Reynard) series, but Ford France wanted French involvement and nominated Rondeau, who had previously only made monocoque sports cars.

'The project therefore became a simultaneous operation, with Rondeau providing the bodywork and Reynard providing kits for the rolling chassis. We built about 40 chassis for 1984, and the cars were called 'Rondeau', not Reynard. The tragic death of Jean Rondeau in a road accident eventually caused the company's demise, but for the next two years Rondeau built complete cars based on our design. They also developed the chassis and I have to say that their aerodynamic package was probably better than ours.'

Talking about the French Connection 10 years later, Rick sounds a little blasé but, at the time, it was a big deal. Reynard had beaten off the opposition to secure the backing of Ford, and Ford is not a company which lightly lends its name and reputation.

Since it was to be a one-make formula, it did not actually matter how competent the cars were in terms of ultimate performance. The Reynards were actually the best Formula Ford cars around, but that does not necessarily matter in a one-make series. The important thing about the Rondeau deal was that Reynard was perceived to be a serious manufacturer which was capable of supplying kits to a consistent standard in quantity, and which was capable of providing proper back-up to service the deal.

For Ford to attempt to introduce a racing category to France was, in itself, a big step given the traditional dominance of Renault and also historical considerations broader than mere motor racing. Reynard received a valuable seal of approval because Uncle Henry was playing hard ball. Had the contract gone to, say, Royale or Van Diemen, the history of motor racing might have been slightly different.

As 1984 approached, the order books filled up, and 128 cars would be sold. The Formula Three project was still firmly in the frame and Paul Owens was still being wooed. In fact, Paul came on board unofficially early in 1984 but, since he had an outstanding legal case against a former employer, his appointment could not be announced until later in the year. With Paul on board the elements were in place for Reynard to move up a notch.

One of the less expected Reynard designs was the chassis for a Cobra 'replica'. Adrian recalls: 'A chap called Adrian Cocking came to us in 1984 and said that he wanted to build a Cobra replica and he wanted us to do the chassis. Adrian did not present himself well, he was a Cockney and rather scruffy, and I had to convince myself that I wasn't wasting my time in talking to him. He had good ideas, though, and what he wanted was a stiff space-frame to carry a big American V8 or a Jaguar V12 as far rearward as possible. It had to have as high a torsional stiffness as possible and to take Jaguar running gear. We did a deal, and Dave Rendall and I designed and built the chassis. Adrian came and took it away and that was the last we heard of it for a while.

'One day Adrian came back asking to buy more chassis with some slight modifications, and we started producing them. Eventually we contracted out the work and took a royalty, although had I known that there would be hundreds of them made perhaps I would have kept the job. Later it was used for a Jaguar D-type replica and Adrian is still making them, under the name RAM, although many kit cars makers have folded. He loaned me one of his Cobras for a time and it was wonderful, a very good product.'

The rapid expansion which Reynard Racing Cars experienced over a period of little more than 12 months meant that Adrian began to spread his talents more thinly (again) and he realised that to be successful he had to create an infrastructure of management and craftsmen-foremen. He says: 'Rick was very useful. We had different styles but he was a very good communicator and we were able to slice up the workload and share the job. His job description had basically been "I'll make 'em, you sell 'em", but he was soon engaged in production planning and product buying as well as selling. We worked as a team with no clear demarcation. It was a bit like doubles tennis where you each have one side of the court all of the time, but you cover the whole court some of the time. Our other key people, such as Paul Owens, have operated in a similar way.

'We ran with one layer of management and one layer of workforce with no problems. The problems arose when we tried an intermediate layer, and it was a long time before I was able to establish a level of competent lieutenants who are, in essence, on the same level as the directors. We try to operate in an atmosphere of free information exchange with a degree of overlap – nobody is confined to a single niche.'

By 1984 the workforce had risen to nearly 30, and joining Reynard on a sandwich course from Bristol Polytechnic was John Thompson. He was not quite on the same terms as current trainees, but he may be accounted the first of Reynard's trainees. Adrian says: 'Until the end of 1983 I did all the drawing myself, but I then took on a school-leaver, a 16-year old called David Hutting, and I brought in Peter Morgan, who is now Production Director, to do sub-contract design work on the Formula Ford 2000 car.

'It was not easy to bring in outsiders because designing is a very personal thing. No matter how close you are to the person you bring in, it's handing over an intimate part of your life. I had been a one-man band who had an instinctive feel for what the market wanted. I knew what it cost to buy parts, how much it cost to make things in-house, how easy it was to make and assemble them, and at the end of the day I knew how much profit I would make.

'I had become what is now called a "simultaneous engineer", although I don't think the term had then been coined. At the time I tended to call myself a "performance engineer".

'The design staff started to grow during 1984 as we began work on the Formula

Adrian with John Thompson, the first Reynard student and now Drawing Office Manager, at the wind tunnel at Southampton University working on a very early Formula Three rolling road model in 1987.

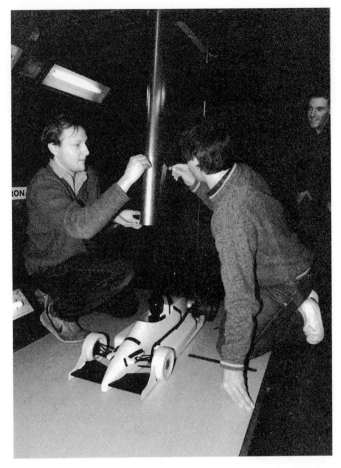

Three car. Then I started to find that when I brought in someone from outside he would do a professional job, as he had done for other people, but we could finish up making something which was too heavy, perhaps, or too complicated, too expensive or too tricky to make. We were beginning to lose the very spirit which had made us successful in the first place.

'We went through a period of unsuccessful design. In 1985 the Formula Three car did not work quite as well as it should have done and the Ford Formula cars were a disaster. I'd brought in people with good reputations, some had more experience than I had. I gave them design briefs and let them get on with it – which is what I would have expected in their place. The experience taught me how not to do things and, in turn, that led me to form the idea that, instead of bringing in people from outside, I should spend time with bright young designers at the beginning of their careers.

'That led to our trainee scheme and what I call the Reynard philosophy. I wanted to train bright engineers in a particular culture. I didn't want clones, I wanted people trained in a way of thinking so they could express themselves without close supervision in a way which was in harmony with everyone else. For that I was prepared to exchange short-term gains for long-term gains because I realised that our chief asset would be our people.

'That was my aim, but what I didn't realise when I started down this route was that the company would evolve its own culture which complemented my thoughts. It was influenced by Rick on the marketing side, Paul Owens on the composites side and by other people from all the facets of our business. The culture grew because the people I recruited were absolutely right for absorbing good ideas and information.'

It is not an idle boast. If you speak to team managers who buy Reynards, they will tell you much the same. When Malcolm Oastler moved on from heading the Formula 3000 project and handed over to John Thompson, the transition was seamless because they operated from the same perspective. It is noticeable that the key people at Reynard voluntarily offer the same opinion.

In both Formula Ford 1600 and Formula Ford 2000 during 1994 Reynards were usually the cars to beat. In Formula Ford 2000 Penistone Racing had Julian Bailey and Gary Brabham, with sponsorship from BP, while Madgwick Motorsport moved up from Formula Ford 1600 with Maurizio Sandro Sala and also ran what was effectively the works Reynard Formula Ford 1600 team, again with backing from BP.

Van Diemen had become Reynard's main rival as Royale and Lola fell out of favour. In the case of Lola it was unfair, as its victory in the Formula Ford Festival later showed, but it was making a car with a front radiator when it became the received opinion that only cars with side-radiators could win races.

Reynards were competitive, but on the whole Van Diemen had an edge in Formula Ford 1600 regardless of which engine was used. John Pratt in a Madgwick-run Reynard was a strong second to Dave Coyne's works Van Diemen in the major championships and it is impossible to know where the slight advantage lay: in the team, the engine, the chassis or the driver.

It was a different matter in Formula Ford 2000 where most of the leading runners used Reynard chassis. Madgwick Motorsport caused a sensation by starting its Formula Ford 2000 cars on preheated tyres, which then were not even used in Formula One. Madgwick built a simple insulated cabinet on a pit trolley, the tyres and wheels were loaded in and were heated by hot air from an oil-fired workshop heater feeding through a length of flexible metal tubing. It was not an original idea – Mike Earle had used it when running David Purley in the 1976 Shellsport Group 8 Championship, but oddly enough nobody else had picked it up.

Preheated tyres gave Sandro Sala a decided edge on the first lap, provided he made a good start, and the first time it was used Maurizio finished lap one with a 300 yard advantage. It also demoralised the opposition, although the oven was so simple and inexpensive that any team could have made one. Instead, there were cries of 'foul!', and eventually the device was banned, but not before it had helped to send Sandro Sala on his way to winning the British Formula Ford 2000 Championship.

Later in the season Madgwick introduced some new ground-effect side-pods which gave an enormous amount of grip and were useful at tight circuits such as Cadwell Park, although they induced too much drag for a circuit like Silverstone. For the 'speed circuits' Madgwick dispensed with the side-pods and used low-downforce wings which were developed in conjunction with the works.

Sandro Sala won the British Championship from Julian Bailey, Mauricio Gugelmin (who switched from Van Diemen to Reynard) and Andy Wallace. Gugelmin took the European series at the last race and Reynard racked up even more championships than in 1983. Through Sabre Fabrications, Reynard sponsored a championship for pre-1980 Formula Ford 2000 cars – and it was dominated by Lola. You can't win them all.

In all, Reynard won 30 championships (see Appendix 1). Two years previously it had barely made 30 cars. The turnaround was remarkable. Perhaps it was the air of excitement which was building around Reynard which led to a slightly unusual deal.

'In my days at the BARC,' recalls Rick, 'I got to know John Webb very well indeed.

Julian Bailey and Gary Brabham in 1984, driving Reynards for Penistone Racing in Formula Ford 2000.

John then ran Brands Hatch and he was responsible for many new ideas in motor racing, including all the Ford Formulae. Not all his ideas took off, but he was a major innovator who changed the structure of motor racing. When I teamed up with Adrian I took him along to meet John and, although he normally dealt with Van Diemen when he had ideas for one-make formulae, he seemed to like us. In 1984 he approached us with a new idea, Formula Turbo Ford. Turbocharging was then all the rage. He wanted to introduce turbos at a grassroots level and asked if we were interested?

'Of course, we were. We took a Formula Ford 2000 chassis and fitted it with bigger wheels, tyres and radiators and plumbed in a 2-litre Ford turbo engine. It was launched to the Press during the official test days for the 1984 British Grand Prix, and Motor Circuit Developments paid for a test programme. Although initially there was quite severe turbo-lag, in the end we got it working pretty well. The only trouble was that the engine did not give the power it was supposed to give, and it was slower than a regular Formula Ford 2000 car. Formula Turbo Ford did not get beyond the prototype car.'

For the journalists who attended the launch, however, there was a clear message: Reynard was a company which mattered. It is of no moment that Formula Turbo Ford failed. The important thing is that Reynard had moved up to stand shoulder to shoulder with Van Diemen, and in itself that was an achievement as plenty had tried and all had failed. It was a company on the way up and it was no secret that Formula Three was the next step.

In retrospect it seems almost obvious that Reynard would establish itself in Formula Three, but historical precedent says otherwise. There were many in motor racing who thought that Reynard had bitten off more than it could possibly chew, but Adrian and Rick had done their homework well. They had selected Paul Owens to strengthen their team and he was to play a major part in the story. It has not always been an easy relationship. Paul is a blunt man and is aware of his value, but the relationship has worked.

Paul Owens

R egarded by many people as the most able and ingenious engineer working in carbon-composites today, Paul Owens joined Reynard in 1984 to work on the Formula Three project. He brought to the company more than 20 years experience in race car design and production and a considerable reputation as a race engineer. Few, if any, have worked with more top-line drivers. Paul is now a member of the board and is Managing Director of Reynard Composites which is located at Brackley, about 10 miles from the main works at Bicester.

'I was born in Salford, Greater Manchester, in 1941. My parents were ordinary

Paul Owens in the Reynard museum.

working class people and I went to a Secondary Modern school where I was much better at practical activities, such as metalwork, than the academic subjects.

'One of our neighbours was keen on motor racing, and he would take me to meetings, and that got me hooked. I was also interested in motorbikes, and when I was 14 I got involved with speedway – the Belle Vue stadium in Manchester was one of the top speedway tracks in the world and it was a major sport in Britain at the time.

'I worked on my own 'bike with a friend and we would push it 20 miles to test it at Belle Vue. It used to take us about five hours to get there, partly because when two kids push a speedway 'bike through a city, they tend to waste time being stopped and questioned by the police.

'It was almost inevitable that when I left school, aged 15, I was drawn to engineering, and I took up an apprenticeship with the Salford Corporation bus company. While buses are a long way removed from racing cars, I received a very good grounding in all aspects of engineering. Salford expected its buses to cover over half a million miles, so every so often they were taken apart and everything was overhauled, which meant we apprentices got experience of everything from electrics to coach building via brake systems and engine and transmission overhauls.

'There was also a development programme going on. They even had a drawing office, and we had to be familiar with the drawings. Then there was day-release to a local technical college and evening classes twice a week. It was a very thorough training and I passed out with my City & Guilds certificate.

'It was through speedway that I met Derek Bennett, who was then a rising star in midget car racing. Midgets were basically four-wheeled speedway 'bikes and were fitted with the same engine – the 500cc JAP. We struck up a friendship and he became like an older brother to me. My speedway riding, which had never amounted to much, fell by the wayside because, after a day's work at the bus depot, I would help Derek at his garage. There was a fairly relaxed atmosphere in the depot, which meant that I could machine things for him.

'Derek and I conceived and built the first independent rear suspension for midget cars, which was very successful, and we made a bit of a local reputation. In 1957 there was fuel rationing because of the Suez crisis and we decided that it would be a good idea to make a bubble car which then were all the rage. We started on a three-wheeler with a motorcycle engine, but it came to a stop when we needed to lay out some money for the body moulds – we simply had none, everything we earned went into racing.

'Derek then built an Austin Seven special, which had a lot of innovations – I learned a lot about rebuilding engines as a result of them. A 750 special was not the most sensible thing since we had to traipse across the country to race, and with the roads and transport we had it took forever. Derek then decided to do a Ford 1172cc special, and we even cast and machined our own pistons. We got good performance from it, but since we were still using the Austin Seven chassis it was not really competitive.

'Despite that, I bought it from Derek and did five races with it, getting a couple of second and thirds but, being an apprentice, I couldn't afford to do any more.

'By that time – we're talking about 1960 – Formula Junior had arrived and we built a front-engined Bennett Special. We built a good engine, but the handling wasn't great, so the next cars Derek raced were all bought from outside.

'The first car I built by myself was a stock car for a customer. It was the first stock car with a space-frame and it was so successful that it changed the way stock cars were made.

'I finished my apprenticeship in 1962, when I was 21, got married, and carried on working on buses during the day and with Derek in the evenings. The full story of those days is told in David Gordon's book, *Chevron: The Derek Bennett Story*, which is also the story of my life until 1978. Derek raced in Formula Three, abroad as well as in Britain, and I'd go with him. It was the days when people like Frank Williams were racing and wheeling and dealing. Everyone has his unbelievable stories from those times and the good thing is that they're all true.

'Derek had enormous success driving Lotus Elites, and this led us to build a car for a customer, Derek Alderson, based on the Rochdale Olympic, a kit car with a fibreglass monocoque. We bonded a space-frame inside the monocoque and fitted a Cosworth engine and independent suspension from an Elva sports racer. Then we took it to Oulton Park to test, and after the two Dereks had tried it and decided it needed a great deal more sorting, I was asked if I'd like to have a go. It was a sort of reward for all the work I'd done on it.

'The car was dreadful, and after two laps I decided that if this was motor racing it was definitely not for me. While I was coming to terms with that, the car snapped away from me, touched the grass and rolled. I was thrown out and I bounced along the grass with the car bouncing along behind me. Then it hit a steel hawser supporting a telegraph pole which sliced it in two. Had I still been in it, I would have been sliced in half as well.

'After that, Derek Alderson decided that he would race a Lotus Elite instead, and he paid for me to work alongside Derek Bennett. We prepared Lotus Elites for them both, but eventually Derek B decided that racing at that level was too expensive, and for 1965 he would build a Clubmans' car. In his usual way he worked it out in his head and then took a welding torch to a pile of tubes. The arrangement with Alderson had ended and I was working for a gearbox company, which meant there were opportunities for machining and other odd jobs, while in the evenings I helped Derek with his cars.

'We built two Clubmans' cars, the other went to Brian Classick. Since we had built two we figured we were now in production and there should be a proper name for them. "Bennett Special" was not good enough for production cars. One day Derek was waiting to be served in a shop and on the wall was a poster showing symbols from the Highway Code and the word "Chevron" leapt out at him. So, in 1965, the first Chevrons were made.

'The Chevron B1 was a great success and other people soon wanted to buy replicas. In the time-honoured way we had become constructors, just as Adrian did 10 years later. We were offered space in an old mill in Bolton, which we shared with a friend of ours who dealt in cars. I took a chance and gave up my job to work full-time for the Derek Bennett Engineering Company and Derek made me the gift of a five per-cent share holding.

'I was on a very low salary, barely enough to survive, and I was working very long hours. This put a strain on my marriage and it finally led to divorce, but I retained custody of my son, Paul, who is now well-known as a writer of computer game programs. The responsibility of bringing up a child meant that I shelved thoughts of racing, while Derek had also decided to concentrate on building cars.'

Paul's contribution to the success of Chevron was considerable, both in the factory and at the race track. The company gained an enviable reputation for the integrity of its designs, and people liked dealing with the unpretentious firm operating from the old mill. Paul Brown, now a designer with Reynard, recalls that when he joined Chevron as a fabricator it was two weeks before he realised that the unassuming man who brought him the drawings was actually the boss.

Mike Earle who, in 1974, was running Marches in Formula Two recalls: 'March totally lost their way in 1974 so far as customers were concerned. You'd phone the works and give your name and be met with something like, "Ah yes, you're customer No. 36, I see you've bought three cars from us, but you've been complaining." If you phoned up Chevron you'd usually be put through straight to Derek Bennett who would say in his broad Lancashire accent, "You want to buy a car, lad? Come up Saturday and we'll make you a pot of tea while we knit one up for you." They were lovely, lovely people to deal with.'

Chevrons won 32 national and international championships, including European titles for Formula Three, Formula 5000 and 2-litre sports cars. In 1973 Peter Gethin won the Race of Champions at Brands Hatch in a Chevron F5000 car, beating works Formula One cars from Lotus, Brabham, McLaren and BRM. They won in Formula Two and Formula Atlantic and today they dominate the 2-litre GT and sports car classes in Historic racing.

Derek took up hang-gliding, and while participating in a competition in March 1978 his glider stalled and he hit the ground head first. At first it seemed he was only concussed, but he slipped into a coma and died 11 days later.

Paul says: 'I was devastated; we had shared so much of our lives. I realised, however, that I had to try to save the company. Because we were based in Bolton, a long way from where the motor racing magazines were based, we did not get much Press coverage. That normally did not bother us, but it did mean that it was easy to assume that Chevron was a one-man band which would collapse without Derek.

'In fact 1978 turned out to be our best year in Formula Two. Derek Daly and Keke Rosberg won races for us, and the future was looking good. Then people started to say that, OK, the '78 car was good, but that had been Derek's car and where was the 1979 car coming from? That was the real problem we had with our Press – people did not realise that Chevron design had been a joint effort involving Derek, Paul Brown, two draughtsmen and myself.

'You can say that it was our fault because we had not been massaging the media machine, and were all happy for Derek Bennett to get the lion's share of the credit. That's the way we operated.

'Since our customers were not entirely convinced that Chevron was still a going concern, I brought in Tony Southgate, who was then the Arrows Formula One designer, to put a well-known name behind our '79 car. Ground-effect had just arrived and Tony had lots of wind tunnel experience. He basically took the '78 car and added ground-effect bodywork because we could not afford a major investment. The result was that we fell between two stools because the '78 monocoque was not narrow enough to use ground-effect efficiently.

'We sold cars, but not as many as we needed to if we were to survive. In 1979 I ran Bobby Rahal in Formula Two on a budget of just $5,000, so it is hardly surprising that we did not win races, although Bobby did exceptionally well in the circumstances.

'In Formula Three the March 793 had started to go well so it took the lion's share of that market. Then the bank demanded collateral if it was to finance future projects. We might have survived, but Derek's sisters, who had inherited most of the shares, were not willing to put up their houses. I would have staked my house, but only for a larger share in the company and that did not happen. We had investors willing to come in, but Derek's sisters seemed to think that Chevron was a gold mine which would keep them in comfort for life and they would not sell their shares. So Chevron folded at the end of 1979, although later the assets were bought by a syndicate, and an unsuccessful attempt was made to keep the name alive.

'I was devastated; I felt that I had lost a large part of my life. Then Eje Elgh – Double-Egg to everyone in British motor racing – who had been one of my protégés, was running in Formula Two with the German Maurer team which had some problems. Eje suggested to Willi Maurer that they should contact me, and so I went to Hockenheim to see if I could sort out the car. I made some improvements and was asked to stay on as race engineer. Paul Brown was also working with Maurer, and between us we made it a competitive car. Maurer wanted me to stay on for 1981 and I said that I would but only if Paul and I could design and build the car in England.

'Eventually Maurer accepted my proposal, and I set up a facility in the old Chevron works, employing some ex-Chevron personnel. The car was made remarkably quickly. Gustav Brunner schemed the outline, and got all the credit, but Paul Brown and I did the detail work and we built it.

'When we turned up for testing at Paul Ricard we astounded the Formula One teams. We had carbon-fibre body panels and underfloors, with the area round the gearbox swept in and streamlined. It was above the quality of most Formula One cars. I had become interested in carbon-fibre, but when I had shown schemes of mine to friends in the aerospace industry they had said what I proposed was a three-year project, whereas I had three months in which to do it; so I found my own way of doing things.

'We had another good year in 1981, but there was mounting pressure from the German side to make the cars in Germany. Willi Maurer, however, let us build the '82 Formula Two car in England. I was Managing Director of Maurer (UK) and equal partner with Willi, but when it came to building cars for 1982 the budget suddenly shrunk and so I had to look for other means of making up the revenue.

'We decided to offer cars for sale, and sold 10 which were built with a workforce of 12 people. Can you imagine that? They won the first two races of the 1982 season, but having tasted success the German side decided to make improvements, and Maurer progressed backwards. It was a classic case of a team not knowing how to build on a win, and it led to a rift.

'After a very good season we looked forward to '83, but the budget shrunk again. Willi took the view that paying the wage bill in Bolton was my worry and I should look for other ways to generate revenue. I said that we'd look at other categories, but there would have to be more investment. Willi was not prepared to do that and, since I did not have complete control over the company, I was not prepared to put my house on the line. The situation became unworkable.

'Paul Brown and I formed a company called Prototype and Composites – we built the world's first composite motorcycle frame – but we were becoming increasingly worried about the supply of money from Germany. Before the overall company went bankrupt I decided to pull out, Willi took his half of the assets to Germany and folded two months later – basically his people were not up to it.

'Meanwhile Gustav Brunner was in charge of design at the ATS Formula One team, another German outfit based in Britain, and Gustav and I are old friends. He'd suffered a broken leg which meant he could not engineer cars at the trackside, so he asked me to go and meet the ATS people at Brands Hatch and I was taken on to engineer for ATS for the South African GP. It was my first time in Formula One, and I was bombarded with good advice, but I ignored it and just drew on my experience, and that worked. Manfred Winklehock qualified in sixth place, the highest he'd ever qualified, and I was asked to join ATS.

'Adrian was talking to me about composites and about joining him, but I was fired up with my new job in Formula One. Then I found that Formula One was not all it was cracked up to be – for one thing the wages weren't being paid. It was a detail and perhaps it is fussy of me to mention it. Come the winter test sessions in Brazil, the team owner, Gunther Schmidt, fell out with Gustav who went and joined Ferrari. That left me in charge of the factory with no designer, one draughtsman and a half-finished Formula One car.

'I wasn't going to be defeated, so we came up with a car using the '83 chassis with a new rear end, different side-pods, wings and underfloor, which was basically my work. Then I was told that I had to use some wings which had been designed in Germany, and they were appalling – they were so big that they hit the engine cover. We went to test in South Africa, and the car was terrible. Finally the rear wing did the noble thing and fell off, and the only spare wings we had were some I'd made. We put one on and immediately knocked 1.5 seconds off our lap times and gained 10 mph on the straight.

'We finished the week second quickest – and all the teams were there. We were one tenth off Nelson Piquet's time in a Brabham with works BMW engines (we had customer units). We were ahead of Williams, McLaren, Ferrari and Lotus, but Herr Schmidt was not happy. He thought we should have been quickest – and it was all my fault. I should not have used the wings I'd made, I should have used the wings he'd had made.

'Schmidt demanded wind tunnel proof of the superiority of my wings, so I tried to book the car into MIRA. It was fully booked, but Adrian allowed me to take one of his sessions and he came along to give help and advice. We had a good test, but to do it I had to spend 48 hours to put a second car together – our one complete car was still in South Africa. After leaving MIRA at six o'clock on a Friday morning, I decided I'd like to go home: I hadn't seen my family for three weeks, I'd had virtually no sleep for a week, and I had just got into bed when the phone rang – Herr Schmidt wished to know why I was not in Bicester. I was fired.

'Come the following Monday I received another call from Herr Schmidt – why was I not in the office? I told him it was because he had fired me. Soon afterwards I joined

Paul with Malcolm Oastler and Rick Gorne at an Indycar race at Rio de Janiero, Brazil in 1996.

Adrian and have been here ever since.' Paul does more than head Reynard Composites, he has an input into the design of cars and transmissions, he has created many of the group's production techniques and he is often called upon to act as a trouble-shooter.

For a time he gave up race engineering to give more time to his family who had been moved from Bolton. At the start of the 1989 Formula 3000 series, however, Lamberto Leoni's Marches failed to qualify and Leoni decided to switch to Reynards provided that Paul would engineer his cars – and so he came out of retirement.

Reynard built a car in two weeks and at the next race Leoni's driver, Apicella, put it on pole. 'We had a good year, and that meant I was well and truly out of retirement. I've been engineering cars ever since in both Europe and Japan. My drivers have always finished in the top three in the European Championship and we won the title in 1991 with Christian Fittipaldi.

'On top of that I have been running this factory which is operated as a separate profit centre within the group. This means that while we supply Reynard Racing Cars, we have to compete for the business. We have also supplied many other racing teams with components, we built the chassis for Vern Schuppen's Porsche-based GT car, I worked with Paul Brown on the Pacific Formula One car, which was built here, and we built the Chrysler Patriot.'

Paul is one of those people whose sheer enthusiasm keeps the years at bay. His zest for life belies his birth certificate and you can understand why he is able to fit in so easily with youngsters like Adrian and Rick. It also helps that he is probably the best in the world at what he does.

This is the first motorcycle that Adrian bought from George Brown in 1969. The side-car Adrian is making is the first actual motorsport chassis that he ever built in his parents' garage. Adrian's first lathe can be seen in the top left-hand side of the picture.

Colourful moments in Reynard's history

Reynard's most recent project, however, is a far cry from the motorbike and side-car. The Panoz was designed and built by Reynard Special Vehicle Projects for the 1997 24 hours Le Mans Sportscar race. Pictured are the prototype road car and RSVP staff.

Briton Mark Blundell is one of many European drivers making their mark in Indycar racing. Mark also drove for Reynard in Formula Ford 2000 and Formula 3000 in the 1980s.

In 1995 Adrian Reynard married Gill Harris on Richard Branson's Necker Island in the Caribbean. Their four children – Stephanie, Max, Sam, and Daniella – joined in the ceremony. Richard Branson, a close family friend, gave away the bride.

A Haymarket publication   6 February 1975 18p

ARCTIC RALLY - SCHECKTER - DAYTONA - ALFASUD Ti

AUTOSPORT

Full review of the 1974 club racing season

Early recognition. As pictured on the front cover of *Autosport*, unknown driver Adrian Reynard leads the Formula Ford 1600 Championship field at Silverstone.

Adrian working on the very first Formula Ford 2000 engine installation at the lock-up garage in St John Street, Bicester, in July 1974. This car was sold to Jeremy Rossiter and displayed at the Racing Car Show in 1975.

Adrian at the 1970 Basingbourne Sprint with Frank and Amy Reynard. He is preparing for the World Record attempts with a 250 cc Royal Enfield motorcycle bought from George Brown.

Adrian with his mother, Daphne, and father, Gordon, alongside his future wife Gill at Snetterton in 1978. He was sponsored by RaceParts UK, who still supply parts to Reynard Racing Cars.

Adrian and Jeremy Rossiter competing in a Formula Ford 2000 race in 1975.

Left At Mallory Park in 1978 Adrian and Rick had their well-documented clash as Adrian tried to pass Rick, outbraking himself in frustration and hitting Rick in the rear. Rick spun and jettisoned Adrian into a parked car. Rick subsequently re-started and continued to finish the race, shaking his fist at Adrian throughout the remaining laps.

Below left The Formula Ford Race of Champions meeting was one of the first major races in which Adrian competed.

Right Adrian's first Formula Three design was debuted in 1976 using a delta rear wing. The car is parked in front of Mike Keegan's Dove at Southend airport, as Rupert Keegan and Adrian pose for the media.

Below Adrian and Rick shared an office – and a desk – for a decade. The current factory was built in 1986, and this picture was taken in 1994 before further extensions were made. This area is now the Drawing Office.

The first Reynard transporter was a Minivan that Adrian renovated with his friend Roddy Smith, who taught him a lot of his early mechanical skills. The picture is taken outside Adrian's parents' house in Knebworth in 1970 after a trip to Elvington in Yorkshire where he broke the World Land Speed records. During these attempts Adrian's sister, Susan, worked as his mechanic.

Adrian and Rick spent a great deal of time together away from the Reynard office. Here they are at a dinner dance in late 1983.

Both Rick and Adrian attend as many races as their schedules allow. Here they are pictured at an Indycar race at Laguna Seca in 1994.

Rick and Adrian relaxing at Jacques Villeneuve's house in Indianapolis during the 1995 season, with Jacques and his manager Craig Pollock.

Left Rick, Adrian and Gill Reynard at a motorsport dinner.

Below left Rick is an expert water-skier, and water-skis regularly with Adrian during the year. He also takes to the ski slopes every season.

Right Adrian barefoot skiing in the late eighties.

Below Adrian is an accomplished pilot and is pictured here with a 1944 Texan T6G (Harvard) at Panshanger in 1989.

Left Rick and Adrian at Tucson, Arizona, test driving a Dodge Viper.

Below left Members of the Reynard race crew in Rio 1996. From left to right: Bruce Ashmore, Malcolm Oastler, Paul Owens, Rick Gorne, Jeff Swartwout (Reynard North America) and Bill Crissan (Reynard North America).

Right Reynard UK staff celebrating outside the Reynard Centre after their first Indycar win of the 1996 season at the first round of the Championship at Homestead. Reynard cars won eight of the 16 races during the season and took 11 pole positions. (*Oxford and County Newspapers*)

Below The assembly shop during a busy winter build of Formula Three and Formula Opel Lotus cars in 1988.

Left An Indycar chassis being worked on in the assembly shop.

Below The Indycar gearbox.

Right Reynard's composites department is based at Brackley, just 15 minutes from the Reynard Centre at Bicester.

Below right An autoclave at Brackley.

Final machining of Reynard components.

Reynard's chief aerodynamicists, Andrew MacAulay and Alan Smith, at the wind tunnel facility in Shrivenham, near Swindon, in early 1996. They are seen developing a 40 per cent scale model of the Championship-winning 96I Indycar.

Chapter Ten

Into Formula Three

'The move into Formula Three was taken with some trepidation,' says Adrian, 'in fact the thing which most focused our minds was that we had accepted a government grant to develop our scheme, so we had to do it.

'Carbon-fibre had only been used in the higher formulae at that time and our idea was to build a simple, low-cost, shell – simple in that it had only two bulkheads and no inner panels, it was like an egg with all the loads going to the outer shell. We had to make it for £5,000 because that was what the market would then stand. Nobody had done anything like it at the time and the moulding techniques were new. In fact it was made in two pieces which were joined together late in the build process.'

The shell incorporated aluminium honeycomb sections and the floor panel was aluminium. Inboard pushrod suspension was used all round, and it was designed to shear on impact in order to minimise damage to the hull. Twenty four cars were built in 1985, which was more composite chassis than any maker had built in a single year, but perhaps that was too many because it meant that Reynard had to spread its technical back-up fairly thinly.

Adrian discovered that it is one thing to go up a class with a car capable of winning, it was another to keep happy customers who had higher expectations than in the Ford Formulae. Budgets were considerably higher and the teams were more professional – and more demanding. Adrian is the first to admit that they did not all receive top-rate treatment in 1985, but you cannot fault Reynard on its ability to learn from its mistakes.

Much of the detail design of the monocoque was the work of Paul Owens who says: 'At first we had some difficulty in convincing people that carbon-fibre was the way to go in Formula Three. People at that level did not know the material and we met resistance.' Reynard certainly did, but the use of carbon-fibre was only one reason. For several years the Ralt RT3 had dominated Formula Three in Britain and overseas. People knew it, trusted it, and established teams had masses of data on the car, and their own special tweaks. They were all important considerations when running comparatively inexperienced drivers.

Then again, most other Formula Ford makers had bombed when they had tried to make the move upwards, and even those few which had enjoyed some success had done so only intermittently. Behind Ralt was Ron Tauranac, who had penned more successful production racing cars than any man in history and whose designs had won Formula One World Championships. His reputation was deservedly high, and buyers like to have a name behind a car – Adrian had been successful only in the Ford Formulae and his input into March Grand Prix was not widely recognised. Paul Owens was in a similar situation, not many people realised how important he had been to Chevron and Maurer.

There was another factor, and that was that ground-effect was banned in Formula Three for 1985, so everyone began afresh. Ralt produced a new car, the RT30, but

Conducting the first full-size Formula Three wind tunnel tests at MIRA in 1985 for a high downforce set-up to be run at Monaco.

some Ralt users stuck with their existing RT3s and converted them to the new rules using an up-date kit produced by Glenn Waters of Intersport. It was a car they knew, and the reasoning went that it was better to begin the season with a known quantity and then see how things panned out.

Paul continues: 'Early in the year Tim Davies was testing a Reynard at Goodwood. He came off at Woodcote corner, the car hit an earth bank, flipped and landed upside down on a concrete barrier. He chopped a concrete post in half and had he done that in an aluminium car, he would have been killed, no question. As it was, he walked away unscathed, and that convinced a lot of people that our chassis was all we claimed for it.'

It may have been a convincing demonstration of the strength of the tub, but orders for the new car came only from teams making the transition from Formula Ford 2000 to Formula Three. Reynard had convinced only existing customers – none of Formula Three 'establishment' had been persuaded. The result was that all the Reynard teams, Swallow Racing, PMC and Madgwick Motorsport were inexperienced. After the first few races, however, David Price Racing discarded its up-dated Ralt RT3s and joined the customer list at Bicester.

At Madgwick Motorsport, Robert Synge and his new partner, Bob Moore, pulled off a coup by securing a works engine deal from Saab. The engines were prepared by John Nicholson of McLaren Engines and they featured a distinctive plenum chamber-come-air restricter mounted low down on the side of the car. This housed a hot-wire sensor which controlled what was claimed to be a very sophisticated engine management system. Much was expected of the cars, but the first time they appeared for a race, at Silverstone, it rained and the water doused the hot-wire sensor. The cars spluttered to a halt and suffered the ignominy of returning to the pits on the end of tow ropes. To make things worse, Saab had invited a large number of guests who were treated to the sight of the cars stopping under their very noses.

Even when that fairly fundamental problem was fixed, the Reynard-Saabs were competitive only rarely. The engines were tall and heavy and the rev band was narrow. Madgwick blamed Nicholson and Nicholson blamed Madgwick, citing the fact that the team was new to Formula Three, with the inference that it was out of its depth. Nicholson was unusually eloquent on the subject, and a damning article appeared in a magazine.

Madgwick sent one of the Saab units to Minister Engines for a rebuild, and Minister had no difficulty in controlling its enthusiasm for what it saw. One story, two accounts, but it did not help Saab which wanted to forget the whole business as soon as possible. It was small consolation that Thomas Danielsson in a Reynard 853-Saab won the relatively short and unimportant Swedish Formula Three Championship.

That story would unfold over the course of the season. In the meantime, the opening round of the British Championship was won by Andy Wallace in a Reynard 853-VW entered by Swallow Racing, with Russell Spence in a PMC Reynard second. It is one of those facts which are easy to record, but it was a phenomenal achievement. Ralt had won every single British Formula Three race since the middle of 1980, and a high proportion of the races in the rest of Europe, so it was the biggest possible upset.

Reynard's debut was as sensational as, later, would be its debut in Formula 3000 and Indycar, and it was made more so by the fact that it was also Swallow Racing's (and Wallace's) first Formula Three race. At that moment the future of Reynard was set: Formula 3000 and Indycar became almost inevitable. The champagne flowed in Bicester.

Many companies have tried to make Formula Three cars. Van Diemen took over the

Andy Wallace testing the high downforce wing on his Reynard 853-VW at Oulton Park. Reynard had discovered that special wings could be developed for specific circuits.

GRD project, but before long it was swimming in the safer waters of the Ford Formulae. Royale tried Formula Three several times and enjoyed brief success only when Tom Pryce drove one of the cars. Dulon abandoned its Formula Three project when its entry was rejected for a major race. Experienced and successful Formula Ford makers such as Elden, Sparton, MRE, Ray and Tiga all tried Formula Three and all failed.

Swallow Racing built its own car in 1987 (designed by former Reynard engineer, Dave Rendall) and failed to win a single point despite it being driven by Tim Davies. Vision, which made successful Clubmans' cars, tried and failed. Anson spent several years trying to crack the formula and ended up with a few place finishes in Britain and a minor European championship – yet Ansons were designed by Gary Anderson who went on to become chief designer for Jordan Grand Prix. Even major players such as Chevron and Lola achieved only spasmodic success in Formula Three, while more than once March went from top of the class to being the dunce.

In the future Reynard would discover that Formula Three is a tough arena in which to be consistently successful, but in 1985 it rode on the crest of a wave. Reynards won the first six races in Britain, and were second in five of them. After six rounds Spence led the series with 45 points to the 34 of Wallace, the 27 of Mauricio Gugelmin (in a Ralt), with Tim Davies in the second Swallow car fourth on 23 points.

All was not sweetness and light, however. The monocoque, about which most initial reservations hung, had proved itself, but the suspension units were sensitive. Andy Miller, who ran the French side of David Price Racing, called it the Reynard Diet. 'Run a Reynard and you spend so much time working on the car that you never have time to eat.'

Rick Gorne, Russell Spence and Adrian Reynard after Russell's victory in an early race in 1985. This victory gave Russell an initial dominant lead in the Championship.

Despite those reservations, Dave Price remains a close friend of Adrian and Rick, and had there been a 1994 Reynard-Renault Formula Three car, he would have built the chassis and run the team.

Spence was run by PMC which had also entered the new Formula 3000 series using a brace of converted ex-works Williams FW08C Formula One cars. Part of the thinking behind Formula 3000 was that it could be a way of using old Formula One cars, but everyone who went down that route hit a fundamental problem: the large fuel cell in a Formula One car meant that weight distribution was not optimum for Formula 3000, which was dominated by developments of Formula Two cars.

Until PMC began to run in Formula 3000, which started later in the season, Spence had the team's entire attention, but when it began its Formula 3000 campaign it encountered so many problems that PMC began to crack at the seams and Russell's performances went off. He was a driver who needed a strong team around him – in the early part of the season he had it, and he won races, but as soon as that support was absent he failed to score a single point.

Before long PMC was wound up and Spence took his sponsorship money and set up another outfit. Obviously the chemistry was not right in this team because Spence did not win another championship point and his huge lead in the series was eroded. That was tough on Russell and it was tough on Reynard.

All was not well at Swallow either. The team had been built around Tim Davies, but it had expanded to include Andy Wallace who, against expectations, proved to be slightly quicker. How much of this edge was because of the effects of Tim's massive accident at Goodwood, and how much it was because Swallow became biased towards Wallace, is something we will never know.

Whatever, Wallace was slightly quicker, Davies felt himself pressured and he perhaps tried too hard because he became involved in a number of accidents, some with Wallace. By mid-season Davies had been dropped by Swallow, when he was still in contention for the Championship, and a potentially brilliant career began to fizzle out.

Madgwick, PMC and Swallow – the three Reynard teams in the British Championship – each had problems which damaged their performance, but the Reynard 853 was quick straight out of the box, while the new Ralt RT30 needed development to get the best out of it. Most of the teams running Ralts were very experienced and, working with Ron Tauranac, they made the RT30 competitive, while capitalising on problems within the Reynard teams.

Tony McAffry, a friend of Tauranac's, says: 'You have got to remember that Ron is ultra-competitive. He was going to make that car work.'

Gary Evans gave Ralt its first win in round seven, Wallace won round eight – and after that Ralts won every race. The Reynards were by no means out-classed, Wallace had a mathematical chance of the title right up to the final round, but he had to be content with second overall while Spence, despite all his problems, was third in the series.

There was another factor. Adrian says: 'We were too cocky; we thought Formula Three was easy. We were so confident that, in the middle of the season, Rick and I took a three-week holiday and went sailing around the Greek islands. The trouble was that we went at the time when Russell Spence needed our support. We thought we had Formula Three cracked, but our going away caused a certain lack of confidence not only with Russell, but with our other customers. It taught us a lesson we've never forgotten.'

Still, Reynards won races in every Formula Three championship in which they ran, and by the end of the season the company was a force to be reckoned with in the class.

After a very successful season in 1984, Reynard took a lot of orders for its Formula Ford cars, partly because of its success and partly because of the fact that Lola stopped making Formula Ford 1600 cars at the end of 1984. Another potential rival, Royale, had gone into liquidation, partly as a result of Reynard's success, so the Formula Ford market was left with only two major players – Van Diemen and Reynard – and Reynard was the outfit around which there was a buzz of excitement.

Rick Gorne takes up the story: 'So much effort was going into the Formula Three car that for our 1985 Formula Ford cars we brought in an outside designer, Weit Huidecoper. In America, Swift had brought out a superb Formula Ford car and we employed Weit to design a car with a similar concept to the Swift. It had push-rod suspension all round and the radiator was mounted in front of the engine with air fed to it by ducts. Weit is a gifted engineer, but was not of the Reynard school of designers and basically the car did not work.'

Van Diemen's 1985 cars were also based on the Swift, but Ralph Firman and Dave Baldwin made their version work and Van Diemens dominated the season in Formula Ford 1600. Reynards, however, continued their dominance of Formula Ford 2000, but most of the leading runners used 1984 cars. In fact, the 84SF had been so good that most people preferred to stay with it rather than risk either the 85SF, about which reports from early season testing had not been good, or else buy the Van Diemen RF85.

They began to have second thoughts when Van Diemen won the early Formula Ford 2000 races but, as soon as the weather became warmer, the Reynard SF84 was the car to have. It seems that the Van Diemens over-heated their tyres, and that was a crucial issue in 1985 because, in an attempt to cut costs, each runner was restricted to a single set of control Yokohamas.

By early summer Reynard 84SFs were dominating in both Britain and on the Continent, and a Van Diemen was lucky to feature in the top six. It was even more rare, however, for a Reynard 85SF to figure in the top six, and some of the teams who had bought them even converted 1984 Formula Ford 1600 cars to Formula Ford 2000 spec, while others ordered brand new 84SFs. Reynard was so stretched that it farmed out some chassis to a subcontractor who used the wrong brazing material. This led to all sorts of problems for some unlucky customers, until the problem was found whereupon Reynard compensated them with new frames.

The star of the Formula Ford 2000 season was the young French-Canadian, Bertrand Fabi, who won the British, European and Benelux titles with Reynards run, respectively, by Penistone Racing and Richard Dutton. Fabi's dominance was even more remarkable given that he was competing against such future Formula One drivers as Mark Blundell, Gary Brabham, Eddie Irvine and Martin Donnelly. With a total of 11 Formula Ford 2000 championships won in 1985, Reynard could be said to have had a good year, but it is noticeable that none of the wins came in North America where people had tended to use the Swift DB3.

In Formula Ford 1600, it was virtually a Van Diemen whitewash, with only Johnny Herbert driving the works Quest able to mix it with the Norfolk cars. In fact, no Reynard driver finished in the top 10 of either of the two main British national championships, and what few successes the marque achieved were in minor championships based at the smaller circuits, and then with 1984 cars.

Rick continues: 'We made over a hundred Formula Ford 1600 and Formula Ford 2000 cars, and luckily we had sold most of them before the season started. When the season did start, we realised we had a flop on our hands. As other people have found, you cannot just copy another design, you have to understand the thought processes of the original designer. In relative terms, we had a dog of a car, and a lot of disgruntled customers, but Hungary was gearing up to stage its first Grand Prix and wanted an inexpensive one-make formula for local drivers.

'We were contacted by a London-based trade company who, in turn, had been contacted by the Hungarian government. The chap who spoke to me had also been in contact with other Formula Ford manufacturers, but I was with him within 12 hours and had concluded the deal in principle before our rivals had left first base. I have no idea why other people do not operate as we do.

'A few weeks later I flew to Budapest and was ushered into a tiny room under a portrait of Lenin with about 20 people cramped around a small table. I presented my proposal and for the next 40 minutes they shouted at each other. I couldn't understand a word, but it appeared to be very heated and it looked fairly gloomy from our point of view. I remember Lenin looking down from his portrait on the wall into a dark, narrow, room full of people shouting at each other, and with me wondering what I had got myself into.

'After 40 minutes of shouting, the room went quiet and their spokesman said: "OK, you've got a deal." Nobody was more surprised than I was, but apparently it's the way they do business. We sold them the entire project: the jigs, the moulds, our unsold cars, the lot, because one of the things they wanted to do was to set up their own manufacturing base. Before long, locally-built cars were being turned out and being raced as 'Hungaro-Reynards' and for all I know they're still making them.

'It did not matter that our car was being beaten by Swifts and Van Diemens in Britain and America because it was a one-make formula, so both Hungary and Reynard benefited. The funny thing is that the 1985 Reynard Formula Fords are the worst cars we've ever made, but they have been among the most profitable. That deal was crucial to us, we were having a hard time with our customers, but we learned our lesson and the 1986 Reynard Formula Ford car, which was an up-date of the 1984 car, was designed in-house by Malcolm Oastler.'

Chapter Eleven _____

Champions

Having upset his Formula Three customers in 1985, at the end of the year Adrian requested them to submit a list of criticisms based on their experience of running the cars. Then he addressed all the comments that he thought were justified, which was most of them. This unexpected move went some way to repairing customer confidence and also to improving the product. Thus the Reynard 863 incorporated numerous detail improvements while retaining the overall concept of the 853. There had been complaints about some areas of quality control, for example, and this was a matter which was given very careful consideration. The situation was remedied by making over 90 per cent of the car in-house.

Despite the 853's promising performance, and the many improvements incorporated for 1986, only two teams in Britain – Madgwick Motorsport and David Price Racing – bought cars and, for various reasons unconnected with Reynard, DPR did not contest the entire season. The customers had voted with their feet.

Reynard's fortunes in Formula Three rested squarely on the shoulders of Perry McCarthy and Andy Wallace in the Madgwick camp, and it was a very strong year in terms of driver talent – the Ralt opposition included Damon Hill, Julian Bailey, Johnny Herbert, Gary Brabham and Martin Donnelly, all of whom graduated to Formula One. Poor Bertrand Fabi was not among them because he was killed while testing his Ralt at Goodwood early in 1986. His death caused the withdrawal of West Surrey Racing from Formula Three for the season, and it had been WSR which had made the Ralt RT30 work best in 1985. That tragedy altered the balance of the season.

Eddie Jordan Racing had poached Maurizio Sandro Sala from Madgwick because Maurizio felt that he had to drive a Ralt, and he seemed vindicated as he won three of the first four races. Wallace, however, won the second and fifth rounds for Madgwick, and a second place in round six elevated him to the top of the table. Since, like all of the leading runners, Madgwick was using Volkswagen engines, the excellence of the Reynard chassis was self-evident.

Reynard's great advantage was the stiffness of its car's tub, together with some wind tunnel development which was novel in Formula Three at the time. Between them, these two elements made the car easier to set up from circuit to circuit. Ralt had traditionally made a 'lazy' chassis which drivers could lean on, and Formula One designers would shake their heads in disbelief: 'It's nothing but brackets supporting other brackets,' they'd say, 'but it works.' Ralts were user-friendly and had seen off some serious opposition to establish a virtual monopoly in British Formula Three, but in 1986 Reynard raised the level of the game.

The season, however, was clouded by controversy over the fuel which some teams used and which stemmed from the interpretation of rules which had not been tightly enough defined. The rule book allowed a higher lead content in the fuel than was available from roadside pumps. Some teams understood that the fuel to be used was regular pump fuel, which had been traditional in Formula Three, while others pointed to the rule book. The arguments need not concern us; the real point is that it affected the history of motor racing.

The difference in fuel could not have amounted to more than a couple of horsepower, and that is the difference between a driver who weighs 10 stone and one who weighs 11 stone – that extra weight has to be carried – and the difference in weight between Maurizio Sandro Sala, who is tiny, and Andy Wallace was much more than a stone. Sala's team, EJR, stuck to standard pump fuel for a long time, expecting that the teams which used additional lead in theirs would be penalised, and the effect was to completely demoralise the young Brazilian. By such things are championships won and lost, as Adrian and Rick had discovered when they took a holiday in Greece.

Wallace was on a roll and had an incredible degree of confidence – he was so confident that he would even discuss with his engineer, Mick Cook, on which lap of practice he should set pole position – and he took 13 pole positions in the season. Since, in Formula Three, there are points for pole and fastest lap, Andy's qualifying pace won him as many points as a win and a third place. From being a good runner-up, Wallace became a consummate winner. By the end of June he was in charge of the championship and thereafter was never seriously challenged for the title. In individual races he sometimes had to cede best, but he took all of Reynard's eight victories in the series.

It was the first time since 1979 that a driver had won the British series using a car other than a Ralt. Ralt actually won 10 races to Reynard's eight, but Wallace evened the score by winning the Macau Grand Prix and the international race at Fuji. It is a scandal that Wallace was never given a chance in Formula One.

Elsewhere, Stephano Modena won the FIA Formula Three Nations Cup at Imola with a Reynard 863-Alfa Romeo (and won three races in the Italian series) and Reynard took the Swedish Formula Three Championship with Niclas Schonstrom. On the whole, however, Reynard made little impression abroad, although Wallace's wins in two of the three most important international races did make people take notice.

The 1986 Formula Ford range was notable for two things: it marked a return to the principles of the 1984 car and was the first major work for Reynard by Malcolm Oastler, who is now a director of the company. Malcolm had joined Reynard as a design draughtsman in November 1985 and he recalls: 'Soon after I arrived I was sorting out the '86 Ford car which was the '84 concept with some of the best features of the '85 car – it was a couple of fag packet sketches with a new aerodynamic package. The Formula Ford 1600 car had its moments, but didn't really go anywhere. On the other hand, we won the Formula Ford 2000 Championship with Bertrand Gachot.'

In January 1986, however, Reynard announced that it had decided to drop Formula Ford 1600 to concentrate on Formula Ford 2000. Rick recalls: 'It was apparent that Formula Ford 1600 was sapping our resources – we were shifting a lot of cars, but there was little profit on each one compared to the Formula Three cars. That was not the major problem, however, it was more a case of servicing the customers. It can take as much time and effort to sell a Formula Ford car as it can to sell an Indycar and a Formula Ford customer has every right to expect equal treatment.

'For many drivers the choice of the right Formula Ford car is the most critical decision of their career – you can get into Formula One without winning races in F3000, as Damon Hill has shown, but you need success at the initial stage or else you may not be able to progress. By continuing to make Formula Ford 1600 cars we were having to service a vast number of customers and there are only 24 hours in a day. We were in danger of selling our entry-level customers short, so we negotiated a deal with Mike Taylor of Fulmar Competition Services. Mike had been a Reynard customer in

Formula Ford 2000, a good driver, and FCS took over the manufacture of our cars, with us supplying about 40 per cent of the components.'

Before that happened, a number of 86FFs had been delivered to customers and a works car was built for Gerald van Uitert who had sponsorship from Marlboro. Despite a new lap record at Snetterton and a second place at Thruxton (which seems to indicate there was not much wrong with the car) van Uitert decided to switch to Van Diemen, a move which did not improve his performance. If in doubt, blame the car.

Thanks to Reynard's connection with Ford (forged when Formula Ford 1600 was launched in France) RRC supplied 15 86FFs to start the category in Finland. Since the first champion was JJ Lehto and the second was Mika Hakkinen, using the same car, the experiment can be counted a success.

Overall production in 1986 was about half of the previous two years, but Reynard's income was still healthy since the company was concentrating on the more profitable areas. Formula Ford 2000 was the company's Happy Hunting Ground once again and Reynards won the Austrian, Benelux, British, Canadian, Dutch and Scottish Championships, the European World Cup and some minor series.

In the British Formula Ford 2000 Championship, Reynard won 14 of the 20 rounds, with Van Diemen and Swift taking three apiece and then only when Bertrand Gachot and Mark Blundell made mistakes. These two, however, dominated the season, with Gachot narrowly winning the British title from Blundell, while the positions were reversed in Europe. Reynards dominated wherever they appeared, with only Paulo Carcasi in a works Van Diemen and Dave Coyne in a works Swift being able to mix it with them.

Reynard stayed on top in 1987 with a new car designed by Malcolm Oastler. 'The '87 car had to be new because there were new regs which put the driver's feet behind the front axle line and we basically just tried to keep the best features of what had gone before, although we took the idea of the integrated oil tank and gearbox housing from the 873 Formula Three car – it was a nice solution at the time. We built a stiffer chassis, with a cast alloy front bulkhead, improved the aerodynamics with a stepped chassis underside, and it won almost every race in Britain for the next three years. We didn't touch it again. Good car, I really like it.'

Formula Ford 2000 was in a crisis, however, with rising costs, and there were times in the early part of the season when the four-car team of Reynards run by Pacific Racing comprised a third of the field. To make up the numbers, a class 'B' for year-old cars (mainly 86SFs) was instituted but, even so, grids in the early races barely made 20 cars. With just three new cars from Swift and the 1987 Van Diemen late in arriving, and not being much good when it did, Reynard had numerical superiority and it was increased as others joined the series or switched chassis. Star of the season was JJ Lehto who won 11 of his 19 starts in Britain and was a clear winner of the European Championship as well.

In Britain an 87SF won each of the 20 rounds and also set pole and fastest lap in a demonstration of dominance to a degree previously unknown in the formula. Clearly the time was ripe for a new category, and by the end of the year General Motors would have thrown its weight behind the Vauxhall/Opel-Lotus series for which Reynard would make the cars.

As Malcolm Oastler says: 'After the first few races even the works Swift team switched to Reynards. We had virtually won the championship by the end of March, so I got on with the new Formula 3000 car.'

Although Reynard had officially abandoned Formula Ford 1600 in 1986 there was sufficient interest in a car for Fulmar Competition Services to build Formula Ford 1600 versions of the 87SF under licence. FCS is run by Alan Cornock, formerly the owner of Royale, and Mike Taylor, whose main business is printing, and the deal came into operation in May 1987 when Cristal Racing was looking for new cars to replace the Quests it had bought, and the young Swiss driver, Alain Menu, was looking for a new team. Alan Cornock brought them together and although the 87FF initially suffered through lack of testing, it was soon giving the Van Diemens a hard time. Indeed, Menu might have won the Esso Championship but for being nudged off in the last round.

In Formula Three the position had changed, and for the first time in several years the choice of engine and engine-builder became crucial. There had always been a choice, but previously there had been a broad degree of agreement, and for some years the John Judd version of the Volkswagen engine had been almost universal.

For 1987 Eddie Jordan Racing put together the right package. EJR was one of the few teams to choose Reynard chassis and, on Adrian's advice, Eddie also chose a new engine-builder, Siegfried Speiss. With Johnny Herbert as his driver, Eddie had a package with no weaknesses.

John Thompson was put in charge of the Reynard Formula Three project with guidance from Adrian until he found his feet. The basic design of the 853 was carried a

The 1987 Reynard R&D Formula Three team was the first time that Reynard had ventured back into running teams since Adrian had managed one in 1979. Phillipe Favre and Steve Kempton drove for the outfit which was set up in late 1986. The Denis Rushen managed team gave Favre and Kempton their only Formula Three race wins.

stage further with a longer wheelbase, narrower track and improved aerodynamics. The latter resulted, in part, from a narrower engine bay which was possible through a new multi-purpose gearbox and oil tank casing which also carried the rear suspension links and anti-roll bar. The new gearbox had Hewland internals in a Reynard casing, so it was not strictly new, but it was the first step towards Reynard developing its own transmission division.

Reynard has tried to pursue a policy of not competing against its customers, but in 1987 it had so few customers in Formula Three that it ran a two-car team under the name Reynard R+D which was managed by Dennis Rushen, who had run Ayrton Senna in Formula Ford 2000 in 1982. Neither of the drivers, Phillipe Favre and Steve Kempton, was an ace, but Favre won a round at Donington, and Kempton won the European Formula Three Cup with Favre setting fastest lap. Reynard R+D gave each driver the highlight of his career, and so justified its existence – but it was a side-show.

The main attraction was Johnny Herbert taking the British Championship. He established an early lead by winning four of the first five races, but other teams got their acts together and the TOM's Toyota engine came on strong at the end of the season. Herbert was a less frequent visitor to the winner's circle from early June, but by then he had a 21 point lead, and his main opposition – Betrand Gachot, Martin Donnelly, Damon Hill and Gary Brabham, all in Ralts, and Thomas Danielsson (Reynard) – shared the wins among them, which made Herbert's life a little easier.

To complete Reynard's triumph, Gary Dunn won Class B for year-old cars in a Reynard 863, while in the European Championship Dave Coyne took the title with his Reynard 873-VW. Reynards also won the FIA European Cup, the French Class B

The Formula Opel-Lotus was one of Adrian's last designs, designed in conjunction with Paul Brown. The cars are still made in the same way today. Many current Grand Prix and Indycar stars drove in the Formula, including Rubens Barrichello and Gil de Ferran, pictured here in 1990.

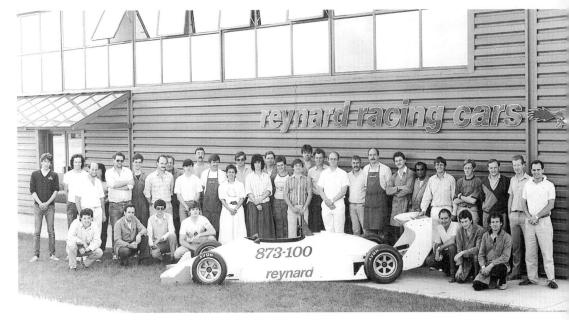

The full complement of Reynard staff celebrated building Reynard's 100th Formula Three car in 1987. Adrian and Rick are pictured with the entire workforce, including Bill Stone who had just arrived back from New Zealand.

Championship, the Cellnet Superprix, the All-Japan Championship and the Japanese Formula Three Association Championship. It was the first time that Reynard had established a significant presence in Japan, which would become an increasingly important market although it is one which the company has failed to dominate to its own satisfaction.

At the end of the season Reynard built a one-off turbocharged 873 for Michael Jourdain in Mexico. Rick recalls: 'Michael organised the Mexican Formula Two Championship and he was interested in promoting a turbo series. He sent over this massive Chrysler engine with a turbocharger fitted – I think it came from a truck – which we had to shoehorn into a Formula Three chassis. It was so big that he had to provide a new engine cover – it looked like a pregnant whale. It went to Mexico and ran a few demonstration laps and that was it.'

A different matter was another outside contract. 'General Motors decided that it wanted to launch a category which was known as Formula Vauxhall-Lotus in Britain and Formula Opel-Lotus on the Continent. General Motors had this lovely new 16-valve engine (designed by Cosworth Engineering) which they wanted to show off. It was a one-make series close in performance to Formula Three, but at a much lower cost. It also had a less sophisticated chassis – it was a combination of aluminium monocoque and space-frame. That was Adrian's baby, he did the concept in three weeks and Paul Brown completed the design in six, which is phenomenally quick. It was a deal we had to compete for, but we won and had the prototype ready in four months, which is an incredibly short time.

'We created new production systems which allowed us to make the cars quickly and cheaply. It was mainly manufacture by computer, and the cars were assembled very quickly. One of the most difficult things to computerise on a limited production scale is welding, so we eliminated as much welding as we could and used a lot of folded panels, honeycomb, CNC punch press panels, and milled aluminium, which can all be generated by computer. It was a very good deal for us because we could build the cars and spares during the summer when business is normally slack. We had a three-year contract, which GM extended by a year, and we made 204 cars to the end of 1991.'

With 95 such cars delivered for the 1988 season on top of healthy orders for Formula Three and Formula Ford 2000, and with a new Formula 3000 car in the wings, Reynard entered an extremely profitable period and Rick and Adrian began to acquire a lot of toys. Adrian already had a Harvard trainer aircraft, and before long would add an airworthy Spitfire to his fleet, with another in need of restoration but still an aeronautical heirloom. His magnificent country house had peacocks on the lawn.

Rick had a couple of Chevrolet Corvettes, one a rare 1954 model (there was only one other in Britain). Then there was the speedboat for their water skiing, about which they are fanatical. In short, they rewarded themselves for all their hard work. Within five years they had taken Reynard from a struggling outfit trying to make a mark in Formula Ford to one setting a new annual production record for any racing car maker. In 1988 Reynard (with 25 FF1600 cars from FCS) would make 266 single-seaters with FCS adding two Sports 200 cars. It is a record which still stands.

Chapter Twelve

Malcolm Oastler

Nobody better encapsulates the Reynard philosophy than Malcolm Oastler. When he was asked to head up the Formula 3000 project he was just 27 years old, and the only complete design he had under his belt was the 1987 Formula Ford car. The 87SF was a superb design, no question, it dominated the final years of Formula Ford 2000, and the Formula Ford 1600 version was still good enough to win the Kent-engine section of the 1993 Formula Ford Festival seven years after being designed. It may even be the best Formula Ford car ever, but it's a massive leap from Formula Ford car to F3000.

If a driver straight from Formula Ford 2000 won his first Formula 3000 race and then dominated the season, it would be sensational – Formula One team managers would never be off the phone. But the mechanics of driving are the same in each case. For a designer to do that is even more remarkable because they are completely different arenas. In Formula Ford, cars have space-frames, but for Formula 3000 Malcolm was designing a composite monocoque. Aerodynamics, stresses, brakes – everything is so completely different in Formula 3000 that it is hard to see much point of contact.

In Malcolm's case there was another factor, and that was that the future of Reynard and all his friends at the factory rested on his shoulders. It's all too easy to write something like 'the Bandersnatch Formula Three car was a flop and the outfit had disappeared by mid-season', but behind those words are redundancies – men out of work and their families having to tighten their belts. In effect, the men at Reynard would do just that in 1988 to friends of theirs who worked a mile away at March Engineering. They were men let down by the fact that the teams designing March's customer cars took their eye off the ball.

Malcolm recalls: 'Sitting down to design the Formula 3000 car was pretty daunting. I lost a lot of hair during that period, just trying to get to the end of it. I knew I was up against three very successful makers, but all you can do is what we did with the Indycar, give it your best shot. You look at all the options, you try to make the best decisions, then you pitch it in and see where it runs. In my case, starting afresh in a new category, I obviously didn't know how it'd run because I hadn't got the previous year's data.

'The same was true for the Indycar, but that was less stressful, because back in 1987 I didn't have the experience I have now. The Indycar was a bigger challenge because the engineering standards are higher, but I had a lot more experience and a lot of good people around me to look after the various areas. The composites department, for example, has improved enormously.'

Malcolm is slightly built and wiry. He talks quickly and has the rare ability to combine humour with precision. When he says he has no ego, you believe him, although he has plenty of self-confidence, which is another thing entirely. Like all good engineers, he is the sternest critic of the cars he has designed, and is generous in his praise when a rival designer delivers the goods.

Malcolm Oastler working at one of the first Reynard CAD CAM stations in 1989. There are no longer any drawing boards at Reynard.

He was born in Sydney in 1960 and grew up on the edge of the city. 'We were the fifth house from the end of our street and beyond that was bush. I suppose my interest in engineering began when I was about 10 years old and I started building mini motorbikes out of scraps of tubing and bits of old lawn mowers. There was a guy up the road who had a Caterpillar tractor business, and welding equipment, and I used to walk up with a couple of pieces of water pipe, or whatever, lay them on the ground and he'd weld them up for me, then I'd go back for the next couple of tubes. Eventually we made this thing, got it to run and, of course, close by was the bush where the billy carts, mini-bikes and go-karts were run.

'By the time I was 15 I suppose I must have made, bought and sold, 14 or so mini-bikes – a bit like Adrian at the same age I suppose. Then I built a go-kart made of bits of old motor bikes which had a clutch I'd made myself and a highly tuned 125cc engine. It went pretty well.

'I got involved with motor racing through drawing. I used to draw racing cars at school – action pictures drawn in pencil. I also made model cars which were usually plastic kits of Australian saloon cars to which I'd add flared wheel arches and so on, and then hand-paint them with all the stripes and numbers. Our local racing magazine, *Racing Car News*, was taking a stand at a motor show, so I rang them up and asked if they would like some models to decorate it. They said to call round, they liked what I'd done and they used them. Then I showed them some of my drawings and they said "We can use some of those," and they commissioned drawings from me.

'That got me on the inside, as it were, and I got involved with a guy called Harry Galloway who was to become to Ralt what Bill Stone had been to March and Reynard. Harry had built a Formula Two car. I'd done a drawing of it for the magazine and he wanted to buy the original. Somehow I got roped in to help him. By that time I was an apprentice with the State bus company – just like Paul Owens – and was on a sandwich course doing a degree at the New South Wales Institute of Technology.

'I helped Harry build a car. Having all the machinery at the bus depot at my disposal helped. Again, that's a bit like Paul. Then for a time I became involved with a Formula Two team: I drove the transporter, acted as a gofer and found that I was able to make some technical input.

'A friend of mine, Edward Vieusseux, bought himself a Formula Ford car, a 1974 Bowin P6, built in Australia by a bloke called John Joyce who'd worked for Lotus in the Lotus 72 era. In fact, it looked like a miniature Lotus 72 with a flat nose and side radiators. Buying a racing car was something I'd never considered because it would have been financial suicide for me. Anyway, Edward had bought a car, raced it and eventually found he couldn't use it. He'd been doing all the work on it himself and it was too much for him.

'After a season he grew tired of that and asked me if I knew anyone who might want to hire it. I put my hand up and and went Formula Ford racing for about 18 months. Most of the cars were four, six, or even 10 years old, like mine was. We used to do an update every year, so they got highly developed. Someone bought a new '83 Van Diemen and did nothing with it – our cars were pretty quick.

'I had a good first season. I won my third race from pole and was runner-up in the national championship. I thought, "I'm all right at this," and figured I'd do a second season and then try to get enough money together to go to Europe. Halfway through the 1984 season, however, I hadn't scored a single point. It was a disaster. I couldn't make a good decision to save my life.

'I ran out of resources, physical, financial, mental, everything – I was knackered. By then I was working full-time for the bus company and a friend and I also had a model car business, so running in Formula Ford as well as doing a million and one other things was just too much.'

While working for the bus company Malcolm showed signs of the ability which Adrian would recognise, and he designed a couple of machines. One was for washing gearbox components and the other was a special valve body test rig. 'We had these Mercedes buses and they used to blow up their gearboxes regularly because they hadn't been designed for going up the sort of hills we had in 40 degree heat. After you rebuilt the gearbox you had to give the bus a test run and if there was any problem with the valve body, and there often was, you had to take the whole thing apart again. I devised a system whereby you could simulate road conditions and gear changes before putting the 'box back into the bus. Saved 'em a lot of money.

'Apart from that it was a quiet life at work. You clocked on at 8.08, had your 42 minute lunch break and clocked off at 4.12, completely unlike working for Reynard. In Australia you have your job and your hobbies and you balance them as best as you can – here I've got a hobby-job, so it's all job. The bus company was pretty flexible, though, they'd let me take time off to go testing and racing, so it was OK. It was never my ambition to be a bus engineer, it was not what I wanted to do with my life, but it was a job and it happened that the bus company was shelling out money when I started my course. That meant that all the time I was a student I got paid.

'Then I decided to take a break and come to Europe for a couple of years. I wanted to get involved in motor racing engineering, and the bus company said they'd keep my job open for me. I sold a few bits and pieces and, instead of the money being poured into racing, it piled up in the bank. I don't know what my plan was exactly. I thought I'd go and see Ron Tauranac, but never got round to it.

'A friend of mine, Steve Farrell, who is now Chief Engineer at Prodrive, had a Formula Ford team, and my younger brother came over with me to work for him. We turned up and Steve offered us both jobs, and that suited me. I worked for Steve for about seven months and did a few races myself in an '85 Van Diemen and discovered

Left Malcolm at Laguna Seca in 1995. He attended as many races as his schedule would allow to act as liaison engineer for Hall Racing, working alongside Gil de Ferran, a position he continued in 1996.

Below Malcolm and Bruce Ashmore at Surfers Paradise, Australia in 1996.

that was not my future. I should have kept to my original plan and not got side-tracked playing at being a racing driver.

'I worked for Steve until the September, sold double-glazing for a month, and then Adrian advertised for a design draughtsman and I started at Reynard the day after the 1985 Formula Ford Festival. I was put straight on to the '86 Ford car, six months later I was designing the '87 Formula Ford car, and a year further on I was designing a Formula 3000. It's a world of opportunity.'

With his incredible track record of success, Malcolm has been approached by a number of Formula One teams, not to mention Carl Haas in Indycar, with offers to make your eyes water. Malcolm says: 'I've got a good quality of life. No real pressures. I get to spend time with my family. Indycar is a nice level playing field and we deal with nice people. I'd only consider leaving if things went wrong here at Reynard and I don't see that happening. No worries.'

Chapter Thirteen _____

Into Formula 3000

R eynard's move into Formula 3000 was bold. It had been an achievement to be first successful newcomer to Formula Three in 10 years, but in Formula 3000 Reynard was pitched against the three most successful makers in modern history: Lola, March and Ralt. March and Ralt had won almost every championship in either Formula 3000 or its immediate predecessor, Formula Two, for the previous 10 years, while Lola had been in the business of making racing cars longer than anyone else and was in the process of destroying March in Indycar.

The fact that there were only three makers (plus Dallara, whose presence with just two cars was hardly noticed) in one the most lucrative production car categories in motor racing tells its own story: Formula 3000 was a tough arena. The rewards for success were potentially substantial, but so was the risk. Reynard had committed half a million pounds to Formula 3000 before the first race, so it was really laying its future on the line.

Despite all its experience, Lola had flopped when it entered Formula 3000 in 1985 because it made the fundamental mistake of using its Indycar monocoque as the basis for its car, and the large fuel cell meant that the weight distribution was not optimal – as those who bought pensioned-off Formula One cars also discovered. Lolas were dumped as people switched to March chassis, but it had recovered from that and had produced an excellent car for 1986. Over the next two years Lola clawed back its share of the market. At the beginning of 1988 it looked strong.

Ralt had begun with a flurry of victories. Indeed, in 1986 it won five of the 11 rounds, which was as many as March, even though they had only about a quarter of March's representation in the field. It began to fall back in 1987, but still won two races. By 1988 Ralt had begun to find life hard largely because its design staff were spread too thinly – the standards in Formula 3000 were rising year by year – and only four Ralts would start the 1988 season, despite having won 12 races in the first three years of the formula.

This relatively thin representation was not unusual. Ralt had never had more than five cars on the grid and, in 1985, had only two yet still won five races. Part of the trouble was that Ralt had a two-car team run from the factory, as it had during the last years of Formula Two. When a manufacturer does that, there is always a potential problem because it is seen to be running against its customers. It is always a difficult situation to manage, but it is not insurmountable.

But the works Ralt team had exclusive use of Honda engines in Formula 3000, as it had in Formula Two, and Honda was dominating in Formula One. In fact, these engines were designed by Neil Walker and John Judd at Engine Developments in Rugby and they were probably not superior to the Cosworths which customers could buy. In fact, in 1986, most of Ralt's wins were taken by the Pavesi team using Cosworths tuned by Heini Mader.

The fact remained, however, that the works Ralts had engines which were not available to its customers and, consequently, there was customer resistance to Ralt. Ron Tauranac's relationship with Honda goes back to 1966 when the Brabham-Honda Formula Two cars he designed were beaten only once, and it continues to this day. There were, then, old loyalties at work, but that did not help Ralt's cause.

Tauranac had designed his first carbon-fibre monocoque while retaining a proven suspension layout and, at first, the marriage was not a happy one as, in pre-season testing, the cars suffered severe traction problems. Neither of the contracted works drivers could be persuaded by Ron that he could, given a little time, sort out the problem and they decamped taking with them £400,000 in sponsorship money. That not only set Ralt back so far as Formula 3000 was concerned, it jeopardised the company's future, especially since, thanks to Reynard, production of its Formula Three cars fell from the usual 80 per year to just 35.

March had won the first three Formula 3000 European Championships and had Japan nicely sewn up, but during 1987 there had been an increasing number of reservations expressed about March's ability to deliver either a competent chassis or even one that was made properly. Teams had flocked to buy Marches at the beginning of 1987 and 37 cars were sold. Some measure of the way they felt about the product they had received was that, despite winning the Championship that year, only 22 cars were sold for 1988 and all but seven of those went to Japan.

So, two of the three main players had problems but, on the other hand, they also had years of working with established teams, building relationships and listening to their requirements. The strength of that network meant that Formula 3000 was virtually a club, and Reynard was not a member. The fact that Rick was able to sell seven cars before the beginning of the season is a tribute both to his powers of persuasion and the faith that people had in Reynard. It was the old story of people believing in Adrian's dreams.

Reynard had done well in Formula Three, but had not dominated and there was not a 'name' behind the new Formula 3000 car. A Formula 3000 car represents a considerable investment, and buying two (as most teams did) was a little like persuading people to hand over a six-figure sum on the promise that it would be converted into gold bricks.

Malcolm Oastler had no track record – most people in Formula 3000 had never heard of him – and the news that the only car he'd previously designed was for Formula Ford was not guaranteed to inspire confidence. Everyone who put down a deposit was acting in blind faith. Some teams, and some drivers, could have been broken had they made the wrong decision.

Adrian discussed the broad parameters of the design with Malcolm, and the young Australian set to work. Malcolm says: 'Adrian chose me because I was there, I suppose. In all fairness, it wasn't just me on the car.'

'It was quite a good car, but we walked in at an opportune time when the Lola wasn't stunning, the Ralt was a bit of a problem and the March was dreadful. At places like Silverstone, where the aerodynamics are important, we were able to run pretty strongly. We got a bit of a drubbing on a couple of the slower circuits, and the Lola became stronger towards the end of the season, but we won the last race. Good car, the '88 car.'

The fact that Malcolm was given such a major commission at the age of 27 was typical of the philosophy Adrian was building for his company. At the end of 1988 he was to say: 'My role is different now, it's much more that of an elder statesman, though since I'm only 37 I'm not sure about the "elder". I think I designed an upright (for the Formula 3000 car) last year, not much more. I'm into sketches now, and my main contribution is holding a weekly engineering meeting, which is a session with no punches pulled. At the meeting we are all on one level, from directors to office boys, and it's an opportunity for us all to communicate. We may spend an hour or more on a particular project which most of the engineers aren't involved in, but they are all engineering topics and I think they benefit everyone because they give everyone a collective motivation – an idea of what the company is trying to achieve.

'I can put over what I believe is important. I'm not saying all these guys are Adrian Reynard clones, because I teach them to think independently and I like them to come up with their own ideas. My guys are good at coming up with ideas, but they are young and maybe they don't always have the experience, so Paul Owens and I act as a filter. We are the old boys who've done it all before – been there, seen it, done it. My role is motivating them and putting them into an environment in which they are productive and happy, and maybe give them a development budget to go and prove their ideas if I think they have merit. We need people who would kill to work with us.

'Take electronics – something I know very little about – I've got guys straight out of school, let alone out of university, who know more about computers and electronics than I do. There's a couple in their early twenties who are brilliant. One is out in Japan supervising the data logging on a car there – and he's only 24.

'I believe in young people, they have so much to offer, and when the day comes that I decide I'm going to do Formula One, I will have a prime staff to carry on the production car side because they already know so much more about it than I do – and they are so much better at it than I ever was.'

This was a particularly astute comment because, just down the road, March Engineering was self-destructing after key people from the production car operation had been transferred to the new Formula One team. It ripped the heart out of the production car side and sent March into a tail-spin which, in turn, jeopardised the Formula One team, which would be sold a few months later.

Adrian was shrewd enough to know that the trick was to keep the two separate, and when he did attempt Formula One, he did just that. The Formula One project nearly bankrupted the company, but the integrity of the production car side was unaffected.

'Most of the dynamic people in Reynard are in their mid-twenties, or very early thirties, and I'm now the old man, but if I had to go and do a project abroad for six months I know the company would work without me. My biggest contribution now is in the drawing office, provoking the designers and setting conceptional briefs. If I was to do an Indycar, for example, I'd have a fair amount to say on what we should do and how we should tackle it. My aim would be to motivate the design team into thinking we would win our first race, and then look for ways of doing it. The important thing is to be thinking in the right way from the start – to have the racer's attitude.

'That's why when I recruit people I try to break them. They get all the worst jobs, but I have to find out how much they really want to do this. I went through hardships. I started from nothing. I'm not saying I want to put everyone else through the same misery as I endured, but I believe that if you can survive the early days, then the rewards are there to be had, and it's that philosophy that I try to instil into people.

'When my designers draw, say, a clutch pedal, I see no reason why they should design a different one for a Formula Ford car from that for Formula 3000. So, one of the disciplines I impose is that we have a common clutch pedal. The same applies throughout our range. There is a massive area of common components, whether it be pedals, brake balance bars, steering or gear linkage parts. So, we have a library of parts which are categorised between common parts for all our cars and special parts which relate only to certain models.'

The above is a distillation of the statement of policy which Adrian shared with us in late 1988. It was an exciting statement because it showed a particular set of problems (how to sell cars, win races, etc.) being approached from a fresh angle. All other racing car manufacturers had approached the market in the same way as most teams and drivers: they'd looked at the formulae, looked at the opposition, looked at their budgets, tried to work out where they could obtain an advantage, and so on.

Adrian did all that, of course, but he (and Rick) had also established a separate set of stratagems – a philosophy which nobody in the racing car industry had thought of. Most people had thought 'racing car', but not 'industry', and that was a major cause of Ralt's demise during 1988. March's downfall came, also during 1988, because it had begun to think 'industry' and not 'racing car'. Adrian and Rick were the first people to consider the entire concept.

In line with their philosophy, the 1988 Formula 3000 car, the 88D, shared the basis of its monocoque with the 883 Formula Three car. It was a new design for 1988, since it had to fulfil a dual role (the fuel cell on the Formula 3000 car was larger); it was made of Kevlar and carbon-fibre, and both the Formula Three and Formula 3000 versions shared a similar suspension layout, with pushrods front and rear.

The aerodynamic packages, however, were completely different to take account of different tyre sizes and bodywork design parameters. At 109 in., the wheelbase of the Reynard 88D was about 7 in. longer than the opposition.

Two Reynard 88Ds were bought by Madgwick Motorsport (Cor Euser and Russell Spence), Eddie Jordan Racing (Thomas Danielsson and Johnny Herbert), Spirit TOM's

Johnny Herbert and Eddie Jordan in 1988 when Herbert drove a Reynard in the European Formula 3000 Championship. He was reigning British Formula Three Champion at the time, and continued his winning ways in 1988 until his devastating crash at Brands Hatch.

Racing (Betrand Gachot and Steve Kempton) while Bromley Motorsport fielded a single car for Roberto Moreno. When Reynard entered Formula Three, all its customers were new to the category – when it entered Formula 3000, again its customers were largely young thrusting teams who were prepared to hitch their wagons to Adrian's star.

In the opening round, at Jerez in Spain, Johnny Herbert set pole position and took his Reynard to victory to maintain the tradition of Reynard winning first time out in every new category it tackled. It takes a sentence to record the fact, but the effect on motor racing was electrifying. Only Lola was able to offer any opposition and, despite their years of experience, the Marches and Ralts were off the pace, while the two Dallaras were a joke.

Teams began to look at their cars and wonder if they had made the wrong choice – the phone lines to Bicester were soon busy.

It was an astonishing achievement, but Malcolm shrugs it off. 'It was satisfying, sure, but it was not a great surprise. We had been testing for three months, so we knew we were on the pace. We thought we deserved to win, it would have been a different matter had we been off the pace during testing and had then won.'

Gregor Foitek opened the score for Lola in the second round at Vallelunga, with Gachot a close second for Reynard. Reynard responded with new anti-roll bars, a new rear wing and aerodynamic plates on the flat undertray ahead of the rear wheels. Relocating the radiators allowed the engines to run cooler – high engine temperatures had been a problem.

Roberto Moreno then won for Reynard at Pau, Silverstone (where Reynards took the top three places) and Monza. Three Formula 3000 victories in a row was then an unprecedented feat.

Pierluigi Martini was a surprise winner for March at Enna Pergusa, but the firm which had won the first three championships was in the doldrums. The car was so tricky to set up that even March's Formula One sponsor, Leyton House, had replaced its Marches with Lolas for the Japanese Formula 3000 Championship. There had been 11 Marches on the grid for the first race in Japan, by the third there was only one.

At Monza both the (replacement) works Ralt drivers, Eric Bernard and Marco Greco, failed to qualify for the first time in the history of the team. Ron Tauranac said: 'The whole thing this year has escalated beyond belief. The Reynard is very quick, there's no doubt, and I imagine that the amount of effort being put in by March, Lola and ourselves is probably up five times. Formula 3000 has always been very competitive, but the drivers are improving and the teams are getting more professional all the time. It is a different ball game from last year, being up at the front.'

What Ron was actually saying was that Reynard had arrived and it was a lean and hungry company which had brought a new level of professionalism. A similar sense of awe was felt at March which for so long had stayed ahead of the game by making a competent product which was only as good as it needed to be in order to win the lion's share of races in Formula Two and Formula 3000. Its cars had improved year by year, but March had never made a quantum leap forward.

March's basic problem in 1988 was that the concept of its car, which was in essence its 1984 Formula Two design, was past its natural life and the 1988 updates had made it even worse. Instead of the new car which was needed, a design which was barely adequate in 1987 was patched up. The March 87B had been touted as a new design but, really, it was a re-tubbed and bodied version of the March 842 and it should have been regarded as an interim design instead of the first of a new generation of F3000 cars.

Normally, the decision to create a new design at March was, more or less, arrived at as the result of a groundswell of opinion – an atmosphere in the works. Someone would say, 'the old bus is getting tired', and someone else would comment that, say, Lola was set to overtake and what could be done about it? By such informal means an idea would snowball, with everyone contributing ideas, and a step forward would be taken.

Reynard had taken the view that if you create a structure within which people can work, the structure need not impede their creative juices, it can encourage them because it gives them security in which to work, and it also gives them a direction for their creativity. A piston will only work within the confines of a cylinder – there it can express its piston-ness and can fulfil itself as a piston. A piston without a cylinder is a paperweight.

March had been successful for years but, in retrospect, it had been more by luck than judgement. It had attracted good people whose instincts, as racers, had kept it on the right course. On this occasion there had been complacency – everyone knew that Reynard was about to come into the picture, but nobody thought that Reynard could win first time out or even make much of an impact.

March had been winning Formula Two and 3000 races for nearly 20 years – it knew the score. A brash newcomer could not possibly hope to come in and wipe the floor with the opposition. Yet that's what did happen, and as one senior man at March put it at the time: 'Reynard moved the goal posts and we were caught completely unawares; whereas, in the past, if there were goal posts to be moved, Robin Herd was normally the man to do it.'

Adrian and Malcolm knew that. March had been the best of a bunch whose standard was not as high as it could have been. In all of Reynard's major moves, it has had the advantage of being the interloper, of being able to study the competition in depth before it has made its move. Its crucial advantage has been the width and depth of that study, of not merely seeing the opposition in terms of machines to be beaten on the track, but also in terms of rival companies to be beaten in the market place.

In early 1989 we spoke to Ron Tauranac, who made some veiled swipes at Reynard. By then his disastrous Formula 3000 season had made Ralt so vulnerable that it had been taken over by March. 'My business was becoming too seasonal, there had been a time when Formula Three, Super-Vee and Atlantic, had dovetailed into each other, because the build season for Atlantics 'Down Under' came in our summer. In Super-Vee we'd been a victim of our own success because we had no-one else to beat. We were getting down to just Formula Three, so we had a problem in keeping people occupied.

'Apart from that, I think some of the problem was the way customers perceived us. Everyone had decided they had to have carbon-fibre tubs without realising that some carbon-fibre construction in Formula 3000 was a long way short of Formula One standards. I have seen a car break up just because it bottomed, and everyone said, "Wow, look at the strength of carbon-fibre, the driver's unhurt," but it should never have broken in the first place.

'Part of the problem was business ethics. I've always built a car and said: "There it is. If you want one, that's fine – if you don't, that's fine, too." We came up against people who'd wine and dine the Press, who'd phone up drivers and tell them they had to buy their cars, who'd offer them special deals, lease arrangements and so on – anything to get the right people into their cars, and I wouldn't do that.

'I'd lately been making a profit of £750,000 a year, but I'd reinvested in machine tools. So, I think I can say that the difference between our product and other people's is that we make things to such tolerances that if you buy something from our parts store it will fit, whereas if you bought almost any production car in the past you'd buy parts and then proceeded to make 'em fit.'

There was some truth in what Ron said at the time. His build quality was then probably better than Reynard's – it was certainly a great deal better than March's. It is the reason why, when Ralt got into financial difficulty, March, which had lost the ability to make a good product, jumped at the chance to buy the company. Robin Herd said at the time: 'Nobody builds production cars as well as Ron,' and as some senior March men also said at the same time: 'We really shouldn't be building production racing cars, because we're no good at it.'

Ron Tauranac said: 'In 1988 we were down to 35 cars from the 80 we'd been used to making, and our profit disappeared when two drivers in Formula 3000 didn't find things to their liking and, instead of waiting for me to sort out the car, they decided to take their sponsorship (£400,000) elsewhere. For a number of reasons, then, our market had shrunk. March needed the extra capacity and we needed more work to keep our people occupied, so it worked out nicely.'

The plan was emerging. March would pull out of the production racing car market to concentrate on special projects, such as the one it had with Porsche to build a bespoke Indycar. All the customer cars would be built at Ralt's Weybridge factory, with the two companies retaining their identities in their traditional markets – Ralt in Formula Three, March in Indycar.

At the time Robin Herd said: 'I have a lot of time for Mr Tauranac, Mr Reynard and Mr Broadley. I think in some ways it's a bigger challenge to build production racing cars than doing Formula One: your budget is tighter, your timescale is much tighter, and you have to give away all your secrets. The most difficult job in the world is to be the Chief Engineer of a production racing car company, because the compromises you have to make are so great. It's much easier to do a Formula One car, because you don't have to consider cost.

'I think to run a successful production car firm, the Chief Designer has to be the owner, because nobody else is going to put up with all the aggravation. That's why we'll leave Ron well alone, but we'll give him back-up on composites, aerodynamics and sales.'

At the beginning of the 1988 season it had been intended to build 10 Reynard 88Ds but, by the end of August, 22 had been made as teams switched cars. Oliver Grouillard summed up the position: 'The Reynards probably aren't much quicker than our Lolas, but the ease with which their drivers set their times is mind-boggling.'

Martin Donnelly, who joined Formula 3000 mid-season from Formula Three, won for Reynard at Brands Hatch. Moreno took the Birmingham Superprix, then Grouillard struck back for Lola at Le Mans and Zolder, while Donnelly rounded off the season with a win for Reynard at Dijon-Prenois. Roberto Moreno ran out as the clear Champion, the first time that any driver had won four races in a single season of European F3000.

The season had been marred by a lot of accidents, mostly caused by drivers. At Brands Hatch every one of the six official practice sessions was stopped by a heavy crash, and the race itself had to be restarted after another shunt. During the race there were more crashes which severely injured drivers, and Johnny Herbert came close to losing a foot when his Reynard was involved in a multiple accident. On hearing the news, Adrian had jumped on to one of the rescue vehicles and was at the scene of the accident very quickly. What he saw distressed him greatly, and it had a profound effect on him.

Adrian recalls: 'Since I was soon on the scene of the multiple pile-up, I saw several of the drivers in acute pain. Johnny himself was screaming at a marshal wanting to know how many feet he had. He was screaming, "How many? How many?"' In fact, Johnny's accident was so severe that the surgeon who treated him could have amputated one foot with a dinner knife – there was no bone to cut through. 'Johnny was in his car for quite a long time: he wasn't trapped, but they were trying to stabilize his condition before they lifted him out, and the front end of his car had sustained three massive impacts.

'The first impact was probably at 140 to 150 mph head-on into a bridge parapet. He then ricocheted across the track and was hit by another car, and then he went head on again into the Armco barrier on the other side of the track. That was the impact that he remembers as hurting – so, after the first and second impacts he was relatively undamaged. Seeing the agony he was in, I vowed that henceforth I was going to make the strongest car that I possibly could.'

'In fact, the monocoque had stood up to the impact pretty well. It was the front of the car which had smashed, and I do mean smashed. We never found some of the components; they had been pulverised beyond recognition. One of the features of our car was that we had a step in the nose – the 88D was one of the first cars to have a raised nose – and that might as well have carried a sign saying "snap off here". Since most of the tub had survived fairly well, I reasoned that it should be possible to increase the margin of safety through design.

'On our 1989 cars we incorporated two elements which improved driver protection. One was that we sat the driver further back – and we already had the driver further back than anyone else – and the other was that we made a flat-bottomed monocoque without a step. This slightly reduced optimum performance, but as an ex-driver I maintain that safety is paramount.'

At the end of the 1988 season Reynard took a couple of cars to Japan and, with Paul Owens engineering, Geoff Lees and Ross Cheever scored a 1–2. Adrian says: 'When we first went over, March was losing its customers, and so we were able to move in on some of their teams and also their agent, Tom Hanawa's Le Mans Company.

'On the back of our first showing, we sold a number of cars for 1989, but we have never really cracked Japan. If I knew the precise reason, we'd have done it a long time ago, but like so many things in motor racing it is not one big reason, rather it is a combination of many small factors. We've won races there every year since we went over, and come close to winning the championship a couple of times, but we have never displayed the consistency which would properly establish us.

'Lola is well-established there and has excellent relations with its customers. It has a good agent, Nova, and it has a good level of teams and drivers. Some teams, too, have works tyre contracts and so the tyres have tended to be designed to suit the Lola. When we first went out there we had been running on a fairly rigid control crossply tyre, whereas in Japan tyres were "free" and tended to be soft-walled radials, although as the years have gone by, European and Japanese tyres have tended to get closer. Anyway, we made a fairly good impression at the end of 1988 and we sold some cars.'

In Formula Three, 1988 was a mixed year for Reynard, the Ralt RT32 was the favoured choice of most teams and Reynard representation was fairly thin in Britain. There seems little doubt that the Ralt was the easier car to set up, and one reason was that it had managed to fit its engine lower in the chassis, bringing down the car's centre of gravity.

Despite that, Keith Wiggins' Pacific Racing provided the young Finn, JJ Lehto, with an excellent package which included the presence of Adrian at test sessions to hone the car to individual circuits. A special chassis with a low-mounted engine was also used at some races.

Lehto won the first two rounds of the British series, but most of the points finishers were driving Ralts. After the third round, Martin Donnelly (in a Ralt) moved to the top of the table, but Lehto was joint leader in the series by the beginning of May and

JJ Lehto won the 1988 British Formula Three Championship driving a Reynard 883 for Pacific Racing. He won eight races from 18 starts. (*Sutton Motorsport Images*)

thereafter was never headed, although he was helped by the fact that Donnelly graduated to Formula 3000.

With eight wins from 18 starts, Lehto was a dominant Champion, but the only other Reynard driver to take a win was John Alcorn, so the season ended with nine victories each for Ralt and Reynard.

Alistair Lyall won the Class B section of the Championship with a Reynard 873-VW, while Jo Winklehock won the German Formula Three Championship and the FIA Europa Cup with a Reynard 883-VW.

Meanwhile, the Reynards made by Fulmar Competition Services were continuing to dominate Formula Ford 2000 in its dying days, and were holding their own in Formula Ford 1600. FCS did a brilliant job and shifted a lot of cars. Its secret was that its motivation was the same as Reynard in the higher formulae – there was good product and dedication to selling and servicing it. The FCS operation gradually became separate from the Reynard story and is outlined in Appendix 2.

1988 also saw Reynard's first sports car, and Adrian says: 'The Sports 2000 was a request from Fulmar Competition Services, we'd never looked at a sports car before, but it was conceived and designed in the usual Reynard fashion. It involved me in terms of the concept, and I was involved in the wind tunnel tests. We brought in an outside contractor to do some of the drawing, but largely the bodywork was conceived in-house. Although the prototype was a little overweight, which broke one of our cardinal rules, it won its first race, which has become a Reynard tradition.'

The car did get down to the weight limit, partly by using Kevlar bodywork, and it was a front-runner in Britain. Alan Cornock recalls: 'Sports 2000 was declining in Britain and all our sums had been done on the basis of selling cars in America. The trouble was that Reynard was represented there by Carl Haas, who was also importing Lola Sports 2000 cars – the upshot was that Lola leaned on Haas. Lola had so much more clout than Reynard since Carl sold its Indycars, and so we sent no cars to America. We just had a couple in Britain and four in odd European countries.

'We'd taken over production of the Formula Ford 1600 cars in 1987, and at the end of 1988 we took over the Formula Ford 2000 cars as well. Reynard supplied us with components, we sourced things like seat belts and steering racks, and we took over the body moulds. We continued to make them until 1992, and built about 150 – one of them even won the 1993 Kent-engine class of the Formula Ford Festival.

'All the single-seaters, including those we made for Formula Renault, were based on the 87SF; we had a consultancy arrangement with Reynard, but most of the development, in areas such as springs, shockers and roll bars, we did ourselves. We had a good run, but finally we needed a new product and Reynard had gone on to greater things.

'We'd still be interested in a new Reynard. I'm sure they could deliver the goods, but meanwhile we're agents for the Van Diemen one-model categories and I still have the rights to all the old Royale designs which are being run in club racing.'

Carl Haas moves into the Reynard story. Carl is one of the shrewdest operators in motor racing and has handled the interests of a number of British racing car manufacturers in North America, beginning with Elva in the early 1960s. It was he who had brought Lola into Indycar on a permanent basis in 1984. Before that, Lola had come and gone from Indycar depending on the requirements of customers. It had first won the Indianapolis 500 in 1966, but had not subsequently consolidated its position until Carl joined forces with Paul Newman, the film star and salad dressing magnate, to run Mario Andretti in 1984.

It was Carl who put together the package which led to the FORCE Formula One team in the mid-1980s, which used works Cosworth turbo engines in a chassis designed by Lola. Carl was to have a profound influence on Adrian and Rick. They all became

In 1987 Reynard Racing Cars received their biggest ever cheque from Carl Haas. The cheque was for £183,000. Note the Toleman backward clock in the background, a present from Adrian's good friend, Alex Hawkridge, then a Group Managing Director of Toleman.

close friends and he taught them many things. Naturally, he worked his own corner and, while Lola was his flagship import, he was happy to represent Reynard in the lower formulae – provided that it did not impinge on his relationship with Lola.

A Reynard Sports 2000 car crossed the demarcation line, which is why it did not get seen in America. There are Reynard insiders who will tell you that he discouraged Reynard from bidding for the Indy Lights contract so that Lola could take a clear run at it.

If such surmise be true, then it means that Carl did his junior company a disservice and, possibly, delayed Reynard's entry into Indycar. The funny thing is that the people at Reynard who will tell you this story admire Carl for doing it, if he did. They like to believe that he did do it because that's what they would have done, as racers. It's a funny old business, motor racing.

For 1989 Reynard aimed to consolidate its success, and it concentrated on just Formula Three, Formula Atlantic and Formula 3000 while building cars for the Vauxhall/Opel-Lotus category and making kits for Fulmar Competition Services.

In the interim, Bill Stone had re-entered the Reynard story. 'I worked for a trailer company in New Zealand for some years. Then I bought a 60-acre farm and bred angora goats and, with Jim Stone, I also set up a used and reconditioned car spares business in Auckland. I drifted away from racing – the businesses were so time-consuming.

'In 1988 we sold the car-parts business, and Maura and I decided to take a holiday in England. I'd kept in touch with Adrian and he'd often suggested that I should work with him again. He was able to persuade me that there was not much difference between taking a holiday for six weeks and working for six months since, either way, I had to find someone to run the goat farm. The upshot was that I went to work for Reynard again, as Adrian's assistant, and after two months, with the backing of his board, he offered me a full-time job – name your price – as Production Manager, with the intention that I should become a director.'

Everyone has his own version of what happened next, and Bill does not escape criticism. Some have suggested that he'd been away from motor racing too long and had lost the competitive edge, but Bill's own account is: 'Paul Owens and I did not get on particularly well and I felt that Rick Gorne resented my return. I can understand Rick's point of view, he had done a fantastic job in building up the company and here I was back on the scene, reaping the benefit of all his years of work.

'I'd accepted the job with the proviso that I had to go back to New Zealand in December to sort out the sale of my farm. Meanwhile, there was work to be done and decisions to be made and I was not there. While I was back home, Adrian called me a couple of times suggesting that I should be in England because I was needed, but we had this agreement. Despite the agreement, my absence did not go down well with Paul and Rick and I can understand that. It's the natural response to the return of the Prodigal Son.'

One might also question the wisdom of an agreement which allowed a Production Manager to take several months off during the build season.

'When I returned to England there was a directors' meeting and I was dropped from the team. My contract was terminated, but Adrian made sure I was not out of pocket – in fact, we remained good friends even if it was not quite on the old basis. Soon afterwards my marriage broke up, but I think that was coming anyway and, indeed, my domestic situation may have reflected in my attitude to work while I was at Reynard.'

Bill suffered a crushing blow, but he bounced back. 'After I left Reynard I set up a fabrication business in Bicester, and Reynard was one of my biggest customers. I also became a subcontractor for a number of kit car makers which were then enjoying a boom. Things were going well and I diversified into carbon-fibre and also built my own kit car, a replica of a WW2 Jeep, but I was spreading the business too thinly. Then came the recession and a lot of my kit car customers folded, owing us money. They took us down with them.

'After the business went, I worked for other outfits, including Ecurie Ecosse, and then became the race team Administration Manager for Andy Rouse Engineering, which built and ran works-backed Ford Mondeos in Touring Car races until the end of 1995.

'While I was still running my own business, however, I became a supplier to Arthur Mallock. I'd built chassis for Arthur when I worked for Arch Motors and again when I was at Sabre Automotive, and we'd always got on well. We were close enough to go on a skiing holiday together, and on our return I met his daughter, Susanne, when she collected us at the airport.

'It was the first time we'd met and I'd known Arthur for over 20 years. To cut a long story short, Susanne and I were married in February 1992 in New Zealand.'

In 1995 Bill returned to Reynard, this time to oversee a Touring Car project for Chrysler, based on its Stratus model. Of course, being a Reynard project, it won first time out.

Chapter Fourteen _____

Business Moves

A new monocoque formed the basis of the 89D Formula 3000 car, which retained its predecessor's suspension layout but had a slightly longer wheelbase, revised nose, different side-pods and a high, ducted, engine cover. The driver was put further back and the monocoque had a flat underside. With Ralt out of F3000, and with March virtually extinct, Reynard made 36 cars and faced serious opposition only from Lola; although, during the year, March was to spring a victory which surprised even them.

Malcolm Oastler recalls: 'We strengthened the car for '89, got rid of some of the bendy bits left over from the Formula Three car, improved the aerodynamics and made it better-engineered and more efficient. Lola, however, improved their efficiency enormously. We won the Championship and seven of the 11 races, but there was a bit of a chink in our armour. In fact we did more development on it than on the '88 car. During the season we came up with a new rear wing, end plates, diffusers and short side-pods – we were kept pretty busy.

'In Formula 3000 the engine and tyres are controlled, so basically you get to play about with weight distribution, lift, drag and the overall aerodynamic package. People talk about suspension geometry, but I think there's more bullshit spoken about that than anything else in motor racing. We've always favoured long wheelbase cars, they're easier to drive and that's good. People will tell you that long wheelbase cars won't go round slow corners – but when a car's in a corner it doesn't know how long it is. You usually get more time from making a car easy to drive than through trick aerodynamics.'

Thomas Danielsson opened the score for Reynard with a win at the first round at Silverstone, and then Martin Donnelly won at Vallelunga. Like many other runners in the field, Donnelly was using a development nose box which then had not passed the FIA safety test, and his win was contested. Even though the nose box had passed the test by the time the protest was heard, Donnelly was disqualified, which is ironic given that the new nose box marked an improvement in safety.

The disqualification resulted in two things: one was that some of the fire was doused in Donnelly, which possibly cost him the Championship, and the other was that Fabrizio Giovanardi and his March 89B inherited the win – it was the last time that a March production car would win a race.

Jean Alesi won the third round at Pau in his EJR Reynard-Mugen, and the top six places were filled by Reynards. At Jerez it was the turn of Eric Bernard and Lola, but Reynards won the next four rounds, with Andrea Chiesa taking Enna Pergusa, Donnelly winning Brands Hatch and Jean Alesi taking the Birmingham Superprix and the race at Spa.

Erik Comas took the last two rounds for Lola, which became strong in the latter part of the season, and he scored as many points as Alesi. Alesi took the title, however, because he won three races to the two of Comas. By such details can a driver's career be shaped.

Jean Alesi won the 1989 European Formula 3000 Championship in a Reynard 89D, taking victory in three of the 11 races. Reynard won a total of seven races in the Championship that year. (*Sutton Motorsport Images*)

In the new British Formula 3000 Championship for one-year-old cars, Reynards won every one of the nine rounds. The Champion was Gary Brabham, son of Sir Jack, whose production racing cars had established the benchmark in the 1960s. And the 1960s Brabhams had all been designed by Ron Tauranac.

In Japan Reynard had a mixed year. By putting the driver further back in the car it biased the weight towards the rear, and using tyres primarily developed for the Lola meant that the rear tyres overheated and the fronts ran cold, which led to massive oversteer. It took time to dial this out of the car, but Malcolm says: 'We won three races in the middle of the season and missed the Championship by a single point. On the last lap of the last race, Ross Cheever had the title in the bag with four corners to go when he got punted off.

'We kept enough confidence among the teams to sell a dozen cars in 1990, but the first cars which went out there had a 'hand grenade' gearbox which used to blow up for a pastime. The car was not that good, anyway, and it finished us for a while. By the end of the year the Japanese confidence level in us was zero.'

Adrian tried hard to crack Japan in 1989 and flew there 25 times. As a result of his impossible timetable, he lost a stone in weight, which is no small thing for a man who is slightly built. He says: 'My hair turned grey and there were even rumours that I had AIDS!'

While Reynard won in Formula 3000, and the cars made by FCS continued to dominate the last days of Formula Ford 2000, the company struggled in British Formula Three. The 893 was a revision of the 883, mainly in the area of aerodynamics. It had a new gearbox and the power train was 22mm lower than previously, which lowered the centre of gravity but which caused problems with the starter motor gear. Although it sold more strongly than any previous Reynard Formula Three car, most of its sales were outside Britain, with a significant proportion going to South America and Japan.

Once again, most of the top British teams chose to go with Ralt – perhaps that should read 'chose to go with Ron Tauranac'. Reynard's hopes rested largely on Rickard Rydell of Sweden, a driver who could be quick over a single lap (which proved that the Reynard 893 was on the pace) but was inconsistent over a race distance.

Rydell won the first round at Silverstone and none other, although he crossed the line first at Donington late in the season and was penalised for a jumped start. Only one other race was won by a Reynard driver, when Paul Stewart took the flag at Snetterton in August, and the season settled down to a contest between the Ralts of Allan McNish and David Brabham, with Brabham taking the title.

Actually it was more than a contest between two drivers since the entire season was blighted by controversy, protest and counter-protest over the legality of the Mugen and Speiss engines which most teams used. But that was true for the few Reynard runners as well as the Ralt brigade. The fact is that Reynard was given a drubbing by Ralt, even while Adrian was in secret negotiations to buy the company as part of March Group plc.

Reynard really lost the season before it began because it had not convinced the best teams to buy its car. Despite successive Championships in Britain – and the British series was reckoned to be the first among equals of the European Formula Three Championships – the Reynard had not shown itself to be so far ahead of the Ralt that established teams wanted to break their long-standing relationships with Ron Tauranac.

In other countries, running on different tyres, Reynards fared rather better than in Britain. Jean-Marc Gounon won the French Championship in a Reynard 893-Alfa Romeo and Thomas Nilsson won the Swedish series with a VW-powered 893. Antonio Tamburini won the Monaco GP support race in a Reynard 893-Alfa Romeo and he was also runner-up, by one point, in the Italian Championship. In the German Championship Heinz-Harald Frentzen was runner-up – he was one of many current Formula One drivers who had a brush with Reynard at an important stage of his career.

The Reynard 893 was a winner, no doubt about that, but you do not prove that unless you get the cars into the right hands. Somehow, the idea went round that the Ralt was the car to have, and that was it. In 1992 the word would go round that a Reynard was the car to have, so people left the Ralt camp – win some, lose some.

With the Ford Formulae cars being made under a different umbrella, Reynard entered a new market with the first carbon composite Toyota Atlantic car, the 89H ('H' for Haas). It was closely related to the Formula Three car, although it had a ground-effect aerodynamic package, and one finished second in the Championship. Simultaneously, it was being rumoured that the next move for the company would be into Indycar, and although these rumours were denied at the time, there was some truth in them.

At the beginning of 1989 Adrian entered discussions with Carl Haas about the possibility of building an Indycar, but these had fizzled out. Then came the possibility of entering Indycar via another route.

While Reynard was having a mixed season on the track, but a very successful one commercially, just a mile away from the Reynard Centre, March Engineering was in deep trouble. For some time March had set the standard for production racing car makers. In Europe in the 1980s it had the lion's share of the Formula Two market, and when Formula 3000 replaced Formula Two, it had dominated that as well. It also had a profitable line in sports cars, a tie-in with Nissan and sold Indycars by the dozen. After

Reynard drivers Heinz-Harald Frentzen, Michael Bartels and Michael Schumacher celebrating in 1989 at Hockenheim after a Formula Three race.

years of struggle, March was suddenly awash with money, and in 1986 it became the first racing car maker to be launched on the stock exchange. It was a very successful launch which valued the company at £14.9 million.

March Group plc, as the overall structure became, brought in outside managers to run it like a sensible business, but motor racing is not a sensible business. March's new management did not understand this; there was a fundamental clash of cultures, and the racing car business was taken away from the racers.

A composites division was established and it lost a lot of money on projects such as the Panther Solo GT car.

March did not have a policy of building a layer of new talent, so when team leaders moved there was no level below them to take their place, unlike Reynard where John Thompson was able to move up to head the Formula 3000 project when Malcolm Oastler moved to other work.

This lack of a culture affected the design of the cars, while a fundamental lack of understanding of customer requirements by the new management led to a sharp decline in product quality. One by one, March lost its markets. Since all this was happening only a mile away, and laid-off workers would keep applying for jobs, the decline was noted at Reynard.

It's smart to learn from your own mistakes, but it's even smarter to learn from other people's before you make your own.

By early 1989 the group was on its knees, there were times when not only was the staff not paid, but individuals dipped into their own pockets to pay outside suppliers to keep the company afloat – in what other industry would that happen? – and trading in March shares was suspended.

The situation was saved only by skilled negotiations by the then chairman, John Cowan, who sold the Formula One team, the Formula 3000 project and the wind tunnel to Leyton House, the Formula One team's main sponsor. What remained was the Ralt operation, the main factory in Bicester, and contracts to build exclusive Indycars for Porsche and Alfa Romeo. The Porsche project was operated from Bicester, under Gordon Coppuck, and the Alfa Romeo project was centred at the Ralt works in Weybridge, initially under the late Maurice Phillippe.

In the summer of 1989 it was known that March Engineering was for sale, along with Ralt, and what remained of March Group plc would become a financial services company. With the Porsche and Alfa Romeo deals proceeding, it seemed an ideal way for Reynard to make the leap into Indycar.

With Carl Haas underwriting the move, Adrian began negotiations to buy March Engineering, mainly to obtain the Porsche and Alfa Romeo contracts.

He was not the only one in the running; Chip Ganassi was also interested. But, eventually, Reynard became the front runner in the negotiations, which were shrouded in secrecy. To keep the sale under wraps, in the documents which were exchanged between the two parties, March was called 'Magenta' and Reynard was called 'Radiant'.

It was real cloak and dagger stuff, except that anyone with an IQ in double figures could have worked out that since 'Magenta' was a racing car maker based in Murdoch Road, Bicester, it could only be be March and a racing car maker called 'Radiant', based in Telford Road, Bicester, could only be Reynard. Apparently, this level of thinking is common in the City of London – it's nice to know that your pension fund is in safe hands.

Adrian agreed in principle to buy March, which would have meant a down payment of roughly £1 million pounds. When Reynard's accountants looked through the March books, however, they discovered that all was not quite as it seemed, and there were a number of outstanding loans between elements of the March group. This made the deal a lot less attractive and, 24 hours before contracts were due to be signed, Reynard and Haas pulled out.

To tie up the loose ends in the story: the racing car division was later the subject of a management buy-out. March Group plc, divested of any connection with motor racing, bought a firm of stockbrokers and then arrived at terms to sell it at a profit to a major bank. An hour or so before the contract was to be signed, the bank called off the deal because it had discovered that a (pre-March) senior manager in the firm had been bleeding it white. This was a crippling blow to the parent company, but a new chairman, Peter Voller, was able to save it from complete collapse.

The March Formula 3000 project, taken over by Leyton House, was never successful and it folded during 1990. Left on a limb, it did not have the culture of Lola or Reynard, so that was more or less inevitable. You can't win in motor racing without a culture to back you.

March Grand Prix struggled after the boss of Leyton House, Aguri Akargi, was arrested for alleged fraud on a massive scale, and it soon folded. The Alfa Romeo

Indycar project faded away, largely because Alfa Romeo could not produce a good enough engine – in fact it was a Ferrari engine with a different name on the camshaft covers to suit Fiat's marketing policy. At one time its outstanding legal case against Alfa Romeo was March's main financial asset. They settled out of court.

The Porsche Indycar project, which showed flashes of promise, was undermined by Porsche's falling sales and the company's disastrous foray into Formula One. Porsche has an engineering culture; it does not have a motor racing culture. So, it can win in sports car racing but it will never crack Formula One.

For many years March had been the most successful production car maker in the world, but it had lost the values which had made it so. The young student who had been so thrilled to strike up a friendship with someone who actually worked at March, had worked himself into a position where he could bid for the company but, with hindsight, it would not have been a good idea.

One can understand Adrian's sentimental desire to buy the company, and one can understand the desire of both Reynard and Haas to get their hands on the Indycar deals. In fact, in both cases, it was looking back to the past.

It is possible that had Reynard bought March it would have taken them both down, because Reynard would have inherited a demoralised workforce, time was running out and the Indycar projects were not as golden as they seemed from the outside.

It would have taken time to instil the Reynard culture into March and Ralt and it would have been a painful process on both sides because, by then, Reynard's philosophy had been formulated and there was no equivalent approach at March or Ralt. One cannot imagine Ron Tauranac taking kindly to having the Reynard philosophy imposed on him. He might have rubbed along with Adrian, engineer to engineer, but one cannot see Ron having any time for Rick Gorne's approach to selling cars.

Had the deal gone through, the position of Ralt would have been uncertain, anyway. Adrian had not decided what he would have done with that particular asset. It was the Indycar contracts which had attracted him, and in itself that shows how flawed the scheme was. You inherit Ralt and you're not sure what to do with it?

For his part, Rick relished the idea of having one factory with rival teams popping out Reynards at one end, Ralts out of the other, and fighting on the circuits. How 'Rick of the Silver Tongue' would have coped as a salesman in that circumstance is a thought to relish. Since the deal did not go ahead it postponed Reynard's entry to Indycar by five years, but it also left the way open for an attempt at Formula One which was very nearly to destroy the company.

A by-product of the interest in March was that Malcolm Oastler was taken off the Formula 3000 project in order to be available for other work within the company (he would have worked on one of the two Indycar projects or, perhaps, on a new March sports car project) and he was replaced by Gary Anderson, who had designed the Anson Formula Three cars of the early 1980s. Ansons had shown promise but required more precision from a driver than did a Ralt, and Anson never got the right person in the car.

With the Japanese market firmly in mind, it was decided to build the 90D with a similar weight distribution to the Lola to optimise the use of Japanese tyres. To do that it was decided to use a transverse gearbox. Then, early in 1990, Anderson left to join the embryo Jordan Grand Prix effort as Chief Designer, and he took two key Reynard men, one the transmission designer, with him. It still rankles with Adrian, who trots out the usual platitudes about remaining on friendly terms with Eddie Jordan, but you can see that the poaching hurt him, and he will never forget or forgive.

That is the story told by Adrian with diplomacy but, according to other people, it was even worse than that. On the day of the 1989 works Christmas party someone discovered that the gear centres in the 'box were not right. He bottled the information until the following day so as not to ruin the party, and then everyone went into overdrive to try to correct the error.

Anderson's defection put a screw into the development of the Reynard 90D and, in particular, its new transverse gearbox. Teams who bought Reynards encountered endless problems with their transmissions, and it cost the company £450,000 over the season to replace broken 'boxes and to develop a reliable transmission: In fact, four distinct gearboxes were made that year and the problem was solved only by the Series IV transmission. By then many teams, particularly in Japan, had lost confidence in Reynard.

One ex-Reynard man to whom we spoke made a point of saying that the only time that Reynard did not win the European Formula 3000 Championship was when an 'outsider' was brought in to design the car.

The intrinsic problems would become clear during the year. Leyton House fielded a car which was usually an also-ran, so the European Formula 3000 Championship was essentially a Reynard/Lola head-to-head. Adrian says: 'We spent the entire year trying to pick up the pieces, so all our efforts went into that. We were fighting a rearguard action instead of making progress.'

Having scored equal points to Jean Alesi in 1989, Erik Comas knew he could take the title and he did, to give Lola its only 'open' European Formula 3000 Championship, and the only one which Reynard had not won since it joined the category. It was not a drubbing, a Reynard was more often than not in the top three, and Eric van der Poele won three races (Pau, Birmingham and Nogaro) while Eddie Irvine led home a Reynard 1–2–3 at Hockenheim. It was actually a better season than most which Lola enjoyed in the Championship, but by Reynard's standards it was a disaster.

In the British Formula 3000 Championship, which was opened up for current cars, Reynards won every round, and several times it took the top six places. The overall winner was Pedro Chaves in a Reynard 90D-Cosworth. It was, however, no more than a side-show.

British Formula Three was a less happy arena, although Reynard spent a lot of money on developing its new car. For a start the company's representation was thin, then there was the astonishing speed of the Finnish pair Mika Hakkinen and Mika Salo, both in Ralts, which caused some runners to switch from Reynard to Ralt. Those who made the switch did not improve – the Finns were in a special class, but then so was Ralt, and it took almost every point in the series.

At the time, the basic problem with the Reynard was thought to be flexing between the tub and the engine and, although various suspension changes were made throughout the season, the car's handling problems were never solved. In fact, the problem was less likely to have been in the mechanical design than in the aerodynamics. Whatever, 1990 is a year which Reynard would prefer to forget except, ironically, it made a lot of money from its Formula Three cars.

Despite the lack of sales and success in Britain in 1989, Reynard's Formula Three sales held up well elsewhere in 1990 and the company set a new record for Formula Three cars made in any one year. Not for the first time, the reason was Rick Gorne's creative approach to marketing, and he says: 'In 1990 we landed a deal with Mexico to supply the national Formula Three series. I'd heard a rumour that the Abed brothers, who ran the Mexican GP, were thinking of a one-make series. I sent them a fax, got an instant response and, armed with a video of the Reynard organisation, I was in Mexico City soon afterwards. I did the deal while I was there, and it was the first time in history that an FIA-recognised formula was run on a one-make basis.

Reynard Racing Cars 1989 Formula 3000 car, the 89D, displayed in the colours of Pacific Racing who ran JJ Lehto.

'We sold them 40 Reynard 903s, and in 1993 we sent them 20 933s – the 903 became the Class B car while the 933 became the Class A car. There is a free choice of engine, the series is tightly controlled, it's fair and it works. It has done well for Mexico and it has done well for us.'

Of the car itself Adrian says: 'The problem with 903 was aerodynamic pitch-sensitivity. We did not then appreciate the importance of pitch and heave sensitivity. This was the essential thing which Dallara got right in 1993 when they wiped us out of Formula Three – because it makes a car easier to drive. Instead, I was focusing on the lift/drag ratio. It was another lesson to learn, but it was a lesson which we did learn.'

One team manager, who began the season with Reynard and then switched to Ralt halfway through, harbours the suspicion that the gearbox casing was flexing. He says: 'I do not know that for certain, but it is certainly an area I would have looked at. My feeling is that Adrian was allowing himself to be governed by economics and he was unwilling to commit money and effort to get things right in detail. We'd bought the cars at the beginning of the season and that was it so far as he was concerned.'

The Reynard 903 was not a bad car, however, because in other Championships and running on other tyres, it was very successful. Michael Schumacher took the German Formula Three Championship in a Reynard 903-VW, and five of the top six finishers in the series drove Reynards. Schumacher also won the prestigious races at Macau and Fuji and would have taken the European Formula Three Cup, but he was disqualified after the finish for changing the type of engine he was using between practice and the race.

In Britain Reynard was seen as a flop in Formula Three in 1990 (Adrian still sees the year as a time when he was thrashed by Ralt), but perceptions change from country to country and Reynard plays on a world stage. Rick had put a lot of effort into finding good local agents, and while Reynards were thin on the ground at home, in Italy Gabriele Seresina sold 21 cars – which was no small achievement in the land of Dallara – and Roberto Colciago won the Italian Championship in an Alfa Romeo-powered Reynard 903.

David Brown, now with Tyrrell, recalls: 'During what was a pretty poor year for us in Britain I was asked to design a new rear suspension. I'd only just finished my traineeship. I had to do it in pencil because the CAD system had not then been installed, and I shall never forget the mixture of elation and fear when I was asked to go to a test at Silverstone where the new suspension was fitted.

'It worked. The driver liked it. I was then asked if I was prepared to design the 1991 car. Of course I was, so Mark Slade and I were set to work on it. You could never get an opportunity like that anywhere else.'

On the other hand, Dallara was making big advances in Italy and was on an upward curve which would see it take a virtual monopoly of Formula Three throughout Europe.

In France, the land of Martini – the racing car, not the vermouth – Hugues de Chaunac handled Reynards, and there Eric Hélary took the series in a Reynard, beating a field largely comprising Dallaras and Ralts, while Niclas Johnsson won the Swedish Championship, with Reynard drivers taking the next three places.

With four out of the five main Formula Three Championships to Reynard's credit, 1990 could hardly be called a year of failure, but everyone likes to win at home, and the

Reynard were presented with their first Queen's Award for Export Achievement in 1990 by Her Majesty's Lord Lieutenant for Oxfordshire, Sir Ashley Ponsonby. Rick Gorne, accompanied by Adrian, accepted the accolade on behalf of the entire British motor racing industry.

British Formula Three Championship was usually perceived to be the most prestigious series. Although that was in the process of changing, Adrian still looks back on 1990 as a very bad year.

The Reynard 90H Atlantic car was even less successful than its Formula Three counterpart, largely because Reynard became complacent after a promising debut year and did not give enough attention to developing it. In turn, that may have had an adverse effect on Reynard's desire to enter the Indycar market, because if you cannot win in Atlantic, your claims to be able to win the Indianapolis 500 begin to ring a little hollow – especially since the Atlantic cars were being sold by Carl Haas, the man Adrian was trying to persuade to take him into Indycar.

Still, come the autumn, Adrian once more entered discussions with Carl with a view to building an Indycar, but again the results were inconclusive.

During 1990 Reynard also won the Queen's Award for Export Achievement, which was a personal triumph for Rick Gorne. His contribution to Reynard's success cannot be underestimated – what happened to all the other hopeful racing car manufacturers who were active in 1982 when Rick joined the company?

1990 had been a year of mixed fortunes. Some of the competition results had been disappointing (Lola scored a 1–2–3 in the Donington Formula 3000 race in the same week that Reynard won its Queen's Award), but the business had boomed and other elements were falling into place which made Adrian's ultimate ambition of going into Formula One seem a distinct possibility.

At the end of the year, when Rory Byrne became available from Benetton, Adrian established a Formula One research project. Unfortunately, however, economic recession was appearing over the horizon. It was a case of a good idea at the wrong time.

Chapter Fifteen _____

To the Brink

During 1991 Reynard attempted to enter Formula One and failed. The attempt not only failed, but came within an ace of bankrupting both the company and Adrian personally.

About the only positive thing you can say about the venture is that it shouldn't have failed. Adrian's thinking was clear, the circumstances seemed right and he made all the right moves. He brought good people on board and did not jeopardise his core business. He had a deal for works engines and, well, almost everything, but had he not pulled the plug just in time he would have lost everything.

The gap between being a successful production car racer and a Formula One team is now so huge that no team which has entered Formula One in the past 10 years has won a Grand Prix. Once-great names, such as Brabham and Lotus, have disappeared. The only team in the 1996 World Championship which has gained even a podium finish and which was not in Formula One 15 years ago is Jordan. That's how tough it is.

When Adrian began to put his plans into operation, which was during 1989/90, things were a little different. When the turbo era ended, the playing field seemed to level out and conditions encouraged newcomers. They came in their droves, and half-forgotten names like Rial, Onyx, Dallara, Coloni and Euro Brun appeared. March Grand Prix was a serious contender, and Lola was in, running its first works-based Formula One team. Everything seemed up for grabs.

It was a time of transition and change, and the Formula One establishment appeared to be nearer to hand than at any time for years. Television coverage had increased considerably during the 1980s, making Formula One an attractive proposition to potential sponsors. The difference between works engines and customer engines was less than for a long time and there also seemed to be no shortage of major manufacturers capable of supplying works engines, since many were building machines for a new Sports Car Championship, due for 1991, which would operate to the same 3.5-litre engine formula as Formula One.

The prospects seemed heady, with companies such as Toyota, Mazda, Nissan and Peugeot known to be building new engines for sports cars. Lamborghini, already in Formula One, but now owned by Chrysler, was apparently poised to become a flagship company for the corporation. BMW, Porsche and Yamaha were all developing F1 engines; Mercedes-Benz was back in racing through the Sauber sports cars; Jaguar was in sports cars, and had been taken over by Ford. The possibilities seemed to be without limit and, moreover, the world's economy seemed to be on an upswing.

That, in brief, is the background to Reynard's attempt at Formula One and, although the project ultimately failed, news of it generated an air of excitement around the company. Unfortunately, that air of excitement did not translate into sales of production cars. Having set record levels for cars built with carbon composites in 1990, the following year was fairly bleak as economic recession hit motor racing, and many sponsors decided that painting their names on the side of racing cars was not their number one priority.

No new Reynard Formula Atlantic cars were sold, there was only an up-date kit for the 90H, but that is par for the course in Atlantic. From 102 Formula Three cars made in 1990 (a record) sales dropped to 36 in 1991. The contract with General Motors for Formula Vauxhall/Opel came to an end during the year and, in any case, since it was a set design, production had steadily declined over the years because, as drivers moved on, they sold their old cars to the next generation. The one bright spot was Formula 3000 and, despite a fairly poor season in 1990, Reynard bounced back with 30 sales.

Overall, sales were still good by most standards, and normally Reynard would have had another profitable year. Unfortunately, however, sales were financing the Formula One project and that nearly caused Reynard to fold.

During the year things became more and more desperate in the works, although that was not the perception from the outside as Reynards won nine of the 10 rounds of the European Formula 3000 Championship.

The Reynard 91D had a stiffer monocoque, and its aerodynamics benefited from some of the lessons being learned on the Formula One programme. For the first time, European Formula 3000 was using only radial tyres and Reynard got the equation right in Europe, while it struggled in Japan as, for most of the season, it tried to come to terms with new rubber on the only car it had in the Japanese Championship.

European teams were more forgiving of Reynard's 1990 gearbox problems than the Japanese (Reynard had taken the matter to heart and had tried to treat its customers fairly), and once again Reynard was numerically superior in Europe. It faced a new challenge in the shape of the Ralt RT 23, the company's first completely new product following a management buy-out of March/Ralt. The company had relocated to Colnbrook, the two arms had been united and the Formula 3000 car bore the Ralt name because Leyton House had exclusive rights to the name 'March' in Formula 3000 for seven years, although that was academic since Leyton House's own Formula 3000 operation had been wound up.

From the beginning of the season, the Reynard 91D looked the best bet. Lola's 1991 car was capable of finishing second on a number of occasions, but it was not easy to drive and several teams switched to Reynard. In that year, Avon produced a new radial tyre and it did not suit Lola, which also had an aerodynamic problem. That latter problem was soon sorted, leaving the tyres, but the car was dialled in over the season.

The trouble was, by the time that Lola had done so it had lost the cream of its customers, so even when it made competitive cars, in subsequent years, it had nobody to demonstrate them. So, Lola lost its European F3000 market, while continuing to win in Japan – to the end of 1995 it had won eight of the previous nine Japanese Championships.

Lola's sudden and almost complete loss of the European market still puzzles Mike Blanchet, but it probably had more to do with Rick's ability to make the right deal with the right team than the Reynard 91D's margin of superiority.

Still, in one race, Marco Apicella was so upset with his Lola that he simply parked it and claimed that it was too dangerous to drive. That did not go down well with his team boss, Jackie Stewart, who had driven some dogs in his time and had never given up. In fact, since Lolas often finished in the points, the car was obviously not far from the pace and it was a case of being close but not close enough.

There was another factor at play, and that was that some teams with the right connections could obtain supplies of fuel similar to that being used in Formula One, which meant up to 20 bhp more in a class where engines are governed by rev limiters.

As it happened, the teams which had the superior fuel – they were mainly among the Italian contingent – were all running Reynards, a factor which made the Reynard appear to be more superior to the Lola than it probably was.

The only Formula 3000 race which did not fall to Reynard was at Pau where Jean-Marc Gounon won for Ralt. Indeed, Gounon also crossed the line first at Enna, but was penalised for allegedly jumping the start. Video evidence suggests that this was a cruel decision, but we are talking about a small circuit in Italy, a land where races are alleged to have been run in ways which gave drivers with a vowel at the end of their surnames an advantage.

The race at Enna in 1991 went to Emanuele Naspetti's Reynard, and he also won more Formula 3000 races than anyone else in 1991. The series, however, went to the young Christian Fittipaldi who was more consistent. That was an especially gratifying result for Paul Owens who was Fittipaldi's race engineer (working with Pacific Racing).

Despite the fact that Gounon had won a race (or two races) for Ralt in 1991, the company did not make a sufficient impression to attract more than one customer for 1992. Things might have been different had Gounon not been penalised a minute at Enna where he had set fastest lap and had finished 45 seconds ahead of the field. The stewards' decision in Italy hastened the end of March/Ralt under its management buy-out team. The word, however, is 'hastened', the company had grown too fat to survive even without economic recession.

Left Reynard won nine of the 10 Formula 3000 races in 1991, and Christian Fittipaldi took the title for Pacific Racing in his 91D. Photographed at Spa are Malcolm Oastler, Andrew Tilley (a Reynard engineer), Keith Wiggins (Team Owner of Pacific Racing) and Paul Owens, Christian's race engineer.

Right Ross Cheever remained loyal to Reynard, continuing to drive for the marque in Japan under the Promise & Reynard banner in 1991, 1992 and 1993. He also competed in Japanese Formula 3000 for Reynard in 1989, 1990 and 1994. He narrowly missed Championship victory in every season.

Reynard had almost everything its own way in European F3000, but in Japan the effects of the disastrous 1990 gearbox were still being felt. Malcolm Oastler recalls: 'We lost all credibility, and for 1991 we only had one car in the series. It was run by our importer, Tom Hanawa, although Tom wasn't importing many cars, and he signed Ross Cheever. That meant that Ross switched from Dunlop to Bridgestone tyres, which put us back until he got used to them. Then Ross won three of the last four races and was second in the Championship again.'

Adrian said in 1993: 'Teams in Japan are very loyal to their suppliers. We also have the problem that not many European engineers want to live and work in Japan, and so we have not been able to persuade our best people to go out there. This has affected us, and the word went round that we did not understand the Japanese market. We could be quick in pre-season testing, but that was not enough. Japanese teams were loyal to the Lola importer, Nova, and Nova working closely with Bridgestone has had the knack of getting the best out of a car over a season.

'We have also been competitive over a season, but our problem has been that most of our wins have been by Ross Cheever who is perceived in Japan to be an excellent driver. Ross has played up that aspect, and who can blame him? He is a star in Japan.

'What we have needed has been a win by a Japanese driver who was not perceived to be on Ross's level. It has been counter-productive to Reynard to have him in our car. In 1994 I think we might crack it, and if we do, we'll have cracked it forever.' As things turned out, Reynard did not crack it in 1994. In fact it made the breakthrough in 1996.

Ross Cheever was out of a drive, and races were won by young Japanese drivers Hattori and Takagi, and Michael Schumacher's younger brother, Ralf.

Paul Warwick, the 21-year-old younger brother of Formula One driver Derek Warwick, won the first four rounds of the British Formula 3000 Championship for Mansell Madgwick Motorsport in his Reynard 90D-Cosworth. It was the sort of performance which was expected of a man who was regarded as an outstanding prospect for the future. He was then killed in an accident at Oulton Park, in the fifth round, through a mix of circumstances none of which reflected badly on Reynard.

The fifth round had been stopped as a result of Paul's accident and not restarted. Since Paul was leading on the lap before the race was stopped, he was declared the winner and, in turn, that secured him the title posthumously.

Formula Three was Reynard's only other market, and there it struggled as Ron Tauranac came up with a very good car in the Ralt RT35. Reynard ran a works team in conjunction with Pete Briggs's Edenbridge Racing, and invested a lot of money in a development car for Gil de Ferran. For the first time in years the British series was more than a Reynard/Ralt head-to-head as TOM's and Bowman entered the fray with cars which were built up to a standard rather than down to a price.

Gil de Ferran took three wins and had an outside chance of the title until the penultimate round. Although it was not a brilliant season it set Reynard on the right course for 1992. The company needed to be set on course since the Formula Three effort had actually lost it money. That was serious because not only were sales down, but the Formula One project was meanwhile bleeding the company white.

At the beginning of 1994 Adrian said: 'Formula One is something I've always wanted to do, I still want to do it, and I will do it – one day. And when we do go into Formula One it will not be just to participate, we will go in when we believe that we have a chance of competing at the front and winning races – the only thing which motivates us is winning.

The unveiling of the 1991 Formula Three challenger, the 913, in front of the Reynard Centre in Bicester.

'The core of any good project is the people. Money is also very important, but if you've got the right people and the money you can do anything. You don't need the factories, the machine tools, or any of the other things which are supposed to be important – you just need the right people, money and the right leadership.

'During the autumn of 1990 I got together with Rory Byrne. We go back to the 1970s when I was building Formula Ford 2000 cars and Rory was Royale's designer. Rory then designed successful cars for Toleman and Benetton, and there were many seasons when his cars were reckoned to be the best-handling in Formula One. Then Benetton brought in John Barnard who established a separate design office close to his home, 80 miles from the Benetton factory, and Rory and some of the other engineers became disenchanted.

'My close friend and mentor, Alex Hawkridge, who had known Rory since the days at Royale, knew what was going on in his mind and he knew what was going on in mine, and Rory anyway lived only a mile away from me at the time. Reynard had enjoyed several profitable years and in 1990, although we had a bad year on the circuits, we had sold 102 Formula Three cars and 29 Formula 3000 cars, not to mention cars for Formula Vauxhall. We felt we were in a position to fund a Formula One R&D programme from our profits, and to build the first car. We figured it would take a year, during which time we could assemble the other elements to make a team, including sponsorship and a factory.

'I spoke to Rory and found that we thought on similar lines, and eventually we decided to go ahead. He gave in his notice to Benetton, we identified the key personnel we would need and we advertised for them. They came from all over, although unsurprisingly many came from Benetton which was located nearby and was then not a happy team. Among them was Pat Symonds whose path had crossed mine many times over the years.'

Reynard established a separate team away from the main factory. Unlike March which had moved some of its best people to the Formula One team, Reynard recruited from outside and preserved the integrity of its core operation. While sales of production cars were intended to provide the initial funding, the idea was that this would be repaid once outside sponsors were on board.

The theory was excellent, Reynard was doing everything right and nobody doubted that the car, when it appeared, would be competitive and that sponsors would form an orderly queue. The trouble was that nobody foresaw world-wide economic recession.

Rick Gorne says: 'During 1990 I was urging that we should go into Indycar. Production car making was what we knew, it was what we were good at. You put in materials at one end, out pops a car at the other end, and you're away. The situation changed when Rory became available, at which point I backed Adrian because Rory had a proven track record in Formula One. We knew that we would have to get a factory engine deal to make the scheme sensible but, since we had all the other ingredients, we thought that would fall into place.'

Adrian continues: 'Including myself there were 19 people on the Formula One team, and we began our research programme starting from a clean sheet of paper with no preconceptions. In all, we spent more than a million pounds to reach the stage of building a wind tunnel model and undergoing testing with it. We had very good data acquisition systems, we wrote our own software, we did our own active ride programme and we instigated a four-wheel-steering programme which finally appeared on a Benetton in 1993. It was a 'first' in Formula One, but was banned under the 1994 regulations. We progressed as far as testing some systems on a Formula 3000 car run for us by Madgwick Motorsport.

'One of my tasks was to find the engine, and during 1991 I did the rounds of major manufacturers, looking for one to become a partner. Nissan and Toyota were not ready for a 1992 start, but they had gone beyond merely thinking about Formula One. Each had 3.5-litre sports car engines on the stocks, but they were unhappy with their treatment in the World Sportscar Championship and were cautious about anything run from Europe. Talks with Piero Lardi at Ferrari also took place about engine supply.

'Yamaha, however, was interested, although it had not had a very good record in Formula One. It had supplied engines to Zakspeed, and then to Brabham, and neither had been successful, although, given the state of those teams, it was not easy to identify where blame for the lack of success lay.'

Despite that, Yamaha had no shortage of wooers, and Mike Earle and Robin Herd were keen to make an alliance. It helped that Robin was the design consultant on the abortive Yamaha OX-99 'supercar' – one of the more ghastly blunders of recent automotive history. Mike Earle was apparently led to believe that the Yamaha engine was his for the asking, if the rest of the elements were in place. Eddie Jordan was also in the frame and, ultimately, he had the misfortune to land the deal. It put a skew into the history of Jordan Grand Prix, an otherwise promising outfit, although it was financially advantageous.

Adrian continues: 'During 1991 Yamaha and Reynard began to move together. I had meetings with their Managing Director both in England and Japan, and things looked fairly bright until they released details of their engine: its dimensions, weight, power and heat rejection figures. We built a wind tunnel model and were dismayed at the size of the radiator ducts we would need. The Yamaha V12 was not that powerful, yet it was big, heavy and, in terms of heat rejection, it was basically a pressure cooker.

'We set Yamaha a target and asked for 700 bhp with reliability for the first race of 1992, and they said that they thought they could achieve that. Rory was not convinced that they could and, even if they did, he felt that the performance of the car would be jeopardised by using the engine – it wasn't just power, it was the whole package, the size, weight, radiator sizes, everything.

'Having been delivered this blow, I then went to see Mike Kranefuss of Ford with a view to using the Ford-Cosworth HB engine. By that time, however, Tom Walkinshaw had become a partner in Benetton and he was pressurising Ford to concentrate on them. In any case, a Ford-Cosworth deal would have been a lease arrangement which we'd have had to pay for, and one of the objectives I'd set myself when thinking of Formula One was to have a major manufacturer as a partner.

'I had spoken to everybody, including Ferrari, Lamborghini, Honda and Renault, but only Yamaha was in a position to be a partner. Renault was sympathetic to us, and liked our ideas, but Renault boss Christian Contzen suggested that our best move might be to buy Ligier. That was a move which none of us seriously entertained.

'I'd also hired someone to find sponsorship and, after six months, he'd come up with nothing. Nothing. We therefore had no outside funding, not even seed-corn funding, and the recession was biting into our core business. Sales were down, property prices were down (I'd moved into a new house and saw its value plummet) and things generally were very difficult.

'I even had talks with some of the then Italian Formula One teams, with a view to our combining, but ultimately these negotiations came to nothing.

'By August 1991, Rory and I had lost faith in the project and from then on I was engaged in a rescue mission, not for the Formula One project, but for the company itself. I should have stopped then, but I kept going hoping that something would turn up until, in September, I grasped the nettle and gave everyone in the Formula One team a month's notice.'

During the year Adrian had to liquidise many of his assets. The Spitfires went, as did the helicopter and the Harvard, and even Rick's beloved 1954 Corvette was sold. At the beginning of October 1991 Reynard's bank said that it could not meet the company's wage bill, and Adrian had to pledge his home as security.

At the end of the month, Reynard's staff wondered why they received cheques instead of the usual direct transfers to their bank accounts, and they were told that the bank's computer had gone down. The truth is that Reynard was so close to the brink that it needed the extra three days leeway for the cheques to clear. Rick says: 'Paul and I were behind the project for Adrian's sake. He had set his heart on it, and we backed it long after it made sense to do so, because of his commitment to it.'

Adrian continues: 'After I gave the Formula One personnel their notice I found jobs for almost all of them. Benetton was happy to take on virtually everyone, since John Barnard had gone to work for Ferrari again. Our arrangement meant that not only were jobs found, but Benetton took on the intellectual property in the heads of our staff. Benetton's 1992 car was effectively a Reynard and I was pleased for that to happen. It meant that our work had an afterlife and the Benetton was a very good car.

'I sold the formal design, the stuff actually on paper and disk, together with the wind tunnel model and the active ride programme to Ligier for £400,000, although it didn't get back all our costs.

'The land that Rick and I had bought for the Formula One factory, together with the planning permission, we sold to Benetton. Rick and I had bought the land for a million pounds, as a joint speculation, and we lost several hundred thousand pounds on the deal. This is something Rick reminds me of occasionally! We also lost money on the factory design which Tom Walkinshaw and Benetton inherited free.' In other words,

The Reynard Formula One car 40 per cent scale model during a wind tunnel test at Imperial College, London.

Benetton's smart new factory at Enstone should have had 'Reynard' on the sign outside.

'It was not all gloom and doom, however, since the project left us with a very good R&D base which benefited our other programmes over the next two years. We also got a lot of good engineering experience, new methodology, and the staff we retained had learned new techniques. There is no doubt, however, that it had pushed the company past the limit of its financial resources. We had worked on the assumption that we would generate a similar level of profit in 1991 to that we had enjoyed in 1990, but the recession meant that we did not.

'We started 1992 practically insolvent and barely surviving. I had my house up for sale, and if I had found a buyer I would have sustained a loss which would have wiped me out personally. It was only the fact that nobody was buying houses which saved me.

'In November 1991 I had not even any idea how we were going to meet the wage bill, and Reynard was saved only when some money from Ligier arrived. There were times at the end of 1991 when I was not sure whether I would have a job to go to the next day. Every asset which could be used as a guarantee was used.

'At about the same time, our contract to supply Vauxhall/Opel-Lotus cars was due to end, but the contract stipulated that General Motors would buy any spares that we had in stock. By the time our contract expired, we had an awful lot of spares! Had it not been for that, we would not now be in business.

'Somehow we managed to survive the winter of 1991/2 and, during it, we drew up a plan of attack. One prong of the attack was that we would build an Indycar, if we could find the right partner. Another was that we would offer ourselves as consultants to major manufacturers. We were to be successful in both.'

There were to be two residues of the 1991 Formula One car. The first was the 1994 Pacific F1 built for Keith Wiggins who had started in Formula Ford and had gone on to win Championships at every level to Formula 3000, every time with a Reynard. Keith thought he had nowhere else to go but Formula One.

In October 1992 Paul Brown was asked to design an F1 car for Pacific. He took as his starting point the Reynard Formula 3000 chassis but, despite what has been written elsewhere, it was a new monocoque with a high nose. One of the design parameters was that the Pacific had to look like a Benetton, and that was reasonable since the 1992 Benetton had been based on the Reynard Formula One car.

Andrew MacAulay was set to work on the aerodynamics. Andrew is a product of the Reynard trainee scheme and, since 1988, he has made a major contribution to Reynard's successes in Formula 3000 and Indycar. He is one of the unsung heroes of the story. In this case his brief was to design an aerodynamic package by eye and so, of course, he used the Formula 3000 wings and so on as his starting point.

Had Keith Wiggins made the approach at the end of 1991 he might have been able to lock into the residue of the Reynard F1 programme, but that had long gone and the intelligence had been sold to Ligier. What Paul and Andy produced was a sensible, cost-conscious, starting point for 1993. Much of it was guesswork, but it was professional guesswork.

Then Wiggins ran out of money and the bits lay around in the factory until late in 1993 when he was able to do a deal with Adrian. He took away the pieces of an already obsolete Formula One car and went racing.

The car was obsolete because, in Formula One, the biggest single area of advantage is not chassis, driver or engine, but aerodynamics. In 1996 Williams was ahead of the field because it was perhaps two or three months ahead in aerodynamics, and it had the will to stay ahead. If Williams did no development for two or three months, it would lose the initiative – the competition is that tight. Williams has a wind tunnel staffed by 19 people to ensure that does not happen.

One got the impression from the Press that the first Pacific was just an up-rated Formula 3000 car, yet Reynard had made a bespoke six-speed gearbox. It was based on the Formula 3000 'box, sure, but it was a different 'box. In pre-season testing at Silverstone, in cold weather, the Pacific was close to the pace as well, which was remarkable, and surprised Paul Brown for one.

Pacific had a reasonable starting point, which was not developed. There were components on the car which were off-the-shelf bits since the project was being done on the proverbial shoestring. The real problem, the one which the armchair pundits did not see, was the lack of wind tunnel testing.

Pacific had no wind tunnel programme save for putting a car in the tunnel at MIRA, which was created for the production car industry. The MIRA tunnel is not a precision tool for racing cars, it has a four-inch boundary layer, which is not much use when you're running cars an inch off the ground and making adjustments in terms of thousandths of an inch. Using the wind tunnel at MIRA for a Formula One car probably did Pacific more harm than good.

Paul Brown says: 'We came up with no more than a starting point, and even that was a year out of date. You normally expect a 50 per cent improvement after your first test in a tunnel, and the Pacific never even had a first test.

'The wings produced the drag, but they did not extract the downforce from that drag.'

The Pacific project was doomed from the start yet, despite using obsolete Ilmor customer engines and not having a star driver, it did manage to qualify for some races. Reynard, and Paul Brown, got some stick for Pacific's dismal showing, but what else did

The DAMS Formula One car was never raced. It was designed by Barry Ward and his team from both Reynard and DAMS during 1994 in preparation for the 1995 Formula One World Championship. A sufficient level of funding was not found by DAMS to complete the project.

Wiggins expect? It's happened many times: when Formula One beckons from the doorway, the brains exit through the window.

Apart from anything else, there is a huge difference between running a Formula 3000 customer car and making your own Formula One car. All we armchair experts can nod our heads and say, 'There is a big gap,' but until we try to bridge the gap, none of us can know. Wiggins was no fool; he's won successive Championships, but even he did not realise how big the gap was.

Later, in 1995, Reynard built a Formula One car for DAMS, the French Formula 3000 team which had also enjoyed great success. At least this time there was proper wind tunnel testing and the car was designed, ground up, by Barry Ward, another product of the Reynard training scheme. It was a proper job and it ran in tests with a borrowed engine.

Having a car is one thing and having the money to run it is another. New regulations came in to protect the driver, and they meant a substantial redesign. Established Formula One teams are used to that, but it put a skew into a newcomer's plans and the project was dropped.

Reynard has yet to make its debut in Formula One, but short odds say that one day it will. In fact, as we will see, had circumstances been just a little different it would have been preparing to make its debut during 1996. However, it would have been under completely different conditions from those which nearly wiped out the company in 1991.

Chapter Sixteen

Back to Basics

Reynard had barely survived, but the plan for recovery was implemented, and during 1992 Rick Gorne was busy as he placed cars in other markets to help save the company. He says: 'When General Motors decided to switch production of the Vauxhall/Opel-Lotus cars, it left us with a void in our capacity so Adrian sketched a revised version of the GM car which we called a 'World Car', because it could be used for one-make series anywhere in the world.

'We did it for ourselves since we had no orders for it, but we built a prototype and went into the market place and sold it. We placed 30 cars in Mexico, where they have Renault engines and race under the name "Formula Reynard" and we have another 30 in Japan where they have Mitsubishi engines and race as "Formula Mirage".'

That was one prong of the attack, but from late 1988 Adrian had been musing about a possible entry into Indycar. 'It was the next logical step. I could have approached a major manufacturer with a proposal to build a Group C car, the category was healthy at the time, but I've always been primarily a single-seater man and I wanted to tackle the single-seater categories first. There have been many times when I could have led the company into something else, but single-seaters are the most pure form of racing car.

'I was toying with the idea of Indycar, but it was a big step to make. Compared with Formula 3000, the investment was so much greater, the technology was higher and the customer base was more remote – all in all it was a bigger risk. Still, I was giving it serious thought and we were talking to Carl Haas. Then, in 1990, we were beaten by Lola in Formula 3000 and thrashed by Ralt in Formula Three. At that point I began to think that if I can't build a car to win in Formula Three, what am I doing considering Indy? It is true that I instigated the Formula One project the following year, but that came about because the material and human resources were available.

'In any case, it is a different matter entirely to commit yourself to Formula One, where you have a good chance of linking with a major manufacturer and attracting large sponsorship. To go into Indycar you have to commit yourself to almost as large an investment and then you have to shift volume to recoup your money.

'I don't think that Carl was getting on very well with Lola and we discussed the idea again in 1990, by which time his relationship with Lola had deteriorated even further, so he was highly motivated. The problem was that Lola had a monopoly of Indycar and Carl was doing very nicely as a result. From his point of view it was a very difficult decision. He could have thrown away a lucrative franchise and ended up with a duff product from us.

'We talked to Carl for three years about doing a car, and each year we were still talking when the time had passed when we could have built one. In 1990 I had gone so far as to produce sketches of an Indycar. It was a personal project which did not involve our drawing office, and had Carl said that he was ready to go ahead, I would have headed the design team.

'Then we decided to do Formula One, which curtailed the Indycar plans. When we were faced with recovering from that adventure, early in 1992, it was obvious to Rick, Paul and myself that we had to put Indy back on the agenda to secure the future of our company. Having gambled all our money on the Formula One project, and having nearly lost my shirt, we agreed that we would not go into Indycar without a risk-sharing partner. The problem then was to find such a partner.

'We pursued three routes. First, I produced a prospectus aimed at wealthy individuals who might like to gamble a million pounds in return for a share of profits over three years. We predicted that we'd build eight cars in the first year, 15 in the second and 22 in the third, and the prospectus was launched into the business world, but it only ever raised prospects of half a million pounds.

'Another string to our bow was to revisit Carl Haas. Our bottom line was that we were going ahead anyway, and if he did not want to be with us, then we would find ourselves in opposing camps. By that time our Formula Ford side had fizzled out and Carl was only selling our Formula Atlantic. Late in 1991 we produced a brand new design, the 92H, which we debuted in the Pacific Championship, which it won.

'In 1992 I engineered Russell Spence's car in the North American Toyota Atlantic series. In true Reynard fashion, Russell put it on pole in his first race, in Miami, and won. In fact, he might have won the Championship but for an engine failure in the last round. I must have flown out to America 12 to 14 times and, since Atlantic races supported Indycar events, I was able to speak to a lot of Indycar owners.'

The Atlantic effort was intended to be a bridgehead for an Indycar effort in 1994 and a deal was struck with Mike Earle who had been a team manager, and a very successful one, since the 1960s. He had founded and run Onyx Racing, which was a March works team in Formula Two and Formula 3000 and, when the turbo era in Formula One ended, Onyx had been one of a number of teams to attempt the transition to Formula One.

Most of the attempts floundered in the planning stage, a few made it as far as building cars and failing to qualify for races, but Onyx not only scored points in its first season, it even won a podium position. By that time control of the team had passed to its sponsor, an eccentric Belgian, who appeared to have limitless funds until he was imprisoned for passing dud cheques. It was back to square one and a new outfit called 3001 International.

3001 International had run Ralts in Formula 3000 in 1991 and had even won a race, with Jean-Marc Gounon at Pau, but for 1992 it had switched to Reynard. When Adrian had been wooing Yamaha for engines for the Reynard Formula One project, Mike had also been in contention and had been a strong challenger with a deal he'd put together with Robin Herd.

In the end the engines went to Jordan Grand Prix, but Mike and Adrian worked out a plan in principle. They would run in Toyota Atlantic in 1992, then 3001 (and its American-based partner) would add Indy Lights in 1993 to prepare for Indycar in 1994. There was even talk of Mike and his partner becoming the Reynard agents in the States.

A base was established in Los Angeles under Martin Dixon, who had been team manager for Onyx Grand Prix, and the drivers were the very experienced Russell Spence and Harald Huysmans. Martin says: 'We were the only fully professional team in the series and we should have cleaned up. Looking at the opposition and organisation was like going back in time. In fact we won the first three races, and people began to mutter that we were ruining the series.

'We thought we had it cracked, the car was very good and Adrian was terrific to work with; very professional and a really nice guy. The trouble was we had underestimated the task of transporting an English team to the States.

'For a start, the motor racing culture is different. If you want something done in England there are dozens of people to choose from, all close to hand, whereas there isn't the same industry in the States. We didn't have enough funding which meant we did not test as much as we should have done. In fact, a lot of our testing was done during practice for the races.

'The people we were up against did not have our resources, they did not have a car as good as ours and their drivers were probably not as good, but they had years of experience and local knowledge and we could not compete with that. I couldn't fault the car, but we didn't get the best out of it.

'Then our engines proved fragile. The 1600cc Toyota has been around a long time and has been stretched to its limit. It does not give local drivers much trouble, but it could not cope with the sheer aggression that European drivers have – again, it's a case of a different culture.

'Late in the season the new Ralt RT40 arrived. It was a very good car, their driver did a lot of testing and we were well beaten. After that I think Adrian had bigger fish to fry and the impetus went out of the project. I think had we had a second year and better funding, we had learned enough to give it a good go – we had learned not to underestimate the opposition.'

Since that experience was shared by Adrian, it gave him a new perspective on racing in America and helped formulate the terms on which he would enter Indycar. On the other hand, the fact that the works Reynard team, with Adrian himself engineering the car, was finally beaten by a Ralt did nothing to inspire confidence in Carl Haas.

During the season, Adrian used his presence in the States to get to know the Indycar team owners: 'On the whole, I got a poor reception: they didn't know me, the company, or what we'd done. They were interested to hear we'd won in Formula Three and in Formula 3000, but it didn't mean a lot to them. Luckily, they also seemed unaware of what we were doing in Atlantic . . .'

That was the background to Adrian's year. Meanwhile, Malcolm Oastler spent most of 1992 in Japan trying to get a grip on the situation there. 'I don't think anyone there is being unfair to us, it's more a case of not having the right people at the right time. We got some confidence back in '92, but the car wasn't brilliant. We'd made it pitch-sensitive again, and the '92 Lola was an excellent car – it was still winning in '94. We won the first two races, then the season started to go downhill and we couldn't really drag it back.'

For the first time in the history of single-seater racing a Japanese maker, Dome, was also a force in the series and won races, but there was no doubt that Lola had produced the better car.

In Europe the perspective was different and Reynards won all the Formula 3000 races save for the last one, at Magny Cours, which went to Jean-Marc Gounon's Lola. That was Lola's first win in Europe since September 1990 and it demonstrates the fickleness of motor racing since, as Malcolm says, the '92 Lola was an excellent car. While Lola won in Japan, virtually everyone in Europe went with Reynard.

Ralt wasn't winning anything in Formula 3000 because it managed to sell only one car and, a few days after the opening round at Silverstone it announced its official withdrawal from the class. Its one driver, Giambattista Busi, was the 1991 Italian Formula Three Champion, a series which had included Luca Badoer (4th) and Jacques Villeneuve (6th).

In 1992, Badoer in a Reynard was a clear winner of the International Formula 3000 series, and Busi failed to score a single point. He had been in the wrong car at the wrong time. In the Introduction we said that most of the 1996 Formula One drivers had raced Reynards at crucial stages of their careers. Among the 'Class of '96' was Badoer, but not Busi.

As usual, Reynard dominated the British Formula 3000 series which was run under the banner of British Formula Two, but that was no big deal since the grids were thin.

During the year Adrian was able to be of service to the Ford Motor Company. Jackie Stewart, who is a Reynard customer through the Paul Stewart Racing team, is employed by Ford as a consultant on matters such as handling. It is not a window dressing exercise because, when Ford prepared to launch its most important new model for years, the Mondeo 'world car', Jackie was reluctant to sign off the design.

Ford was one or two months away from Job One (the first car to roll off the production line) but Jackie was not happy with an aspect of the steering. He and Adrian happened to meet at Silverstone in the summer of 1992, and Jackie tried to explain precisely what the problem was. Each time that Adrian suggested a possible cause Jackie said, 'No, they've looked at that; they've measured this; they've put instruments on that.' Ford had a team of engineers working on the problem. It was a problem which only Jackie perceived, and nothing that the engineers did solved it to his satisfaction. Ford doubted that there was a problem at all.

Adrian takes up the story: 'Jackie was able to describe the feeling very accurately and I analysed it as 'non-linear hand-wheel torque'. This is a fancy way of saying that when he drove round a corner he could detect a change in the load on the steering wheel.

Left Luca Badoer was a dominant winner of the 1992 Formula 3000 Championship. (*Sutton Motorsport Images*)

Right Paul Stewart Racing used Reynard chassis in both Formula Three and Formula 3000. Adrian and Jackie Stewart have a strong mutual respect for each other, and can be seen here chatting on the pit wall at Silverstone during a race weekend in 1992.

None of the test engineers had picked this up, but Jackie wasn't happy with it. I wasn't sure whether he was being over-fussy.

'The day after Jackie and I discussed the problem I took a plane and, unannounced, I arrived at the Ford test track in Belgium. I drove the Mondeo, but could not find a problem with it. Ford couldn't find a problem either, and we wondered whether Jackie was being over-sensitive. To cut a long story short, we spent many days driving round the Scottish Highlands with Jackie driving and me taking notes. Then I drove and he took notes. Then we drove other makes of car. Then we got back into the Mondeo and made adjustments to the damping, steering and anti-roll bars.

'I made Jackie undergo "double-blind" tests, and eventually I could feel the problem he had described, as could one of Ford's engineers, Richard Parry-Jones, later a Vice President of Ford, who had once been a rally driver. It was almost a subjective thing, when you turned into a corner the car just did not give you a consistent feel and you couldn't be sure why. After trying a lot of changes, and running further double-blind tests with Jackie, we found something which isolated the problem, and we suggested a solution. It was a modification of an existing part, which cost no more to make, and Ford was able to incorporate it into their production process with a minimum of fuss.

'I think had it not been modified, the Press would have said things like "the steering feels imprecise." As it was they voted it International Car of the Year and Jackie earned his consultancy fee. And so did I!'

Having put a great deal of effort into Formula Three, Reynard reaped the benefit in 1992 and Gil de Ferran in a Paul Stewart Racing 923-Mugen scored nearly twice as many points as Phillipe Adams, who was the runner-up in a Ralt. De Ferran had been the leading Reynard user in 1991 and his development work on the 913 was carried over into the 923.

For once, however, Reynard was helped by that mysterious commodity, the received wisdom of the team owners. Ralt had introduced a new car, the RT36, which used a carbon composite tub for the first time. Many owners decided that the Ralt was 'too new' and threw in their lot with Reynard.

At least, that was the story in the Press. A source close to Ralt at the time maintains that the real reason was that the March management wanted a younger image. Ron Tauranac was 'yesterday's man', so he was taken off the Formula Three project and assigned to the Formula Atlantic car, while a very capable young designer, Andy Thorby, was brought in to design the RT36.

One can understand the thinking behind this. If March/Ralt was to have a long-term future, then it needed to bring on fresh blood. Ron was already officially an Old Age Pensioner, and not even he is immortal. Besides, Thorby already had a good reputation in Formula Three, while he was unknown in North America where having Ron's name on the Atlantic car could help sales.

Whatever the rationale, it was a mistake. Tauranac did not endorse the RT36, and team managers lost confidence in Ralt. Motor racing is supposed to be a highly technical and rational sport, but the fact remains that it is frequently subject to wholly emotive decisions because, as it turned out, the RT36 was a pretty successful car.

In fact, despite its many wins, the RT36 was not a good customer car. One team manager said: 'It was OK if you were running a Formula One-style operation, but you can't run a customer car if it takes half an hour to change the battery.

'You don't get many words out of Ron, but he does know how to engineer cars for customers. The Ralt RT36 should have been billed as "Ron Tauranac with Andy Thorby". Andy could have done the main work, with Ron just helping him out, showing him how to make a customer car that works within the limits of the testing available, the expertise of the teams running them and so on. Instead, we finished up with a so-so car with no name to it, which was not a customer car.'

Reynard has had its share of taking the brunt of customer prejudice, and for this reason it stresses that its cars are first and foremost Reynards, without emphasising the name behind a particular car. Credit is always given to individual designers, as occasion arises, but the 'name' behind any car is Reynard with the implication, correct as it happens, that there is an entire team at work.

The same has always been true with Lola. Everyone knows that Eric Broadley is Lola's founding genius, but you'd be hard-pushed to put an individual designer's name to most of the cars which Lola has made – the names of John Barnard and Patrick Head, for example, meant little to the world at large while they were cutting their teeth designing cars for the junior formulae in Huntingdon.

Like Reynard, Lola has trained many designers and engineers and, like Reynard, it takes its pick from bright young graduates. By contrast, to read most Press reports, you would have thought that Ron Tauranac had always worked alone without a succession of talented assistants, including Patrick Head. That was fine to a point, but as soon as Ron was taken away from Formula Three, customers felt let down. The guru had gone and his followers were devastated.

The same thing happened to March in the Indycar market. For several years Robin Herd was the visible personification of March in America and he lived there for half the year while other people designed the cars back home in Bicester. When he suddenly left the scene at the end of 1986, to concentrate on Formula One, American customers felt cheated, and sales slumped.

Gil de Ferran won the 1992 British Formula Three Championship in a Reynard 923-Mugen, driving for Paul Stewart Racing. He scored nearly twice as many points as Phillipe Adams's Ralt in second place. (*Sutton Motorsport Images*)

Then again, it was known that March/Ralt was not making money, and if you are not making money it is not long before you are not making cars. In 1991 March made 62 Ralt RT35s (to Reynard's 36 Formula Three cars) and still lost money. Part of the reason was that it was over-staffed, and part that it had been relocated to an area near Heathrow where factory rental was incredibly high, and it did not have the tight cost controls to which Reynard (and Lola, and Ralt under Tauranac) operated.

You cannot imagine Rick Gorne shifting 62 Formula Three cars in a season and making a loss, yet by the end of 1992 March/Ralt, under its new management, had made a loss of £1.25 million. It was bought out by two entrepreneurs, Andrew Fitton and Steve Ward, who had once done rallies together.

Even so, when the 1992 British Formula Three season started, those team managers who had defected from Ralt began to question their wisdom when the young Dutch driver, Marcel Albers, set pole position in the opening round of the British series and won the race. He was on his way to a win in the second round as well, until slowed by a misfire. Then Albers was killed in the next race, which weakened the Ralt contingent and changed the balance of the season.

Albers' death also meant that we were deprived of seeing a potentially great battle between him and Gil de Ferran. Albers had set pole in the first race, but de Ferran had taken fastest lap, and those positions were reversed in the second round. It would seem that there was little to choose between either Albers and de Ferran or the Ralt and the Reynard.

At the end of the season Reynard had won 10 races to the six of Ralt in Britain, but in Germany the score was Reynard 11, Ralt 15 and Ralt also won the prestigious race at

Monaco, so the RT36 can hardly be called a failure. According to a Ralt insider it was, however, fussy to set up: the Italians didn't like that as a matter of principle, while the Japanese were unable to undertake all the testing that the RT36 needed to get the best from it. These are the sort of considerations which a maker of customer racing cars operating on an international stage has to take into account. Each country has a different motor racing culture.

On the back of a fine 1992 Formula Three season, when it won both the British and German Championships, Reynard expected to dominate the category in 1993. Certainly, orders rolled in and the position looked healthy, but if Reynard had won two major Championships in 1992, so too had Dallara – in France and Italy.

Dallara has been around since 1978 and often its ambitions have outstripped its resources. It had run cars in Formula Two, Formula 3000 and Formula One, but having not succeeded at the higher levels, Dallara decided to concentrate on Formula Three. If it was under-resourced by usual Formula One standards, it was handsomely set-up for Formula Three and it was the first Formula Three manufacturer in history to have its own wind tunnel, and that was not the only ex-Formula One technical resource it brought to the scene.

At the end of 1992, at the Macau Grand Prix, Adrian and David Brown saw the new Dallara and realised that the Italians had made a quantum leap. The Reynard 933 was a move forward, but Dallara had leap-frogged the opposition and come up with a slim, slippery car which had pitch-sensitivity well under control.

Under most circumstances, that would not have mattered a great deal, at least so far as the British series was concerned. British teams had traditionally bought British cars. There had been some perfectly good Formula Three cars made abroad, particularly by Martini and Dallara, but none had been so superior as to outweigh the advantages of dealing with people teams knew. The factories were close to hand and there was also a common language.

For 1993 Ralt had produced an update of the RT36 but, despite many fine performances during the previous year, teams were still suspicious of it and, besides, changes within the March/Ralt organisation did not inspire confidence. Only one leading team, Edenbridge, bought Ralts and, ironically, that was to set the seal on Reynard.

When a new British team announced that it was to run Dallaras, it caused a small ripple of interest because the make had made only occasional appearances in Britain before. In any case, its two drivers were not expected to perform much above midfield.

At the first round of the Championship, Reynards filled the top six places, but come the second round, at Thruxton, people suddenly took notice of the two Dallaras. For a start, Steven Arnold, whom nobody rated highly, put his car on the front row of the grid. The other, driven by Warren Hughes started well back after gearbox problems in qualifying, but then Warren sliced through the field to finish sixth and he was, by a long way, the fastest man on the track. By the fourth round Edenbridge Racing had dumped its Ralts, bought Dallaras instead, and Oliver Gavin immediately scored a second place.

Reynard won the first five rounds, but after that Dallara took every race and, as the season progressed, more and more teams made the switch. Reynard had filled the top six places in the first race, but Dallara took the top six finishes in the last one.

The Dallara was slimmer and so was quicker on the straights. It was more predictable in the corners and so was less likely to 'bog' the engine. It used its tyres more efficiently and was more consistent over an entire race distance. Unlike most Formula Three cars, it could be driven aggressively, whereas the narrow power band of Formula Three engines, which carry air restricters, had always needed delicacy and precision. All in all, the Dallara 393 was a superior product.

One seasoned team manager believes that the Dallara was actually too good. This sounds like an odd thing to say about a successful car, but his reasoning is that drivers in Formula Three are in a learning category and that a car as competent as a Dallara does not teach them enough. That is a back-handed compliment if ever there was one.

Reynard responded to the Italian invasion and produced a new aerodynamic package, including smaller and lower side-pods, but these were additions rather than a new concept. David Brown, who headed up the project, says: 'We simply could not believe the stories about the amount of wind tunnel testing Dallara was doing, nothing like it had ever happened in Formula Three before.

'We were not good enough in the area of aerodynamics to compete with Dallara, that's accepted. Then Andy Miller of Paul Stewart Racing was able to demonstrate that there was flexing in the gearbox casing. All we could do at that time was to weld a plate over the casing.

'The worst thing was that the weight distribution wasn't right and we over-loaded the rear tyres. If we dialled that out by making adjustments to the suspension, we had nowhere else to go in terms of fine tuning.

'It was unbelievable the way we lost Formula Three. In a matter of weeks, we'd lost everyone who could afford to dump their Reynards and buy Dallaras and, since the cost of a car is not the biggest item in the budget, that meant most of them.'

It was the first time that a major British single-seater series was lost to a foreign interloper and, for Reynard, the irony is that it occurred in a year when, for the first time since entering Formula Three, all the indications were that it would wipe Ralt off the map.

The Reynard 933 was not a bad car, but the Dallara was better. In no other industry can a leading company lose its entire market in a matter of weeks, yet that is what happened. The cost of a chassis is usually a surprisingly small percentage of a team's budget, which has to cover a workshop, wages, engines and engine rebuilds, transportation, spares, tyres, testing, and so on. It becomes even smaller if you can sell your Reynard to, say, a hill climber to offset part of the cost of your new Dallara. If your Dallara then wins, you have no difficulty in selling it to someone who wants to do Class B (for year-old cars) the following season.

By the end of 1993 Reynard decided to leave the customer Formula Three market. It did not doubt that it could make an effective response to Dallara, but it would require so much effort to win back customers at a time when its efforts were needed to be focused on Indycar. The 1993 season had shown how fickle the market can be, and if Reynard leap-frogged Dallara in 1994 and was swamped with orders – *I want one and I want it yesterday* – it would have put a skew into the company's production plans during the most important year of its history. There are times in the production racing car industry when success can be as embarrassing as failure.

Instead of looking at the customer market, Reynard began to negotiate with Renault for a works deal. Renault was preparing an engine for Formula Three and the idea was that Reynard would design a car exclusively for Renault to be run in the British and French Championships. That way investment and costs would be predetermined and so would production. In fact, the plan was to farm out production if the deal went ahead.

In North America, Ron Tauranac's Ralt RT40 wiped the floor with the opposition and, ironically, it sowed the seeds of its own demise, since the '93 car was so good that hardly anyone bought the '94 car. Seventeen RT40s were made in 1993, but only 10 in 1994, and it was the only outlet which Ralt had. Still, it wiped Reynard out of that particular market. 1993 was not good for Reynard in the intermediate formulae.

By the admission of Andrew Fitton, Managing Director of Ralt/March, the RT40 succeeded not because it was a vastly superior car, but because Ralt spent more time and effort servicing its customers. That is a double-edged statement because, over the winter of 1992/93, Ralt had all but lost its Formula Three market, so almost the only customers it had to look after were in the Toyota Atlantic series.

In European F3000 in 1993, Reynard established a monopoly for the first time in the category's history. John Thompson's Reynard 93D was not the only type of car used in the series, however, because Pedro Lamy won a race, and finished close runner-up to Olivier Panis, driving an uprated 92D. Lamy's car was identical to the 1993 model save for the fact that it did not have the new sequential gearbox. Third place in the Championship was taken by David Coulthard.

Despite having no representation in European F3000, Lola continued to reign supreme in Japan. Malcolm Oastler says: 'Our '93 car was good, but since the '92 car had been a bit difficult, we were short on representation. The 93D was a big improvement, but not many people got to see it. The car was a bit difficult to set up on Japanese rubber, but Ross Cheever won two races and missed the Championship by one point – again – but we've never really had an excuse.'

In fact, Reynard had made an advance, but nobody in Japan seemed to care about that, or about the fact that Lola had taken a step backwards. Its 1993 car was overweight, and teams experienced numerous problems with the sequential gearbox.

The natural response of European teams in that situation would be to chuck Lolas and buy Reynards, but the Japanese simply brought out their '92 cars and used them instead. In 1994 some teams achieved success with up-rated '93 cars which were considered to be marginal in 1993. Others continued with 1992 cars. Many of the cars which race in Japan cannot really be called '93 or '94 cars – they are hybrids which teams have assembled.

Chapter Seventeen

Edging Into Indy

During 1992 Adrian had used his time between engineering the Toyota Atlantic car in America to feel his way into the Indycar scene, but he found that he had his work cut out. 'An exception was Jim Hall. He didn't know me from Adam, but I knew all about him – I was photographed alongside his Lotus at Watkins Glen in 1963, remember.

'I put it to him that he was an innovative engineer who had taken risks with his own Chapparal sports car designs; he understood engineers; he had employed John Barnard in Indycar before John became a superstar Formula One designer; and I was happy to call the car a Chapparal if he wished. He listened with interest, but was not quite convinced. He went on to the back-burner for the time being.

'It was obvious that it was going to be a difficult sell, not least because Carl had all the owners tied up, he had been dealing with them for years and they all knew him. We could still have gone in with Carl, but I perceived a number of difficulties, the main one being that he demanded what I thought was too much control over the project.

'If he had come in with us, he would have wanted to control the marketing of the cars, and his own team demanded a high level of preferential treatment. He had that from Lola, but some other Lola customers were not too happy about it. Newman/Haas is essentially the Lola works team, which receives all the latest tweaks ahead of the customers.

'Apart from all the other issues, it was quite a brave move to go against Carl, and therefore we had to find someone who was prepared to take the risk with us. At Phoenix on 4 April 1993, Carl and I eventually agreed to part. It was an emotional moment for me because I'd valued his company as a friend and I knew, deep down, that he still believed in us. I had to accept his commercial reasons, however. He knew he was going to sell 30 or so Lolas a year, and we were an unknown quantity.

'During 1992 I'd visited Chip Ganassi, who had said that at least he would consider buying a Reynard Indycar and, further, he and I had got on very well. After we split with Carl, Chip seemed to me to be the best prospect and he was very easy to deal with. I told him how much money we'd need and presented him with a business plan. The idea was that he would be a shareholder in the American distribution company, Reynard North America, but that it would be essentially controlled by Reynard Racing Cars in some specific areas.

'These were: fair treatment of customers; Reynard would be able to define the extent of the works deal for Ganassi; we would have a say in the choice of personnel for Reynard North America. Finally; we wanted price capping so that Reynard North America could not charge extortionate prices for cars or parts.

'These were the areas which I thought would give us a stable business platform in the USA, although Chip could invest in Reynard North America and enjoy profits from it. It was a much better plan than we could have negotiated with Carl, and it gave us a distributor with intimate knowledge of Indycar. Chip would also lay down deposits for 12 cars, and that was a risk for him because if they were not delivered, or failed to sell, he would not get the deposits returned.

'We met at Long Beach in April 1993 and we had the deal done within a month. It was probably the smoothest major deal we've ever done. A few weeks later he came to my house and we spent all night working on my word processor drawing up the contracts. I ran them off; we signed them; he went back home and the money came. It was as simple as that. I then turned to Malcolm Oastler and said: "Malcolm, design us an Indycar."

'We sat down together and drew up our brief. Prior to that, the only time that Malcolm had even seen an Indycar was when he went to Indianapolis for "Carburation Day" in 1992. We decided that we didn't want to produce a complicated car. In fact, we even specified the same sort of wheels as Lola used, so that existing Lola teams could save money on wheels if they came with us. We also didn't want to produce a car which was so radical that it was liable to be outlawed, because we couldn't afford that.

'Then we had to ensure that we could obtain engines. Carl Haas thought he had Cosworth tied up exclusively, and he bet me, at 50–1, that I could never get my hands on a current Cosworth engine. I shook his hand for $1000, but I haven't yet called in the bet.

'Above all, I wanted to make it a safe car. In fact, I wanted to make it the safest car

When Adrian and Rick closed the deal with Chip Ganassi, they felt it was one of the smoothest deals they had ever completed. They hired a Beach Starship aircraft to visit potential customers in the American market to sell Indycars when Reynard was still an unknown quantity. A total of 13 cars were sold for the 1994 season despite the fact that only eight had been predicted.

that's ever raced at Indianapolis. I'd seen the remains of Nelson Piquet's car after his terrible accident in '92, and it affected me as much as Johnny Herbert's crash in 1988.'

How well Reynard succeeded in this was demonstrated at Phoenix in the second race of the 1994 season when Jacques Villeneuve's Reynard T-boned the stationary Lola of Hiro Matsushito at 150 mph. The Lola broke in two (as it was designed to do) and the photographs show Villeneuve's car driving through the middle of it, its nose cone like a knife. Matsushito sustained only bruising, shock and a dislocated shoulder, while Villeneuve did not even suffer that.

Adrian continues: 'We put together a small team consisting of some people in-house and some from outside. One of the first decisions to make was whether to have a longitudinal gearbox or a transverse gearbox. We decided on the former, and it was designed by Barry Ward who had designed our Formula 3000 'boxes. Barry was then only 26, but he is a product of the Reynard training scheme: he'd been with us for three years and was already at a level where you could entrust him with an Indycar transmission, or more.' Barry it was who, two years later, designed the abortive Formula One car for Jean-Paul Droit's DAMS team.

Malcolm Oastler takes up the story: 'As I've said, sitting down to design the 94I caused me less stress than the Formula 3000 car because I'd got so much more experience and the company was so much stronger as a whole. In any case, a certain amount of the car is designed for you by the regulations which tell you how wide, or how high, the chassis has to be at certain points.

'Then there are the dimensions for the wings, the driver's pedal box and so on. By the time you've been through the regs you've got half the car already. Then you see how best to shuffle the things around in the envelope.

'Indycar is actually easier than Formula 3000 in one important area – the installation of the engines – although, with turbochargers, the plumbing is a nightmare. In Formula 3000 you have to make allowances for seven different types of engine: there are three "high crank" engines and four "low crank" engines, which means problems with mating the gearbox and so on.

'In Indycar, the Ilmor D and Cosworth XB are completely different engines, but they share similar dimensions and the same angle between the two banks of cylinders. So, although we have to use different mounting brackets and so on, it's no big deal. Both companies were very helpful to us. I know that it's ultimately in their best interests if we get it right, but they both went out of their way to be especially helpful. Of course, since their engines are so similar as an overall package it makes life easier for us: in each instance the gearbox casing comes from the same casting – it just gets machined differently.

'When we later had to fit Honda engines to our cars, much the same was true. There was very little difference in the exterior dimensions. In fact, the only special installations we've had to do were on a Toyota engine for 1996 because the Toyota is that much shorter.

'Having a troublesome gearbox is the worst way to start with a new car when you want to get out and running with it. If we'd bounced in with a troublesome 'box it would have set the whole programme back, as we discovered in Formula 3000 in 1990 – which is why we chose a relatively simple longitudinal transmission. We had a transverse 'box, which is based on our Formula 3000 transmission, and to have used that in the car would have been fine, engineering-wise.

'The trouble is that it would have meant dismantling the exhaust system and taking off the underbody just to change ratios – an hour-and-a-half job. We couldn't go to customers and say, "Here's your new Reynard and, by the way, it's going to take all day to change your ratios." That's not the way to introduce yourself to any new category, let alone one with strict limits on the time you can go testing. With the longitudinal box you can change ratios in half-an-hour; no problem.

Adrian continues: 'During the month of May I visited Indianapolis and I saw Rick having a deep conversation with someone who turned out to be Bruce Ashmore, Lola's chief Indycar designer who was also the engineer on Mario Andretti's car for Newman/Haas. We talked about our project and he said, "I wouldn't mind having a meeting with you in England sometime. Chip Ganassi has been talking to me about the project and the possibility of my joining his team as an engineer." It blew my mind that someone as experienced as Bruce could take us seriously.

'In early June, Bruce and I met at The Green Man pub near Silverstone, by which time he had spoken at greater length with Chip. He felt his future was limited at Lola; he was not particularly happy working with Newman/Haas, and his contract was about to expire. I was flattered, sceptical, excited – a combination of emotions – but after our meeting I decided that he had the right personality to integrate with our existing design team.

'Bruce is a star designer who isn't "starry", and I thought he could bring a lot to our design, and could save Malcolm from falling down any holes. I saw him as both insurance – although we were arrogant enough to believe that we could win anyway – and as a familiar figure who could represent us in America.

'The upshot was that Chip hired him to work for Reynard North America. It was Chip, not us – although, naturally, we were in agreement – and it was Chip who negotiated his salary and so on. Bruce had twin loyalties when working in Indycar, one was to Newman/Haas, the other was to Lola, but Lola was happy to release him.

'Soon afterwards, Bruce came here to work with Malcolm on the car. He made some valuable inputs, particularly on the aerodynamic side, but he generally approved of what we were doing, both in the design and in our approach to the market. In particular, he approved of our longitudinal gearbox, which was a relief since Lola was known to be designing its 1994 car around a transverse 'box.

'All Indycars are compromises, since they have to cope with slowish street circuits, road circuits and high-speed short, and long, oval tracks. A transverse 'box gives a slight advantage on street circuits because it allows the creation of more under-car downforce by getting more air to the underside of the rear wing. It also allows better weight distribution, but it is at a slight disadvantage on the speed circuits. Ideally, you'd use both types, but we did not want to pioneer so radical a move in our first year.'

Some Chief Designers would have thrown a wobbly had someone of Ashmore's stature and experience been appointed, just as they were about to enter a new category, and they would have taken to a day-bed with a severe case of bruised ego. Malcolm has no such problems and says that he and Bruce rub along extremely well. Besides, they have different functions within the project and Bruce is based in America, where he is employed by Chip Ganassi (Malcolm looked after Jim Hall's team) so, in typical Reynard fashion, it is a case of complementary talents.

Carl Haas, however, took a different view and slapped in a lawsuit, claiming that Ashmore was appropriating Newman/Haas intellectual information. There have been cases of designers who have left one team for another, having carefully packed duplicate copies of blueprints or computer disks, but you cannot erase a man's talent or experience from his brain, so Haas's action came to nothing.

'It was frustration on Carl's part,' says Adrian, 'it was Haas protecting Haas information. It certainly was not Lola protecting Lola information. It was settled by Bruce writing a letter. We had rattled Carl's cage, that's all.'

Bruce had been a Lola man all of his working life. In fact, he was born five miles from the factory exactly two weeks after Lola had startled the motor racing world by scoring a 1–2–3 in the 1100cc race at the 1959 Goodwood Easter Monday Meeting. The son of a farmer, he had no interest in motor racing and had intended to read engineering at university until he saw Lola advertising a vacancy for an apprentice.

It would not be until 1993 that he met Adrian, but their paths had nearly crossed several times over the years. When Adrian raced against Mike Blanchet in Formula Ford 2000, Bruce was the junior mechanic on Mike's car. When Reynard had its disastrous showing at the 1982 Formula Ford Festival, Bruce had designed the Lola which won. He progressed to Indycar design and, when Nigel Bennett left to join Penske in 1988, he took over as Chief Designer and his cars won four successive Championships, 1990–1993 – he was the Main Man.

He says: 'When the approach was made, I was ready to accept because I had been based at the Lola factory in Huntingdon when really I wanted to live and work in America so that I could be more closely involved with the teams. Adrian gave me that chance. What I particularly liked during our discussion was that he constantly emphasised that I would have to fit in. He said, "If you don't fit in, I won't employ you."

'I don't think that Malcolm Oastler was particularly happy when I arrived. It was a bit of a character test for him, but I made it clear to him that he was the Chief Designer and I was the new kid on the block. I think that he was wary of me for a long time, but now we work very well together.

'So far as I was concerned, the problem with Lola was that everything was based in England, and Lola is very concerned about secrecy. One thing that Adrian constantly asks is, "What are we doing next?" The point is that you can't be secretive once you've made your car because it's in the open, it's history. The real secrets are what's in your head.

'When I worked for Lola, I was close to Newman/Haas, but not with the customers. Lola almost seemed to take the view, "We're the geniuses who designed the car, now you find out about it."

'Adrian takes the view that you should be able to tell the customer everything, and show the customer everything. You share what you've got, and what you know, because that way you help your customer to find out everything about the car, which makes life easier for him – and you are also more likely to keep him as a customer.

'Reynard North America is based in Indianapolis, where a lot of Indycar teams are based. If a team goes testing in the morning and has a problem, by the afternoon when it wants an answer to its problem, the factory in England has knocked off for the day. Lola had only about 20 per cent of its drawings on CAD, whereas the Reynard is designed completely on CAD and our systems are linked. We can give the American customer what he wants when he wants it. We can show them everything and they appreciate that.

'It seems obvious. Everyone knows there's a time difference between England and America, but Lola was not meeting the problem. It was part of my thinking in 1993, and I was delighted to discover that Adrian felt the same. The fact that we have a base there makes a huge difference.'

Reynard's move into Indycar was as auspiciously timed as its other major moves. In the mid-1980s March had a virtual monopoly in the category, and this had led to vast profits, but also complacency. Customers were not amused to take delivery of bodywork which one of the racers back at the works had examined and rejected, but who had been over-ruled by a bean counter. At least one team found the word 'Rejected' writ large on

Reynard North America take a mobile spares unit to every race. This is also fully equipped with up-to-date CAD CAM equipment for the teams' use. Staff from both the American office and Bicester attend every race.

The key players are in constant touch. From left to right: Adrian Reynard, Paul Owens, Bruce Ashmore, Malcolm Oastler and Rick Gorne in America during the 1995 season.

Michael Andretti's first chassis was delivered to the team on time and was on the pace immediately. Michael finished fourth in the 1994 Indycar Series with two victories to his credit.

the inside of a bodyshell for which it had paid a considerable number of dollars. When Lola was able to offer an alternative, backed by impeccable standards of product quality, customers were only too happy to make the change. In turn, Lola established a virtual monopoly, and while the company did not make the same mistakes as March, American team owners faced different problems.

One was that Lola had a monopoly and customers do not like dealing with a monopoly in any sphere. In motor racing, having only one supplier means that you cannot easily buy the extra advantage that all teams seek.

The other was that Carl Haas, Lola's agent, was running his own team in conjunction with Paul Newman. Newman/Haas had reintroduced Lola to Indycar in 1984, it had been responsible for Lola's renaissance and, naturally, it enjoyed a special relationship with the works. Newman/Haas received new tweaks from Lola before anyone else, which was perceived as an unfair advantage, although the downside is that not all new tweaks work and they can waste valuable time and effort.

Chip Ganassi, a former Indycar driver whose career had been terminated by a major accident, knew that he had a great opportunity, yet to succeed he had to put together a package which included a star driver, and stars tend not to like taking risks on an unknown car. On the other hand, in Formula One, the reigning Indycar Champion, Michael Andretti, was having a torrid time with McLaren. There were many reasons for this, but the essential point is that by mid-season, he was ripe for wooing, and Chip Ganassi paid court.

Chip was successful, and he also secured Cosworth engines. That focused the attention of a lot of people and, before long, many American team owners knew Rick Gorne's phone number by heart. Rick was not the only person speaking to team owners, and many were surprised to find that Carl Haas was suddenly prepared to utter words which had previously not passed his lips – words like 'discount' and 'special deal'. Rick, who admires Carl almost to the point of hero-worship, revelled in the competition. One side of him was mortified at every lost sale, another side was delighted at being able to lock horns with so shrewd an operator.

Despite keen competition, Reynard did something that no new maker in Indycar has ever done before – it sold its entire initial batch of cars. Adrian's 1992 business-plan/prospectus had predicted eight cars, but 13 had been delivered by the end of April. The first was delivered to the day, and from the beginning of testing Michael Andretti was on the pace. It was a two-way equation: Reynard gave Michael a car he could believe in, and Michael, returning to his natural environment after a bruising spell in Formula One, gave Reynard the benefit of his awesome talent.

During winter testing he traded fastest times with Nigel Mansell's Lola – first, one would have the edge, then the other. Michael returned to Indycar as though he'd never been away, and the stage seemed set for a great battle between the two drivers and the two companies.

Chapter Eighteen

The Chrysler Patriot and Other New Directions

While Indycar was one part of the rescue package, another was for Reynard to offer its expertise to major manufacturers as a consultancy. Consultancy had been a buzz word in the motor racing industry for years. The expertise which many manufacturers have in carbon composites, for example, should be saleable to other industries, and the idea of generating money in this way is attractive. In theory, it should buffer the effects of a poor season and spread work throughout the year instead of just in the build season.

The reality, however, is that consultancy can drain the core business, which is winning races, and the demands of most other industries cannot take account of the build season. Consequently, successful consultancy projects have tended to be few and far between. Team Lotus had a major input into the carbon-fibre racing bicycle with which Chris Boardman won a gold medal in the Barcelona Olympics, and racing car engineers have also made, of all things, carbon-fibre brief cases.

The late Ayrton Senna had such a one. It was very expensive but, he claimed, impervious to any impact. He was singing its praises to his team-mate Gerhard Berger, who decided to put the case to the test, and threw it out of the window. At the time they were travelling in a helicopter.

These side-projects have been the exception rather than the rule, but a breakthrough came with Reynard's work on the Chrysler Patriot which, in turn, has led to the establishment of Reynard Special Vehicle Projects. RSVP is a separate entity, although one which can tap into the Reynard Group's expertise, and is involved with projects outside of the automotive industry.

Major manufacturers have often formed alliances with specialists, hence the Mini-Cooper, Lotus-Cortina, Sierra-Cosworth and Renault 5 Gordini. Reynard Special Vehicle Projects has a wider brief and, among its initial projects, is a seat for airliners. Although a link between airline seats and a racing car company may not be immediately apparent, a successful racing car company has the best possible qualifications for the job.

You want your seat to be light, yet strong. Who has the best expertise in making light, but strong, structures? If you are going to introduce a new design, then it must be an improvement on existing designs, and racing car companies are honed to make improvements on a weekly basis.

RSVP was possible only because of Reynard's success in Indycar. The cash that it generated permitted the formation of a consultancy arm without jeopardising the main effort. March Group plc had tried consultancy and had failed because it had not properly assessed its own strengths and weaknesses. Reynard's strength has always been the depth and width of its thought.

In July 1996 a 'think tank' praised the achievements of the British motor racing industry and said that other industries would benefit if they formed liaisons with racing car manufacturers. The report said that it was not just the level of engineering excellence which would be beneficial, but the whole approach.

Honda long ago realised this. It went into motor racing not merely to gain prestige, but to educate some of its brightest young engineers. The traditional Japanese hierarchical system meant that they were waiting to progress to seniority at the very stage of their lives when they were potentially at their most creative. Taking them out to work in Formula One did not upset the hierarchy because it was a separate entity.

Setting them to work with teams like Ralt, Spirit, Williams, McLaren and Lotus meant that they had to respond at the same speed as racing people. If a problem arose it was to be solved there and then – you didn't call a committee meeting for the day after tomorrow. John Wickham, whose Team Spirit first took Honda into modern Formula One (it had been there in the 1960s) said: 'The idea is to get them to think in the English way, not in the Japanese way with its deference to seniority.'

Honda recognised a particular problem to be overcome, one which was rooted in Japanese culture but, regardless of country, large manufacturers tend to create their own cultures and it is often beneficial for them to form an outside alliance with a company which operates in a different way. The Chrysler Patriot is a prime example of that.

It may seem odd to call the Patriot a successful consultancy project since, after a lengthy testing programme, the project was scrapped as unworkable. From Reynard's point of view, however, it was successful because Reynard fulfilled all its requirements. In any case, it provides a graphic illustration of how the motor racing industry can operate.

Adrian recalls: 'After the Formula One project nearly wiped us out we needed more than Formula Three and Formula 3000 to promote growth, especially since economic recession was hitting both markets. We had a very good prototyping facility, and we had shortened product lead-time by devising new manufacturing techniques. I felt that this ought to be of interest to major manufacturers, so I drew up a list and made them a presentation. In some cases they were cold-calls, in others I had a personal contact.

'One such contact was Tony Richards, a Director at Chrysler, whom I'd met when I had visited the Lamborghini plant to look at their Formula One engine. Tony forwarded my letter to Chrysler in America, to "Liberty", their prototype and advanced concepts division. Liberty is a wonderful place, it's a facility separate from the main factory where about a hundred young designers and craftsmen consider and build new ideas. It's like the "Skunk Works" which the Lockheed aircraft company used to have, where people were given free rein to push back the envelope of design, and to do it quickly.

'That's how we work at Reynard and, as soon as the company reaches a given size, I intend to break it down into smaller units in order to maintain our speed and flexibility.

'Liberty was run by Tom Moore, and he wrote to me suggesting that he might have something for us. He came to visit us with Tom Gale, Chrysler's Director of Product Development, and Bob Lutz, President, and they were pretty impressed by what they saw. At the time we were nearly bankrupt and had very few machines. Not having the kit to impress them with, I emphasised that we were able to make all our cars from very little: we were lean, we were efficient, and we made the best of our resources – we conjured advanced racing cars almost out of the air. I did not know at the time, but that was precisely the attitude which Chrysler had taken on board during the previous few years when restructuring the company to meet the competition from Japan.

'I then visited the Liberty plant and was told about their new concept, which was to build a car with a turbine engine fuelled by natural gas, and which would produce

From left to right, Adrian Reynard, Tom Gale and Chrysler's Chairman, Bob Eaton, at the launch of the Chrysler Patriot at the Detroit Auto Show in January 1994.

energy that could be stored in a flywheel. This principle is familiar to anyone who has owned a toy friction-drive car, but here we are talking about systems which were initially developed for space craft and satellites.

'In space there are solar panels which produce electricity which, in turn, drives the flywheel via an electric motor. When energy is needed, as when a satellite is in darkness, the process is put into reverse: the flywheel then drives an alternator which feeds electrical power into the system.

'Chrysler believed that this had applications for the road cars which will have to be built to meet the more stringent emission laws which some governments have in the pipeline. Battery technology shows no sign of being able to meet these goals in the immediate future, whereas this concept was a low-emission system using natural gas which is available in most households on tap. Since the flywheel and gas turbine were known technology, the problem came down to applying them in a new environment in the most efficient way.

'Chrysler showed me a scheme which utilised four hub-located electric motors with a big fuel tank down the middle. They had conceived it as a racing car – motor racing had the right image and it is a perfect place to force technology – and they asked if we could build them one of these. Naturally I said that we could.

'That was late in 1992. I came home and started to draw a few schemes, and then Al Turner (the executive in charge of the project) said that, to demonstrate its potential, Chrysler would like to build an endurance racing sports car – something that could compete at Le Mans and Daytona. At the time, sports car racing was in a trough. Group C had just been axed, while alternatives such as GT and World Sports Car racing were being proposed, but had yet to be finalised. I toyed with the idea of designing a GT car, but we would have had to build quite a number for them to be homologated.

'Al Turner and I went to see the main people at Le Mans and said: "Look, you could have Chrysler here, but the concept is a hybrid and the engine does not conform to your existing regulations – for a start it won't have a clutch. I can guarantee to design a car which meets your main regulations if you can be flexible over your fuel and engine rules." They listened and they were very positive.

'Al then went to IMSA, and they were positive as well because they wanted the kudos of something like this in their series. We hit both organisations when they were in a low – had they had healthy and oversubscribed categories, perhaps they would not have been so receptive.

'Chrysler had wanted something with a roof because it styled better, but I went back to them with a WSC design which had the turbine-alternator, the flywheel, the fuel tank and one electric motor with a transmission – I had no faith that electric motors operating on each of the four wheels could be made viable, bearing in mind the fail-safe systems you'd have to build in, and bearing in mind the time-span Chrysler had allowed. Besides, four-wheel-drive is not allowed under WSC rules. Chrysler wanted a car on their stand at the Detroit Motor Show in the first week of January, which gave a delivery deadline of 28 December 1993 – and by then it was February 1993.

'Until then it had been an exchange of ideas, but what kicked off the project as a reality was a visit to our factory early in the year by Chrysler's Vice President Engineering, François Castaing, who was once the Technical Director of Renault's Formula One programme. He decided that he liked us, and we were brought in as collaborators. There was, however, no formal agreement, no contract and no purchase order, which left me in the dilemma of not knowing how much of the company's resources to commit, because up until then I had been doing everything by myself.

'After the Long Beach Indycar race in April, Rick, Malcolm and myself called in on Chrysler and hammered out the deal. At that time I had one piece of paper showing the rough layout and, while we left with an agreement, we left without having the deal confirmed. That gave us eight months to design a new car from scratch using new technology which nobody then understood in that particular application. Further, we needed a turbo-alternator, which was not then in existence.

'In May I took the plunge and decided to go ahead anyway, and I briefed Paul Brown and a team at Reynard to design the car. I decided that we needed up-to-date Le Mans technology, so went to see Nigel Stroud who had designed the Mazda Group C car which won Le Mans in 1991. He came in as a contracted freelance to head up the project alongside Paul Brown.

'The idea was that the gas turbine would run at maximum revs (100,000 rpm) all the time to achieve its greatest efficiency. When the car was under braking, the turbine would switch to powering the flywheel which would rotate at a maximum of 80,000 rpm and store the energy.

'That energy could be drawn off, via an alternator, to supplement the power from the turbine to the electric motor which was actually propelling the car. In rough terms, if the turbine was producing 500 bhp, which was our aim, the flywheel could provide an extra 200 bhp for 10 seconds, 100 bhp for 20 seconds, or 50 bhp for 40 seconds.

'From the start I had decided that there should be one motor, and it should be at the back. It revved to 24,000 rpm, and the remarkable thing is that its maximum torque is at zero rpm – it has superior torque to a typical 4-litre normally aspirated engine and it remains constant throughout the range.'

There exist a number of public transport systems in the world which use flywheels to store energy. Trams charge up every time they stop, and the system does away with the need for overhead cables. A tram is a fairly stable environment, however, and a gyroscopic system had to be designed into the Patriot's flywheel. Had it not, the centrifugal forces generated by the flywheel would have flipped the car onto its back had it gone more than 15 degrees from the horizontal – as on the bankings at Daytona or, even, if a car went high over a kerb.

Adrian continues: 'My contribution was to go through the design as it progressed and freeze various elements. Eventually we would assign a space to, say, the turbine and send the drawing to the engineers handling that aspect and ask them to provide a machine within that envelope. We worked with a series of envelopes, and what was left over was what we built the car around. It was illuminating that, despite the fact that our partners were dealing in space technology, none of them had the same determination that we had to get the weight down.

'We offered Chrysler prototyping facilities and a short lead time, and we effectively designed and built a new car from scratch in six months. It was not just that we were dealing with technology which was entirely new to the automotive industry, but we also had to build a wind tunnel model and run an intensive programme at MIRA.

'Since it was going to be at the Detroit Show, it had to look attractive, and Chrysler's Chief Stylist, Jack Krane, came over and we incorporated some of his suggestions so it could be signed off. As an example, we lowered the roll-over bar by two inches: it made it illegal for racing, but it satisfied Chrysler's immediate requirement for it to look good on an exhibition stand.

'Until the last month, we had sketches but no firm drawings from subcontract suppliers. It was only in December 1993 that we began to receive the major components from America. While Paul Brown, Nigel Stroud and I were working, often by guesswork, Paul Owens was involved in the design of the monocoque. He also had an input into the design of the gearbox, and he worked with Nigel on the back end of the car.

'Paul got the chassis buck in the middle of November, he delivered the complete chassis in the first week of December and the bodywork arrived a week before the car left. We had planned to finish on Christmas Eve, but because Chrysler wanted it in their own colours, the paint had to come from the USA and it was of a different type from that which we normally use, and that added four or five days to the build time.

'Nigel Stroud, Paul Owens and Mike Shirley assembled the car themselves. They refused any extra help, except for one fitter, because they didn't want to spoil other people's Christmases. Apart from Christmas Day itself, they worked throughout the holiday and delivered the car on 28 December.'

That is what we mean when we say that you don't have to race cars to have a racer's attitude.

Before the Patriot was unveiled at the Detroit Motor Show, it was photographed at Donington Park, apparently being test-driven. It was moving, but the clue is that it was photographed on a slope.

Reynard supplied more chassis and spares, and for nearly two-and-a-half years Chrysler persevered with the concept, but could not solve one basic problem. The flywheel constantly left its moorings and broke through its carbon-fibre casing. A discus, 2 ft. in diameter, weighing 157 lb. and spinning at 80,000 rpm is a potentially lethal object which could spoil your day. In fact, it was tested in a lead-lined pit with a lid weighing several tons on top. Even then it melted the lining of the pit.

While the Chrysler Patriot will become a footnote in the history of the automobile, the experience of working with a major manufacturer was certainly to Adrian's taste,

The Chrysler Patriot was unveiled by François Castaing, Chrysler's Vice President Engineering, who announced the technological advances of the Patriot.

and it marked a significant new step for Reynard. In 1994, soon after delivering the prototype, he said: 'For the future, I have consultancy firmly in mind, but the past has taught us not to expand too swiftly, because you can be caught out by the rise and fall of the economy. Working with Chrysler, I have been able to understand those areas which they do supremely well, and those which we do well, and how we can co-operate. In the case of the Patriot, we were able to build a prototype from scratch in a timescale that nobody else in the world could better.'

That was not an idle boast because, before long, he would be discussing a project with Ford, which turned into the Ford Indigo, and one with Chrysler which would lead to work on racing Dodge Vipers and a partnership to create the Chrysler Stratus which would run in the 1996 American Touring Car Championship.

'At the beginning of 1994 we restructured our group under a holding company, Reynard Engineering Group Ltd – so we consisted of Reynard Composites; Reynard Racing Cars and Reynard Manufacturing. At present, 90 per cent of the work of Reynard Composites and Reynard Manufacturing is supplying Reynard Racing Cars, but they have the capacity to expand independently. As it is, they have to tender to supply us with product at the right quality and right price.

'Reynard Composites, for example, has built carbon-fibre monocoques for the Vern Schuppen Porsche-based road car and the Pacific Formula One car; and among other projects was a body for Mazda for a special car which could have the engine in the front, middle or rear, and be front-wheel drive, rear-wheel drive or four-wheel drive. Paul Owens's contribution to the Chrysler Patriot was that of an active subcontractor – it went far beyond his receiving a set of drawings and being asked to make something up from them.

'We now have Reynard Special Vehicle Projects to handle outside consultancy. It is a separate entity owned partly by myself and partly by its key personnel under a stock-sharing scheme, although the distribution of shares in the company is not without conditions.

'There is no logical limit to what we could do. As examples, I progressed some way towards the design of a carbon-fibre helicopter, but was finally defeated – at least for the time being – by the expense. Another project, which may never come to fruition, but which shows the way in which we are thinking, was one which was proposed by The Hon. Ian MacPherson.

'Ian is the son of Lord David Strathcarron, who was once a racing driver and who is now a motoring writer – he's the President of the Guild of Motoring Writers. Ian suggested a basic sports car – a motorcycle on four wheels, which would be, in effect, a Lotus/Caterham Seven for the next century. His proposal was that we would invest time in design and he would invest time in raising capital. He calculated that we would need £5 million to do the job properly, so that we could set up a factory to make them.

'We came up with a mid-engined monocoque design, and Ian's sums suggested a break-even point of 400 units a year, and that with a fully homologated "turn-key" car. In fact, we worked around an annual production of 500 cars. It hasn't happened yet, and perhaps it won't happen.'

Chapter Nineteen _____

Reynard Goes Stateside

The beginning of 1994 saw Reynard in a completely different mode of operation from any other year in its history. To begin with, for the first time since 1985 there was no Reynard Formula Three car.

The company had tried to form an exclusive relationship with Renault which would see Reynard build five cars. That way, production would be controlled and, with Renault backing, the cars could be built up to a standard and not down to a price. Of course, it would also allow Reynard to maintain a bridgehead in the formula should it want to re-enter the customer market at some point in the future.

Had the plan gone ahead, Reynard would have designed the car, while Dave Price would have built the monocoque in his factory, DPS Composites, in Dorking; and Dave would also have run the British team. It would have been the first time that Reynard had farmed out a chassis to an outside company, which indicates the pressure there was on Reynard Composites to prepare for Indycar.

David Brown had drawn 80 per cent of the Formula Three car and the moulds were made. Reynard was fairly confident of landing the deal.

Negotiations dragged on throughout 1993, but a mutually satisfactory deal could not be agreed and the project fizzled out. Dave Price says: 'I kept going over the budget figures and found that they did not make sense. I phoned Rick, who said, "I've been doing the same and was about to phone you with the same conclusion."

'The Renault engines went to West Surrey Racing which ran a second team of Dallaras. In the event, that proved to be the best possible result because the Renault units were off the pace. Since the engines were in Dallaras, run by a top team, alongside WSR's Mugen-powered Dallaras, it showed that they were at fault. Had we had the engines in Reynards, it would have been the car at fault, or the team, or the drivers – anyone but Renault. We all had a lucky escape there.'

Absent from Formula Three in 1994, at least after the first four races, was Ralt. The new owners had commissioned a completely new car, the 94C, from a former Formula One designer, and it was terrible. It simply did not work, and the team withdrew. The plan had been to run a two-car works team and then sell cars on the back of the success which would undoubtedly come.

For so long Ralt and March had been part of the background to the Reynard story, yet within a short time of the withdrawal of the Ralt Formula Three team, March existed only as sets of old drawings in one of Andrew Fitton's offices, and Ralt had moved to humble premises in Oxfordshire where Steve Ward continued to build a few Atlantic cars and to service existing customers.

Ron Tauranac flew out to Tokyo and clinched a deal to design and build a racing school car for Honda. It was precisely the sort of deal which Andrew Fitton had as part of his future plans. In 1996, Ron moved on to the Honda British Touring Car effort and, within weeks of his arrival, Honda had scored its first ever win in the series.

Successive managements of March/Ralt had undervalued their biggest asset. It is inconceivable that, had Ron still been the name behind the Ralt Formula Three cars, Dallara could have established a monopoly in the category. Dominance, perhaps; but not a monopoly.

Reynard had battled against Ralt in Formula Three for years. First one company had the upper hand, then the other. It is ironical that the respected opponent was finally defeated, not on the track, but back in Ralt's own factory.

With Reynard out of Formula Three, it faced 1994 centred on just two open markets, Formula 3000 and Indycar, as did Lola. The two supreme production racing car makers met head to head in three arenas: Indycar and European and Japanese F3000. Lola had numerical supremacy in Indycar and Japan, while Reynard had the lion's share of European F3000.

Motor sport's controlling body, the FIA, had made threats to scrap Formula 3000 altogether, or at least introduce a one-make substitute, because costs had escalated. The number of Championship rounds was down to nine in 1993 and would sink to eight in 1994 because circuits found it too expensive.

In the first season of the Formula, 1985, Christian Danner had won the Championship on a net budget of about £80,000 and there had been 11 rounds. Admittedly, that had been an unusually low budget, and most people's was at least twice that amount, but by 1994 a typical budget was £600,000 per car.

The grids were still full, and it was still the main stepping stone to Formula One, but interest in the category had waned. That much was evident by the tiny crowds and by the fact that cars rarely carried backing from one major sponsor, but were covered with many names, like in Formula Ford. Even then it was hard to see what the sponsors were getting for their money, since television coverage was confined to satellite stations, which did it poorly, and not even the specialist Press seemed to be able to get pumped up about the formula.

Formula 3000 had been in crisis for some time, but rumblings from the FIA caused all the teams involved to do the unthinkable. They sat down to thrash out the problem together with chassis and engine suppliers, and agreed a package to reduce costs and stabilise design for two years. They then presented their ideas to the FIA and won a temporary reprieve.

As part of that move, Reynard actively promoted an up-date kit for its Formula 3000 car, to convert a 93D to a 94D. Previously you could update cars by buying bits and pieces from the factory, but this was a positive promotion of a kit. Reynard also produced a front suspension system exclusive to the Japanese market. The main difference was in the steering geometry, which made the car easier to drive; but it was not offered to European customers because it was more expensive.

Although they were fierce rivals, neither Reynard nor Lola wanted a one-make formula, especially one which froze the overall specification for three years. From a constructor's point of view it was not a good thing – whoever got the contract could be damaged. Once you have designed your car for such a series, you make 10 designers redundant. When the contract comes up for grabs again, you look around for your design staff and find that you laid them off three years ago.

The bright young guy that you nearly kept, but had to let go, is now somewhere else. He has not been brought on through the ranks by working in the design office as an assistant and then being present at test days and races, honing his talent by engineering a customer's car and progressing its development in preparation for next year's car.

On the other hand, if you allow an open formula then costs escalate because the customer has to pay for the R&D of the companies involved. Costs in Formula 3000 unquestionably rose when teams did deals with Reynard, Lola, or whoever, to have works engineers attend their cars. On the other hand, each one who did so was after that extra advantage and they were happy to pay for it.

When the 1994 European Formula 3000 Championship began, Reynard had lost its monopoly among teams – a couple switched to Lola – but that did not reflect in the results sheets, as the top six places in the opening round at Silverstone were filled by Reynards led by Franck Lagorce. It was business as usual. In fact, for the second year in succession a John Thompson design won every round in the series with 'Jules' Boullion taking the title from Lagorce and Gil de Ferran.

There you have it in one paragraph. In an eight-race series, Reynard won every point-scoring place except for one fourth and one fifth. The trouble is that it sounds so easy, but if motor racing was easy all those outfits which presented Formula Ford 2000 cars alongside Reynard at the 1975 Racing Car Show would now be in Indycar.

The quality of any win is determined by the quality of the loser. If you or I stepped into a boxing ring with Mike Tyson and we floored him, we would be true champions. If Tyson took us apart with one punch, it would mean nothing. When Reynard beat Lola, it meant something.

Of course, every single driver and every single team had stories to tell, but then they always have, at every level. There is this engine problem, that brake imbalance, wild driving by Fernando Fandango, sponsors not fulfilling their contracts, and so on. The fact remains that, in Europe, Reynard drivers won all but five points in the Formula 3000 Championship.

The Lola T94/50 was by no means a bad car, and it frequently showed pace, but it was under-represented and, if it had a fault, it was that it did not allow its drivers to make best use of their tyres in qualifying.

In Japan, however, things were not so rosy and, despite pre-season optimism, Reynard still did not crack the Japanese market. For the first time since it was inaugurated in 1973 a non-British car (the Japanese Dome) took the title. There was no particular reason for this. Dome had not made a startling technical breakthrough – rather it had made a car which worked in harmony with its Japanese Dunlop tyres.

In fact, Dunlop underwrote Dome, which ran a single car for Marco Apicella, and car and tyres were developed in harmony. The entire operation was as focused as a Formula One team – indeed, Dome was preparing to go into Formula One. Makers of production racing cars cannot be as focused as that.

Dunlop created its tyres for that one car, and other teams which used Dunlops had to use the tyres which Apicella chose. As it happened, only one of the five Reynards in the series ran on Dunlops, and John Thompson says: 'We could get the best from them, but after five laps they were rooted.'

That is the way it is in Japan, and John did not regard it as an excuse, merely as an explanation. Like everyone else at Reynard, it merely served to strengthen their desire to crack the Japan Championship. In fact, Reynard took a couple of wins during 1994 while most teams which ran Lolas enjoyed their best results with developments of the 1992 car.

Before the end of 1994, the FIA announced that, from 1996, International Formula 3000 would be a one-make, one-engine category, and interested parties were invited to apply, no previous experience necessary. The last bit was true – one company, which had run cars in Formula 3000, and had restored historic cars, did apply.

Reynard did not want a one-make formula but, naturally, it responded. For the first time, the roles of Rick and of the design team were reversed. Rick had to sell a concept and then, if it was accepted, the designers would have to fulfil it. It would occupy his time over the coming months.

That was part of future planning. The immediate problem over the winter of 1993/4 was the entry into Indycar. Apart from taking on the old rival, Lola, there was the matter of Penske, which had assembled a three-car 'Dream Team' with Al Unser Jr and Emerson Fittipaldi, each a former Champion, plus Paul Tracy, who had won five races for Penske in 1993.

Lola had more strength in depth than anyone else, with Nigel Mansell, the 1993 Champion, Mario Andretti, Scott Goodyear, Robby Gordon and Raul Boesel heading a list of more than 20 drivers which included former Champ, Bobby Rahal, with works Honda engines. Honda, however, was the unknown quantity since it was making its debut in the category and was at the bottom of its learning curve.

Reynard was the outsider; apart from the fact that it was new to the category. Its only likely front-runners were Michael Andretti and Mauricio Gugelmin, and Gugelmin, a refugee from Formula One, had yet to win an Indycar race. There was also Vasser, who Adrian had tested with at Sears Point shaking down a Reynard Atlantic Car. As when Reynard had entered Formula Three and F3000, it was largely the outsiders who gave the company a chance.

That's how the field seemed to shape up at the beginning of the season, but Jacques Villeneuve, son of the great Gilles, had other ideas. He was making his debut in Indycar, having graduated from Toyota Atlantic where he had driven a Ralt.

Despite Adrian's hand-on-heart assurances that Reynard was not going to try anything radical in Indycar, it did. Of course it did – it is in the nature of the beast that it would. The particular gimmick was a gearbox casing delivered to teams just before the first race of the 1994 season which featured 'cooling fins' which just happened to be turning vanes. While carrying out the important function of cooling the transmission they also, a mere coincidence, generated downforce. The Indycar technical commission was not convinced that the vanes' primary function was cooling and when the cars so fitted arrived at Surfers Paradise there was a run on hacksaws as the vanes were removed. Nice try.

At Surfers Paradise Reynard maintained its tradition of winning first time out, and the only glitch was that Michael Andretti did not set pole. It was an odd race which was delayed by the weather and a great number of crashes, and it was foreshortened since the final laps were run in near darkness. At the end of the day Michael Andretti emerged the winner. He had had his share of luck, including clipping a tyre barrier without damaging his car, but he had returned to Indycar in the best possible way.

Each of the six Reynards in the race ran in the top six at some point, and four of them finished in the points (4th Jimmy Vasser, 6th Mauricio Gugelmin, 7th Teo Fabi). Although there was an element of luck in Andretti's win, it was not luck that every Reynard ran in the top six, and four finished in the points – and they used both Cosworth and Ilmor engines. Reynard had arrived.

The race was transmitted to the Reynard Centre in Bicester via satellite, and virtually the entire workforce turned up to watch it. Other racing car companies provide a similar service, but for once the Press picked up on it and *Autosport* ran a piece on the 'unsung heroes' of Bicester. There was a photograph of champagne being sprayed and there were quotes from various workers. When almost everyone in a factory can find time on a Sunday to watch a race, when they have been working impossible hours for months, there is something special going on.

Adrian speaks of culture and philosophy; they are fine words, but motor racing is full

Michael Andretti won the opening round of the 1994 Indycar World Series at Surfers Paradise, Australia, continuing Reynard's tradition of winning the first race of every new series entered. (*Sutton Motorsport Images*)

of people with fine words. The Reynard workforce voted with their feet and demonstrated the effect of his ideas.

A few days after the race Adrian sent a fax to Chip Ganassi and it read:

22 March 1994

Dear Chip

What a fantastic triumph of vision, faith, determination and teamwork. As you said, we close the first chapter with the joint satisfaction of a really difficult job well done. We have all witnessed a true partnership at work with teams of aligned people working together to beat the best in Indycar racing.

Thanks, partner, for allowing us the opportunity to continue the Reynard tradition; now you are part of our story and we are pleased to be part of yours.

It will continue, no doubt, to be a difficult task ahead – the Indycar Championship win. I feel that we are now more able to tackle the problems that may arise. This weekend has strengthened the bond between us and demonstrated that we can negotiate in a constructive and fair manner on difficult and confused issues. Let us all learn from our experiences and endeavour to be more professional in this business and ever respectful of each other's contribution.

Thank you Chip. See you at Phoenix.

P.S. I was once asked to jot down ten of the most important characteristics of a race car builder. They are not all relevant to RNA (Reynard North America) business, but I enclose them for your interest:

Ten pre-requisites to design, build and sell racing cars and stay in business.

1. The company must have an engineer proprietor; engineers can learn about money and business.

2. The culture must be simple, easy to understand, allowing rapid change with minimal admin.

3. The environment must be a good place to work, catering for the fulfilment of personal careers as well as corporate goals.

4. The right attitude is vital; there must be no prima donnas in the team.

5. Well-conceived, economic and effectively applied R&D is everything.

6. This is a risky business. Make a good profit when times are good and put some aside.

7. It is a young people's business; early recruitment and training is a great investment.

8. NEVER . . . get complacent, give up, give financial credit, believe the Press or hold your breath for someone to say 'thank you'.

9. The power of a good team is greater than the sum of individual people; surround yourself with great people and empower them.

10. Service, product quality and value-for money are customer-perceived qualities; listen to the customer constantly.

Michael Andretti in the pits during a race on a one mile oval track in 1994.

References to the fact that 'we can negotiate in a constructive and fair manner on difficult and confused issues' and the hope that the two sides could 'learn from our experiences and endeavour to be more professional in this business and ever respectful of each other's contribution' indicate that the Reynard/Ganassi relationship had not always been smooth. Nor had it, and it would become very tricky in the future, but at Surfers Paradise each side had delivered what it had promised.

After Surfers Paradise the result at the Phoenix one-mile oval was a little disappointing, with Jimmy Vasser being the highest Reynard finisher in fifth place, but Malcolm Oastler was not phased by that. 'The most telling thing was that Jacques Villeneuve, in his first oval race, was on the front row of the grid just two hundredths of a second off Paul Tracy's pole time. That showed we had got it right. We had showed that the car worked well on street circuits and short ovals, where you would expect us to be at a disadvantage because of the route we took with the gearbox.'

Later, Malcolm would admit that there was a world of difference between speed in qualifying over a few laps and sustaining that speed over the course of a race. For Reynard, much of the problem came down to the fact that, about half the time, the engineers often worked at circuits where they had not been able to test, and therefore teams were having to guess what the optimum settings were. On some of the one-mile ovals, which require very subtle car set-ups, this was a major disadvantage but, of course, things should get better year by year as each team builds up a data file on its Reynards.

It was during the race at Phoenix that Jacques Villeneuve's Reynard T-boned Hiro Matsushito's Lola at 150 mph, and it speaks volumes for both makers that the worst injury was Matsushito's dislocated shoulder. Adrian, however, was not complacent and said: 'We will be carrying out a thorough examination of Jacques Villeneuve's damaged car, together with a freeze-frame video recording of the accident, so that we can assess how our car reacted to the impact. There is always room for improvement and we must always strive to make further gains in driver protection.'

'When we began, my mandate to Malcolm was that we didn't want any injured drivers, and I think that our tub has the thickest laminate of any Indycar tub. Stan Fox gave us a very good crash test at Indianapolis where we were able to measure the g loads. He did 62g head-on into the wall, just crushed the nose a bit and then stopped. The wings weren't even damaged, they just flopped back. It was real progressive impact absorption.'

At Phoenix the Penske team appeared with 'shark fins' on the rear bodywork and, sure enough, 'shark fins' were soon appearing on other cars. Malcolm is highly amused: 'One of these days I'll put a bath tap on a side-pod and if the car wins, you'll find bath taps everywhere. The Reynard teams added their own fins, we didn't supply them, but it gave them the opportunity to sell more sponsorship space – some did and there's nothing wrong with that. Look around you, all this has ultimately been paid for by sponsors.'

After the brilliant showing at Surfers Paradise, Malcolm was confident of a good result at Long Beach, another street circuit, but the Reynards were not happy there. The basic problem was putting down the power out of the slow corners, and it was a matter of weight distribution rather than aerodynamics. In a 50 mph corner the aerodynamic package provides only 300 lb. of downforce on a car which, with driver, weighs about 1800 lb., whereas at Indianapolis cars generate about 3000 lb. downforce.

Malcolm says: 'Weight distribution is something we can put right; no problem. It's a mechanical problem, and a case of not having data from last year's car. We'll have that information for 1995, and it'll be good information. There are a few poor teams in

Indycar, but we've only worked with very good people. I thought that the whole scene was wonderful: good teams, good drivers, good racing.'

At the beginning of 1994 Adrian was musing aloud: 'If you really wanted to win the Indy 500 badly enough, and you had the money, you would go to someone like Cosworth and commission a push-rod engine. There's a loophole in the rules which would allow you to run to the same capacity and boost as the 'stock block' formula. You'd finish up with 150–200 bhp more than the opposition and you'd wipe the floor with them. Of course, it would probably be banned or restricted afterwards, but it might be in some company's interest to do that for the sheer prestige and publicity of winning at Indy.'

Adrian was not the only person who had read the rule book, and Roger Penske had already gone to Ilmor, in which he is a partner, and to Mercedes-Benz, and the result was a push-rod Ilmor engine for the Indy 500 which had 'Mercedes-Benz' on the cam-covers. The Penske team dominated qualifying, but Jacques Villeneuve qualified fourth fastest, with Michael Andretti fifth.

In the event, only one Penske-Ilmor/Mercedes-Benz finished, but it was in the top slot. Not far behind, however, was Villeneuve's Reynard, winner of 'Class B' as non-Mercedes-Benz users called themselves. It was Jacques' first time at Indianapolis and it was only his fourth Indycar race.

As Adrian had predicted, the pushrod engine was banned for 1995, but Mercedes-Benz recouped its investment through massive publicity.

Michael Andretti crossed the line behind Jacques, but was issued a penalty which placed him sixth ahead of Teo Fabi's Reynard and behind Bobby Rahal's Penske, Jimmy Vasser's Reynard and Robby Gordon's Lola. Four Reynards in the top seven – not a bad debut at the Brickyard.

Lola had its share of misfortune, however, and three of its strongest runners – Nigel Mansell, Mario Andretti and Raul Boesel – retired, so the result was not a clear-cut case of Reynard having outstripped its old rival. Malcolm is the first to agree: 'The Lola was a good car.' In Mansell's case he had the bizarre experience of circulating slowly, in second place, under a 'full-course yellow' and having a rookie blast out of the pit lane, hit the back of his car and land on top of his cockpit. Lola had more than its share of misfortune.

As the season went on, the Penske team was dominant and the threat from the Newman/Haas team, representing the Lola works, was strangely muted. Part of the reason was that Mario Andretti had announced that he would retire at the end of the season, so for him the season became the Arrivederci Mario Tour. If Mario, coming to an end of one of the most distinguished careers in motor racing history had lost a little of his edge, it was entirely understandable. Fans everywhere prayed for him to end the year unharmed.

Mansell's position was a little more complicated. In May, Ayrton Senna was killed and, according to sources close to Newman/Haas, his attitude changed. He had public, and private, rows with his team-mate Mario Andretti, he lost interest in testing, his race performances lacked fire and on two occasions he simply quit. The charitable view was that Senna's death had disturbed him and he was suffering from profound shock and a realisation of his own mortality.

Most people, however, thought that the realisation of his worth to Formula One made him lose complete interest in Indycar. As one team member said: '1993 was the honeymoon year, 1994 was the divorce.' With Senna dead and Alain Prost retired, Mansell was the only World Champion still racing, and Formula One was perceived to be in need of his pulling power. Bernie Ecclestone was soon brokering a deal whereby

Mansell could return to Williams. Not only did Mansell's racing edge become blunted but, from mid-season on, he refused to test.

Robby Gordon and Raul Boesel in other Lolas suffered cruel luck when apparently on course for wins. Overall, however, the season belonged to Penske, whose cars are designed and built in Poole, Dorset.

Malcolm says: 'Where the Penskes were brilliant was their ability to race – they used their tyres better in racing conditions, whether it was with a full load of fuel or when the tyres were worn. We were often right with them in qualifying, but they generally raced better and where it was most apparent was on the short ovals.'

It was not apparent to most observers that Penske also had two clear technical advantages – one was in its suspension, with an extra spring which helped to adjust ride height, the other in a new viscous-coupling differential built by Xtrac and also used by Tyrrell in Formula One. So close was the Indycar series, and so closely matched were the three chassis designs, that these apparently minor innovations were enough to tip the balance.

It has to be said, too, that Penske was focused on Indycar. During the post-season discussion, the word 'focus' kept cropping up, as it had when discussing Dallara in Formula Three and Dome in Japanese Formula 3000. As Malcolm says: 'We won more races than the other production car maker, Lola, but we were also racing against Penske, and Penske beat us.'

Over the course of the season, however, Reynard did come up with aerodynamic modifications which made the car less pitch-sensitive and hence more competitive over the length of a race. Another was the development of a 'shortitudinal' gearbox which was 20 lb. lighter, 2 in. shorter, and had a much quicker gear shift. Malcolm says: 'The internals are made by Xtrac, it's a case of having stuff designed for the job and not using what's already around.' Unspoken, but none the less lingering in the background, was the word 'focus'.

The new transmission was first run in the last round, at Laguna Seca, and was carried on to the 1995 car.

The season ended: Reynard 3, Lola 1 and Penske out of sight with 12 wins. The three Penske 'Dream Team' drivers filled the top three places in the Championship, with Reynard's top scorers – Michael Andretti and Jacques Villeneuve – in fourth and sixth places.

Michael won at Surfers Paradise, and on the street circuit in Toronto, while Jacques, who won the 'Rookie of the Year' title, took a superb win on the Elkhart Lake road circuit. By the end of the season, people were talking of Jacques as a future Formula One star, and even hard-bitten followers of the sport became misty-eyed at the thought of him in a Ferrari bearing the number 27, which will always be associated with his father.

It is slightly ironical that Reynard took its wins on street and road circuits when it had believed that its best performances would come on the long ovals, but let's not forget Villeneuve's superb second place at Indianapolis on his, and Reynard's, first run there.

Reynard had done better than anyone could have expected, given all circumstances, even if it was partly because Lola suffered more than its fair share of ill luck. Reynard had not been so rash as to make promises about performances, but it had made promises about customer service, and these had been fulfilled.

The speculators who, in 1992, had been offered a share of the action, and had turned it down, must have been feeling pretty sick. Under the predictions of the prospectus, they would have made a profit had only eight cars been sold in the first year of Indycar,

Jacques Villeneuve drove a Reynard Indycar in 1994 and 1995, claiming the 'Rookie of the Year' title in 1994, and the overall Drivers' Championship title, and Indianapolis 500, in 1995. He still remains close friends with both Rick and Adrian.

and Reynard sold 13. Year two of the plan predicted 15 cars, yet Reynard was to sell nearly double that number in 1995.

From the outside, it appeared to be a case of Reynard being ever onward, ever upward, but behind the appearance of apparent harmony, there was strife.

Not long after the company's successful debut at Surfers Paradise, Carl Haas began to woo Rick Gorne. He came a'courting bearing promises of gifts – substantial gifts – and Rick was tempted. To draw an analogy, Rick and Adrian had been in a marriage for 11 years and it had hit a stale patch. In supporting Adrian's dream of going into Formula One, Rick had invested a lot of his own money in the factory site, and when the Formula One project floundered he was hit hard.

Then there was the fact that he admired Carl Haas, almost to the point of reverence. So, when Carl suggested the odd dinner-date, Rick was receptive and, on more than one occasion, he did not tell Adrian until after the date.

Adrian says: 'Not long into 1994, Carl suddenly saw how vulnerable he was. I think that he did not give us much chance of success because he'd seen us operate in Toyota Atlantic, but that was with the B Team. When we went into Indycar we hit it with the A Team.

'The easiest form of response in that situation is to poach your rival's key personnel, and I don't blame Carl for trying – he's also made his overtures to Malcolm Oastler. If you are successful in your poaching, however, it means that there is something wrong with your target's relationships or job satisfaction and working environment. That is why, between us, Chip and I were able to get Bruce Ashmore on board.

'Malcolm is not unhappy. He could earn a lot more money elsewhere, no question about that, and he's had his offers from a lot of people besides Carl. It is my job to create an environment which he does not want to leave.

'Money is not the bottom line. It has its place, of course, but it's not the be-all and end-all. My friend, Richard Branson, operates in the same way. He does not offer fantastic salaries, he offers opportunities. Don't get me wrong, we pay good money, but you could earn more elsewhere, although you would not get the same job satisfaction.

'If money is your prime motive, so be it. If that is your prime motivation, you're not a Reynard person. We aim to offer a quality of life and I am confident that our key people share that philosophy – I should know, I hand-picked them.

'On my part, I have instituted a profit-share for the entire workforce and a shareholding scheme for key personnel. In 1995, everyone who had been on the strength for six months or more shared a bonus of £400,000. That is 10 per cent of our profit, and the arrangement is so structured that it cannot be reduced if I were to decide to pay myself a million pounds. It cannot reduce the bonus.

'It also allows anyone on the staff who cares to do a simple sum to know how much profit the company is making, and that's no bad thing.

'Having said that, in 1994 Rick was unhappy and it was something we had to talk about. We had some very candid, very painful, discussions with no holds barred. He laid it on the line for me and I laid it on the line for him. I don't mind admitting that some of the things he said shook me to the core. One thing which was clear was that I had not appreciated his feelings and I needed to raise my own game.

'He was tempted by Carl's offer, and who can blame him? He was going home to his little cottage, and Carl was offering him the whole of the US of A. We both knew, however, that a move would have torn him apart, because he'd invested so much of his life into this company.

'We don't have to go into all the details. Some of them are very personal, but the upshot is that the relationship was born again, stronger than ever!'

Chapter Twenty

Off-Track Racing

Until the end of 1994, the story of Reynard is broadly linear – student builds Formula Ford racing car, it is good so student becomes constructor. There are ups and downs, good times and bad, but he survives and progresses from the Ford Formulae to Formula Three, from there to Formula 3000 and so to Indycar. There are a few diversions and wrong turnings along the way, but that is the way in which the basic story can be plotted. Over a different time-scale, it parallels the story of many a racing driver climbing the ladder of success.

From the end of 1994, however, the story fragments because it was then that Adrian bought a house in America and took his family to live there for a year. He was going to have to spend the best part of six months there in any case and there were also significant tax advantages in the arrangement.

Adrian says: 'Apart from anything else, it showed that the company could operate better without me being in the office. I had gradually been pushed into a role – it was me who was initialling every single invoice, for example – and the break allowed the factory to reorganise without me, while it released me to do some creative thinking and, as a result, I was able to initiate a number of projects which, otherwise, we would not be undertaking.'

That meant that Adrian was no longer present to select the trainees, and the job devolved to Peter Morgan who had joined the company to manage the Indycar project and had taken over as Production Manager. Peter says: 'We have formalised the selection process, and applicants are now interviewed by myself, a senior engineer and someone who has been through a traineeship.

'We hope that everyone who goes through it will be offered a job at the end. There have been very few people who we have not offered jobs to. In addition, we now offer three places to engineering undergraduates who have to do a year in industry as part of their degree course; three summer placements to engineering undergraduates, as well as work experience to local school children.

'Basically, all these people get some experience of the whole business, apart from assembly – that has to be done by experienced people.'

Then Reynard, together with TWR and Prodrive, has sponsored a B. Eng. degree at the Oxford Brookes University (formerly the Oxford Polytechnic) which is, in effect, a degree in motor racing engineering. Taking this into account along with school work experience, summer placement, degree course industrial experience and, finally, the trainee scheme with a job waiting at the end for almost everyone who undertakes it, we're almost talking cradle-to-the-grave.

Peter continues: 'My own department has changed, as well, since Reynard is no longer selling Formula Three and F3000 cars. Gone are the days when a guy would arrive in a van from Paul Stewart Racing to pick up spares. We either deal with branches of the group, such as the Chrysler Stratus project, or with Reynard North America which handles all the Indycar spares, and the Le Mans Company in Japan – nothing, these days, is sold over the counter.'

The question of spare parts caused some problems in the Reynard/Ganassi relationship, since during 1995 Reynard believed that Ganassi was not meeting his commitment to order them in sufficient quantities to service the Reynard teams properly – that had been a crucial part of the Indycar strategy. Lawyers became involved, and there were moves to dissolve the partnership, but the situation was defused by Chip putting in orders. It was an expensive process, and time alone will tell whether the relationship was damaged beyond repair when, in 1998, the contract between the parties expires.

As Adrian went Stateside with his family, an intriguing proposal hung in the air. In the summer of 1994 he'd met at The Green Man pub near Silverstone with Paul Stewart and Rob Armstrong, and the one item on the agenda had been Formula One. Paul and his father, Jackie, were of the opinion that Formula One was expanding into the Pacific rim and there were many companies there with the potential to become sponsors. Reynard and PSR provisionally agreed in broad terms to pool their resources, and made a joint proposal to Ford who, at the time, turned it down. The idea, however, remained on the back burner.

Another thing hanging in the air was an interest in Touring Car Projects. During 1993, Reynard had made a pitch to both Renault and Ford, the idea being that the company would design and build the cars which would then be run by associated teams. Had the pitch been successful, it was intended that Paul Stewart Racing would run the Ford team and Madgwick International would run the Renaults. That had come to nothing, but it had put Adrian back in touch with Bill Stone, who was team co-ordinator for Andy Rouse Engineering which was building and running the works Ford Mondeos.

Released from the pressure of the day-to-day running of the business, Adrian concentrated instead on following up other opportunities.

As for the Formula One project with Stewart Grand Prix, Adrian says: 'Paul came back to me in the middle of 1995, when I was in America, but at that time they did not have an engine deal and there were so many other things happening that I let it go. In fact, at the time, the decision seemed so obvious that I did not even bother my fellow directors with it.

'I could have kicked myself when Stewart landed Ford engines for five years, but that was a late development – there was no whisper of it when I turned down the chance. It has not altered our relationship with PSR, and I have been happy to make suggestions to them about the people they should recruit, even if they haven't always agreed with me.'

While the Chrysler Patriot project ultimately came to nothing, Reynard had kept its side of the deal, and doors were open. As a direct result of the Patriot, the Reynard Group was entrusted with two projects. One was making carbon composite bodies for the Dodge Vipers which have been seen in competition (Reynard also did a small amount of chassis consultancy work on the racing Vipers) and the other was to assist in the development of a car for the American Touring Car Championship which would get under way in 1996.

In the middle of 1995, Bill Stone returned to Reynard to head up the Chrysler Stratus Touring Car project. It was under different circumstances from his previous return. He was a Project Manager, not a potential director. 'My boss is Adrian,' he says, 'and neither of us has any problems with that.

'As soon as I returned, the Press was full of speculation because, shortly afterwards,

Bill Stone (right) is head of the Chrysler Stratus Touring Car project. He spends a great deal of time in America overseeing the project.

Andy Rouse Engineering, where I had been the team co-ordinator, lost the contract to prepare the works Ford Mondeos. The Press assumed that I'd played a part in that, and they speculated that Dick Bennetts would be in charge, I would run the team and Paul Radisich would continue to be one of the drivers.

'You can understand that to an extent – three Kiwis in one team. It may yet happen, but at present we have our contract with Chrysler. As for me being in some way instrumental in Andy losing the works contract, that was pure speculation.

'It was clear to me long before I left that I had become redundant at Andy Rouse Engineering. Andy had retired from driving and was looking after the team, so he and I were more or less doing the same job, and we parted amicably.

'In any case, Adrian had first spoken about the Stratus project in November 1994 and we kept in touch over the next few months. In June 1995 he phoned to say that it was on, and I flew out to Detroit in July. I was given virtually a free hand to assemble my team, and had six weeks to do it in. We had a deadline of March 1996.'

Chrysler actually has a bigger input into the Stratus than most other companies involved in Touring Cars. It is quite usual for a manufacturer to farm out its entire project to a racing car company, as Renault has done with Williams and Volvo has done with TWR. Other manufacturers like to form an alliance and keep quiet about it. Simtek, for example, made a substantial contribution to BMW's ITC programme in the early 1990s, but this was not widely known.

It had been many years since Chrysler had actively been involved in motor sport, and François Castaing knew that, regardless of the expertise that Chrysler had within its own ranks, there is more to motor racing than just good engineering. Give a rule book to a road car engineer, and give the same book to a racing car engineer, and you are liable to get different results.

The road car engineer will take the rules as limits which must be complied with. The instinct of the racer is to look for loopholes or, at the very least, stretch the letter of the law to the very limit. It is the difference between an accountant who is a thoroughly competent professional and the accountant you want to prepare your books for the tax inspector.

Bill continues: 'I brought in Pete Duffy to head up the design team, although Paul Brown has worked on the chassis and has done all the aerodynamics. It was one of the few times that a designer was appointed without Adrian's say-so, because he was in the States.

'Touring Cars have advanced tremendously, even in the relatively short time that I've been involved with them. To be successful, you need a designer with single-seater experience and Pete's includes spells at the Leyton House and Simtek Formula One teams. Touring Cars are nothing like their road versions. For a start, the roll cage is virtually a space-frame on which body panels are hung; then there is a six-speed sequential gearbox, and so on.

'For the next 16 months I flew to Detroit on average once a month. The first thing we had to get right was communication, in terms of a racing culture. Chrysler did not have a racing culture, it had a culture based on design by discussion at meetings. You'd raise something like the alternator bracket to 10 people around a table and they'd go away and discuss it. You'd go back a month later and find no agreement had been reached and you were still without an alternator bracket.

'But they were bright young guys who were willing to listen, and before long they were running with the ball. In fact, the whole programme has caused a tremendous amount of excitement within Chrysler.

'Chrysler has made a commitment to the American Touring Car Championship, and our role is to give them support. We have supplied kits of parts, which they have assembled, but all the work on the engine has been done at Chrysler.

'The Stratus has a forward cabin, which means that the engine bay is small. So, there is not much leeway in positioning the engine, but having the 2-litre unit from the Chrysler Neon situated at the front has worked out pretty well, and the handling is as good as any Touring Car. One thing which a Touring Car needs is good traction, and that's what the Stratus has.

'You'll notice that Vauxhall won races with the Cavalier, which had the weight right over the front wheels, but struggled when it introduced the Vectra where the engine is right back against the firewall.

'If we do have a slight handicap, it is on engine power. Most of the opposition has about 295–300 bhp. You look at people like BMW and discover that they have five or six years of engine development behind their Touring Cars.

'Our debut was at the very first race of the American Touring Car Championship at Lime Rock, the day after the US 500 and the Indianapolis 500. Reynard had won both those, and I was a bit haunted by the Reynard tradition of winning first time out. The field was not huge, but there were cars from Toyota, Honda, Ford, BMW and Mercedes-Benz. They were all privateers, but the quality of the machinery was good.

'They had a "double-header" at Lime Rock and we won both of them. The first went to David Donohue, son of the late, and great, Mark Donohue, and the second to Dominic Dobson, the former Indycar driver who is part-owner of PacWest, which is running the cars in the States. In fact, we won the first three rounds.'

It was an achievement which went largely unrecorded in Britain, although Russell

Bulgin devoted his column in *Autocar* to the fact that, over a single weekend, Reynard had won at Michigan, Indianapolis and Lime Rock. Russell has a humorous style which infuriates some readers, and makes him required reading for others, but on this occasion he was straight down the line in his admiration for the achievement. It was a remarkable one, Touring Cars do not often win on their debuts.

Russell Bulgin's *Autocar* column, dated 12 June 1996, read as follows:

Reynard Racing Cars scored four victories on Sunday 26 May. Three you know about – the Indianapolis 500, the US 500 and a win first time out for the Reynard-engineered Dodge Stratus in the new North American Touring Car Championship opener at Lime Rock. And the fourth? Nobody from Reynard had to sprint to Heathrow and jump on a plane with bits of race car poking out of their baggage.

This – listen up now – is a very big deal. Three Reynards were involved in accidents at Indy. Seven cars were damaged in a startline shunt at Michigan – less than a week before the next race in Milwaukee. Four drivers at Michigan – including winner Jimmy Vasser – competed in their T-cars. Come Sunday night, there were 10 cars in need of rapid repair four thousand miles from Bicester's loftily-labelled Reynard Centre.

You imagine panic calls from race teams to Reynard HQ. Skilled blokes in shop-coats working all-nighters. An autoclave pressure-cooking carbon fibre around the clock. Fabricators ratcheting up the overtime. The Oxford FedEx franchise turning record profits.

Doesn't happen. Reynard has a subsidiary in the States. Reynard North America holds a cache of spares. RNA's Jeff Swartwout sorted out the teams' immediate requirements on-site in Brooklyn, Michigan. Parts were sent out on the Monday after the races, true. But this was just a regular consignment pre-ordered for Milwaukee: one underfloor, one sidepod, four wishbones, some pushrods. Nothing major.

Reynard, then, coped with a major racing incident without troubling the factory back home. The parts – each individually bar-coded to facilitate stock control on either side of the Atlantic – were there. Waiting. Ready to go.

We know all about the British motorsport industry, set tight upon a wafer of real estate spreading due north-west of London that *Time* magazine christened Carburettor Valley. We know all the high-tech brilliance it is capable of, week in, week out. What is easy to forget is that the design innovation and engineering flair required to be globally competitive is worthless without exemplary back-up. Which is why, during the nine-month season, Reynard is primarily a service – and not a technology – business. And that's the victory which matters most.

Bill Stone continues: 'Pete Duffy left us to join Benetton in mid-1996. He wasn't here long enough to absorb the Reynard philosophy, but we are continuing to develop the car and are making new kits for 1997. It is possible that cars will be sold to privateers; it is even possible that they will race in Europe, since Chrysler has re-entered the European car market. It's been a good relationship.'

Paul Brown says: 'We have had a partnership with Chrysler and a true partnership is a rare thing. Chrysler wants to do as much as it can in-house, to give its engineers projects which will improve the breed. Our job is not to do things for them, but to show them how to do it.

'We are really only interested in a true partnership, and are hoping for a long-term relationship which will cover all of Chrysler's motor sport activities, including drag racing and sprint cars.

Read the American magazines about Chrysler's involvement in racing and you get the odd reference to Reynard. You would expect this when dealing with such a partnership. Reynard's success will be measured like that of any good master craftsman, when he can say to the apprentice, 'That's good.'

Another product of Adrian's year in America was the Ford Indigo, which was unveiled at the 1996 Detroit Motor Show where, as virtually a two-seat Indycar for the road, it caused more than a little excitement. As is customary with such products, however, the name of Reynard was barely mentioned, although it was a Reynard project. In fact, Adrian says: 'It was actually built by the British motor racing industry, and DPS, G-Force and Hewland all played key parts.

'It began when I asked Jackie Stewart, who has good relations with major companies, how I could advance Reynard with such people because I think we're a very good company. Jackie introduced me to Neil Ressler, who is one of the senior Vice-Presidents at Ford, and he is all about advanced engineering – a brilliant guy. Neil came to our factory in '94 and liked what he saw, but he could not identify any business we would do together.

'Then I got a call from a friend of mine at Cosworth who said: "We're doing some work for Ford and they're thinking about doing a sports car. Why don't you go in there and see if they'll do a Reynard sports car, in the same way that Carroll Shelby did the Cobra?"

'I put it to Neil that we should do a Cobra for the 1990s, but he said they'd got their own programmes and ours wouldn't fit. So I went away a bit discouraged, but Neil said to keep in touch.

'I was in the States, but over the phone I got a young student we have here to package the engine that Cosworth was building. I went back to Neil and showed him some alternative layouts, but he said: "Don't waste your time. We've got a guy here called John Coletti working on things." I asked to meet John Coletti and he showed me what they were doing – when Neil Ressler passes you down the line at Ford, it's like you've been sent by the gods.

'Once I understood what they were doing, I could go away and come up with a Reynard design which was a bit more special. Then I went back to Neil and left all the drawings with him, now using Ford's new V12 modular engine. Again, he was not encouraging, but three weeks later, just before the Indy 500, I got a call from Dave Velliky, who is the Director of New Concepts, who said, "Come and see me."

'I was there next morning and Dave said: 'We've cancelled our in-house sports car, we'd like to go ahead with yours. Can you build us one by the Detroit Show? I went with a price in pounds – and they wanted to pay the same in dollars. Dave was tough, but I accepted the challenge. Up to then, everything had been done just by me and my student.

'From the States I tried to put together a team of people. I phoned around and got John Piper, who'd never designed a complete car before – most of his work had been in transmissions – and got him on stream with Nigel Stroud and John Love, who was Project Manager.

'We initially sketched out a front-engined car with a transaxle at the rear, which Ford liked because all their road cars are front-engined, but at a key design meeting in Detroit we were able to put the engine in the back. From that stage we decided to use an Indycar gearbox.

'The next five months were frantic. We took half a dozen people to Detroit and used Dave Price to do composites, G-Force to do the buck work and Hewland to do the transmission. Then we inherited the responsibility of a show car as well, so the contract became bigger and more difficult.

'We delivered the "show car" and the "go car" just about on time, and before the "go car" went out Andy Wallace shook it down at Silverstone. The car was built by Reynard and the British motor racing industry. It was a miracle that it happened. I was responsible for the concept, but it was largely done outside of the main company.'

There was talk of putting the Indigo into production, but it came to nothing. John Love and John Piper were on board, however, and another project was in the air with Panoz. That led to the formation of RSVP which is looking after the Panoz Esperante, and Nigel Stroud is also involved as a consultant.

Adrian says: 'I was at a race meeting in '95 when a chap called Peter Thompson said that there was a little company called Panoz which had built a great car, but had difficulty in marketing it, and was I interested in helping them, using the Reynard name?

'I was free of the office and living in the USA, so I went over to Atlanta and found an incredible little company, staffed by about 10 people, who had used Ford parts to make a roadster – a little car with cycle wings. Don Panoz runs a big pharmaceutical company and his son, Danny, started this company. I recognised like spirits and loved the car.

'We got talking and soon were discussing another design they had on the stocks, called the Esperante. This was going to be a front-engined two-seater coupé which took a lot of parts from the new Mustang with its 4.6-litre dohc engine, and they were going to repackage these parts with an aluminium body.

'They asked, "Would you like to help us with this? We want to race them." We decided they could race at Le Mans, Sebring and Daytona, and Don said go away and prepare us a proposal.

'I thought that they should use a carbon-fibre chassis and body, a transaxle mounted at the rear, and said, "Let's go for a GT1 win at Le Mans" – typical Reynard, try to win first time out. We knew it would be quite an expensive operation since the cars would have to compete with McLaren, and we were determined that they would look as good, be stiffer, lighter, more aerodynamic yet be a fraction of the cost. We also thought that perhaps we could sell some as replicas.

'Don Panoz let us run with this idea, and then commissioned us to design the car. Then we said we had done wind tunnel testing and could get more downforce by changing the shape. He said, "Fine, change the shape." We developed a really high performance GT1 car, which can be raced at Le Mans. The project is now quite big because we're going to build seven cars and we're talking Indycar prices plus.'

As we've said, the Ford Indigo and Panoz Esperante led to the formation, early in 1996, of Reynard Special Vehicle Projects under John Piper as Technical Director. RSVP is owned by Adrian and key personnel and, unlike Reynard Composites, which is a subsidiary of the Reynard Group, it is a separate operation in its own facility, albeit on the same industrial estate as the Reynard Centre.

Writing only months after RSVP's formation, it is hard to say a great deal about it since it is exploring unchartered waters for a racing car company. In essence, RSVP handles everything at Reynard which does not bear the Reynard name.

By mid-1996 it had completed a lightweight, high speed, evaluation vehicle for a major road car manufacturer. It was also working on aircraft seats for Virgin Airlines. The design specifications and the rigour of testing demanded by the CAA, meant that this would have a long lead-time with no guarantee of production. It will not be ready for production until 1998 at the earliest, and if it does meet all requirements, and is produced, it is likely to be manufactured as a joint venture with Virgin.

As a first step towards the quality assurance needed for CAA approval, Adrian asked Glyn Jenks and the staff of Reynard Manufacturing Ltd to instigate ISO 9002, the

In 1996 Reynard received their second Queen's Award for Export Achievement, presented by Her Majesty's Lord Lieutenant for Oxfordshire, Mr Hugo Brunner. During his speech to the Reynard employees in a formal ceremony on 4 July, he expressed his admiration of the company's continual achievements.

international quality standard. It is a testimony to their dedication and already high process standards that this was awarded in September 1996, just six months after Adrian's request – a world record for ISO 9002 implementation.

From July 1996 RSVP began work on Ford Mondeos for the 1997 British Touring Car Championship. As a completely separate enterprise, RSVP's relationship with Ford did not affect the relationship Reynard Racing Cars had with Chrysler.

Then there is the Panoz Esperante, which is scheduled to run at Le Mans in 1997. 'Lotus Seven for the 21st Century' was on hold, but by no means dead.

Having attracted world-class clients within months of its founding, the future looks bright for the new venture which, within seven months, had 24 employees and was growing rapidly.

Taking on McLaren in GT racing is nothing if not ambitious, but it would be either a very brave, or foolhardy, commentator who would dare to suggest how that might pan out.

Early in 1996, Reynard received its second Queen's Award for Export Achievement, another triumph for Rick Gorne and, indeed, for the Reynard philosophy. One hesitates to use the word 'philosophy' because it is so often used when 'policy' would be more apposite yet, in this instance, philosophy is the correct word. It permeates the entire group of companies, and people refer to it unprompted and without embarrassment. It is not the boss's hobby horse, it is real and it works.

It is the reason why the key personnel are so loyal to the company, why they refuse mega-buck offers from elsewhere and why they will say, disparagingly, 'So-and-so is not a Reynard man.' It is the reason why Bill Stone can happily work for a man who was once his partner, and why hundreds of bright graduates apply to work for peanuts under the trainee scheme.

Chapter Twenty-One

On-Track Racing

In European Formula 3000 in 1995, Lola had better representation than in previous years and there was clearly very little between the two chassis, since Lola took a win and two second places. It was generally agreed that victory in the series was really due to Super Nova, which had spent the winter setting up its Reynard 95Ds to be user friendly, and its two drivers – Vicenzo Sospiri and Ricardo Rosset – headed the final table with Marc Goossens (Lola) and Kenny Bräck (Reynard) in joint third place.

Mike Blanchet, MD of Lola Cars, reckons that there was little to choose between the Reynard and the Lola, and it was a shame that it was the last year of the open formula because Lola had clawed back some of the ground it had lost in 1991 when some of the best teams had switched to Reynard.

If Lola had had its best showing for some years in Europe, in Japan in 1995 Reynard finally got the break it had been hoping for – wins by a young Japanese driver, Toranosuke Takagi. Ross Cheever had won many races for Reynard but, too often, the Japanese had seen that as a win for a superstar driver, not for a superior chassis.

Vincenzo Sospiri and Ricardo Rosset dominated the European Formula 3000 Championship in 1995 for Super Nova Racing. Pictured is victor, Sospiri. (*Sutton Motorsport Images*)

Ross was not seen as a superstar when he raced in Europe, but John Thompson says: 'He's one of the quickest drivers I've ever seen. In fact if I was setting up a Formula 3000 team tomorrow, my first call would be to Ross, and my second would be to a good broker to insure the car. The sad thing is that he has not had a drive since the end of 1994.'

The whole of the Japanese series changed early in the year when an earthquake devastated the city of Kobe. It destroyed the factory of Dunlop Japan which had backed the 1994 Champion constructor, Dome. That, in turn, meant that Dome was absent from the Formula 3000 series, and its plans to enter Formula One were blighted.

We see a story about an earthquake on the television news and forget it a week later. Meanwhile there are factories and homes in ruins, and a footnote to the calamity is that motor racing history is changed.

With Dunlop absent, Bridgestone was more relaxed in its approach, and that made a subtle change to the Championship as a whole. Saturo Nakajima entered Tora Takagi in a Reynard, and he won several races. Indeed, he was favourite for the Championship, but there was a multiple pile-up early in the last race which eliminated Takagi and most of the Reynard runners, and Toshio Suzuki came through to take the title in a Lola.

Takagi's performances, however, gave Reynard credibility and led to a spate of orders for 1996. For the first time, Reynard had a significant presence in Japanese Formula 3000, with up to 12 cars on the grid (eight of them new for 1996, the rest being up-dates) and in the early races of 1996 wins were taken for Reynard by both Tora Tagaki and Ralf Schumacher, the reigning World Champion's younger brother. Andrew Gilbert-Scott, winner of the 1983 Formula Ford Festival in a Reynard, was also showing well in a 96D, but Lola was by no means completely overwhelmed.

The 96D had a curved rear wing cross-tube, like on many Formula One cars. It was done at the request of the importer, and wind tunnel tests showed that it was mainly cosmetic. It was neither better nor worse than the previous arrangement. But, that's what the customers wanted and, if it went against the grain to fit it, it at least helped to ensure greater representation in Japan.

After eight years of effort, in 1996 Reynard finally won the Japanese Formula 3000 Championship, and did so in style, winning eight of the ten rounds. Although Ralf Schumacher clinched the series, from Reynard's point of view the fact that three Japanese drivers – Naoki Hattori, Tora Takagi and Katsutomo Kaneishi — each won races was of more long-term importance. Further, the Reynard importer, Tom Hanawa's Le Mans Company, won the Team Championship with over twice as many points as its nearest rival.

During 1995 it was announced that Lola had won the contract to service Formula 3000 in Europe from 1996 for three years. Japan decided to stay with an open formula for the foreseeable future.

John Thompson says: 'It came as a bit of a surprise to us since we had worked with the FIA to draw up the regulations – and since we'd been given a sneak preview of them, we felt we were favourites. Lola undercut us.'

Adrian says: 'I can only assume that Lola was desperate for the work. It would have cost us £48,000 to have made all the parts to build a car, and we submitted a tender of £70,000 per car. Lola came in with a bid of £53,000, which means that they are making very little on the sale of cars.

'If we were not in Indycar, I may have considered making a cheaper product, but I think that a company is entitled to a profit margin. Besides, had we competed with Lola on price, it might have compromised our capacity to build successful Indycars.'

Mike Blanchet says: 'We made our bid in line with what we understood to be the

FIA's intentions. In the first year we will not make money, or lose any, on the cars we sell. The profit will come from the second and third years plus, of course, from spares. You have to look at a three-year formula in its entirety.

'It was not only important for us to win the contract as a manufacturer, but from the point of view of our engineering staff. We operate as a team with people being able to transfer from one project to another, so we have not had to lose anyone because it's a one-make formula.

'A slightly different matter is Japan which is operating its own formula. The market there is not large, maybe 12 cars a year, because Japanese teams like to develop their own cars, so you'll find a lot hybrids like a '94 car running in '96 with the team's own side-pods and wings.'

Reynard lost its Formula Three market to a superior product, but it lost the greater part of its Formula 3000 market in a battle of tenders. From its debut in 1988, Reynard had dominated European Formula 3000, and its off-shoots like British Formula Two, and had won the Championship six times in the seven years it competed. It is hard to think of any other business where a market leader can be legislated from its position virtually overnight.

If you make tennis racquets, and a rival produces a superior product, you grin and bear it – and set about trying to come up with something even better. You do not find the controlling body of lawn tennis telling you that you can only sell your racquets as long as they are cheaper.

Early in 1996, we spoke to Max Mosley, the President of the FIA who said: 'You've got to ask yourself what's the purpose of Formula 3000? Is it to educate racing car manufacturers or is it to bring on drivers for Formula One? So far as we are concerned, its primary purpose is to bring on drivers for Formula One.

'As it was, you had manufacturers competing on a race-to-race basis, with each one trying to make a more competitive car, and the competitors were having to foot the bill for the manufacturers' research and development costs. You can either have that, or you can have the competition before the season starts by asking manufacturers to submit a tender.

'The difference in cost to the driver is going to be less than half what it was under the old system. When they were paying the R&D costs, the number of drivers was restricted. In 1996, Formula 3000 will cost about the same as Formula Three, and I hope that we will get a better selection of drivers.'

In the middle of the year we spoke to a Formula 3000 team manger who said: 'Costs are very little down on 1995, although things should improve in 1997 and 1998 because the cost of the cars will come down since you don't have to buy new ones, although the cost of spares still isn't cheap and there's no way around that.

'Everything that you use on the car, even a Gurney flap, has to be a Lola part. You cannot make anything yourself. So far as I am concerned, it makes the whole thing boring. You cannot work for your special advantage, because there isn't one to be had.'

He was not the only team manager to feel that way, and Jean-Paul Droit's printed comments were even stronger. Others, however, felt that the new rules were allowing drivers a better chance to display their talent.

For Indycar in 1995, Malcolm Oastler designed new side-pods to improve the engine cooling on the 95I – in 1994 cooling was adequate, not brilliant. In all there were about a hundred detail changes, and they ranged from strengthening the uprights and some areas of the tub, to performance-enhancing changes such as a new underfloor, new front wings and front suspension geometry. Overall, the new aerodynamic package made the car less pitch-sensitive, and during winter testing, Reynard 95Is were lapping under the record on a wide variety of circuits.

As Malcolm said before the '94 season, 'Once you've done a year in a series, you have a data base to work from. Things must get easier.'

By the end of 1994, Reynard had lost the Rick Galles team to Lola, but had increased its overall representation in Indycar for 1995. From six cars on the grid at most races (with 14 made) Reynard would make 27 cars in 1995 to the 30 of Lola. More to the point, Reynard faced 1995 with a much stronger line-up of drivers, although Michael Andretti left Ganassi after his one-year contract to fill the place at Newman/Haas just vacated by his great father.

Alan Mertens, formerly an Indycar designer with March and the 'mer' in Galmer, maker of the car which won the 1992 Indianapolis 500 for Rick Galles, explained his reasons for choosing a Reynard for PacWest, for whom he is Chief Engineer: 'The first thing is that Reynard has established itself competitively in the series, with potential for the future. The attitude of the company is very aggressive and upbeat. It's very supportive of its customers and has denied us nothing – and our demands have been very great. I'm very confident that we have made the right choice of car and people.'

The new gearbox, introduced late in 1994, gave some problems in early season, but an intensive programme sorted it out before the end of May.

For the first time in many years there was a choice of tyres as Firestone re-entered Indycar, but this did not affect Reynard and Lola users. Both cars seemed equally happy on either type of tyre. The team that it did affect was Penske, who were contracted to Goodyear as one of the company's official test teams. Initially, however, the Penske PC24 was very unhappy on Goodyear's '95 rubber.

At first, Team Penske was puzzled by its apparent retrograde step, having dominated in 1994, but back-to-back tests with a PC23 showed where the problem lay. What had happened was that Goodyear had changed the construction of its tyres between winter testing and the start of the season.

The Penske PC24 was by no means a complete flop, and Al Unser Jr won four races and finished a strong runner-up in the series. In fact, since Emerson Fittipaldi won at Nazareth, Penske finished the year with five wins, which was more than any other team, even if it did suffer the ignominy of failing to qualify for the Indianapolis 500.

Nick Goozée, who heads up Penske's English facility, says of Team Penske's darkest hour: 'We had a serious aerodynamic problem which had been masked in 1994 when we were running the push-rod Mercedes-Benz (Ilmor) engine. Then we had over 1000 bhp, and our drivers had to brake for corners, but running with 850 bhp meant that the circuit should have been flat-out and we discovered a problem.'

When its drivers failed to qualify with their PC24s, Penske acquired Lolas from the Rahal-Hogan team to attempt to qualify but, even with all of its vast resources and experience, it could not get its drivers on the grid. Nick says: 'We would like to have bought Reynards, in fact we owned a Reynard, but in the time available we had to buy from another team. The Reynards we were offered had not been maintained to very high standards. We'd helped out Bobby Rahal the previous year, when he'd been running Honda engines, and he returned the favour.'

Since a Lola sat on pole position and one finished third at Indy, Penske's failure to qualify its Lolas demonstrates the subtle process that teams undergo when they take delivery of new cars and dial them in during testing. Penske did not have the time to come to terms with its new cars, so the greatest team in the history of Indycar, and two drivers who are both former champions and two-times winners of the 500, were bumped from the grid by lesser teams and lesser drivers who had been able to form the right relationship with their cars.

The headline from race day itself was that Jacques Villeneuve in a Reynard won on

En route to his 1995 Indycar Championship title, Jacques Villeneuve won the Indianapolis 500 at only his second attempt. (*Sutton Motorsport Images*)

only his second attempt – but he had been second (and winner of 'Class B') in 1994. What made the youngster's win the more remarkable was that he had been penalised two laps for technical infringements, but had made them up under 'full-course yellows', and had come through to win what, in his terms, was the Indianapolis 505.

Naturally, there was rejoicing from the Reynard camp at that. It was the turning point of the season, because before the race the honours had been fairly evenly shared, with Reynard and Penske each taking two wins and Lola taking one. Although he had not been a race winner, Scott Pruett actually led the Championship for Lola before Indianapolis, but then Villeneuve moved ahead and stayed there.

The rejoicing, however, was controlled since, on the first lap, Stan Fox had crashed his Reynard and photographs went down the wire to newspapers all over the world showing him slumped in what remained of his cockpit with his legs out on the track. They were among the most horrifying pictures of a motor racing accident of recent years and, to look at them, one would have said that Fox would have been lucky to have survived in any condition at all. On the evidence of the photographs, nobody would have given him much chance of walking again or even of keeping his legs.

Even while the race continued, Adrian and Malcolm were examining the wreckage. For Adrian it had been a replay of Johnny Herbert's terrible accident in Formula 3000 in 1988. His distress over that was so profound that, when we interviewed him a few months later, we could not bring ourselves to include his comments in the article we wrote – it seemed too much like an intrusion on private grief.

Malcolm, too, has talked of the responsibility of 'sending these guys out strapped to a 240 mph ground missile,' and has been clearly shaken by some accidents. There was much soul-searching as they examined what remained of Fox's Reynard. When a car hits a wall at anything between 180 and 240 mph you have to think in terms of an aircraft flying into a building. You don't expect survivors, but not only did Stan survive, miraculously, he did not even sustain broken legs.

Malcolm says: 'It was the worse sort of accident, because Stan went into the wall head-on, normally on an oval you hit it at an oblique angle.'

What had happened was that, in the course of a four-car pile-up, Eddie Cheever's Lola had T-boned Stan's car and had punctured the monocoque, which had compromised the integrity of the structure. Stan then hit the wall with his car in a condition whereby it could not absorb the forces as it had been designed to do. It was a freak accident. In fact, it had been two separate, if connected, accidents, but it had happened.

Another accident involved Mark Blundell at the new oval circuit at Rio de Janeiro in 1996. There was a brake failure on Mark's car and the design of the track meant that he hit a wall head-on at 195 mph. He survived without serious injury and was racing again before too long, but as Malcolm says: 'One minute you're chatting to a guy on the grid, a guy you've known for years, and the next minute he's hitting a wall at 195 mph.' His look tells you everything – he's a laid-back guy, but not when it comes to driver safety. Blundell's accident shook him rigid.

As the newcomer to the Indycar scene, Reynard had been circumspect about throwing its weight around and expressing too many opinions. After Stan Fox's accident, however, Adrian and Malcolm decided that they would take the initiative and incorporate Kevlar into the 1996 chassis, to lessen the possibility of another puncture, and they began to quietly lobby other teams about other safety ideas.

There was no big fuss about it, but engineers chat at race meetings, or share a beer after practice, and that's as good a time as any to float an idea and see if anyone objects to it. There are ways of getting things done without drawing up petitions. Engineers will see the sense in any logical proposal.

A case in point is a modification which is planned for the Reynard 97I which will feature a transverse gearbox, because a change to the under-car regulations will permit that without compromising the desirability of being able to change gear ratios quickly. It will feature a six-inch long magnesium alloy box which will mirror the front-end sacrificial structure, whose function is to absorb energy. It will help to protect drivers in the event of them going into a wall backwards.

Once the idea is stated, it seems blindingly obvious, but nobody else thought of it. Perhaps it is a case that, coming fresh to Indycar, Malcolm can bring a different perspective.

Cockpit safety will improve in 1997 as a result of Malcolm's lobbying, but there was nothing that he, or anyone else, could have done about the crash which claimed the life of Jeff Krosnoff at Toronto in 1996. Jeff's Reynard ran over the rear wheel of another car, was launched into the air and wrapped itself around a tree – 30 feet up – at 180 mph. Yet Jeff might still have survived had he not sustained head injuries.

Malcolm has his own list of circuits which he thinks should be laid to rest because they cannot offer drivers an acceptable degree of safety – when a car weighing 900kg is travelling at 230 mph and hits a wall, the energy the monocoque has to absorb is awesome. Time alone will tell if his private crusade succeeds, but driver safety is no mere slogan with him.

Another thing which Reynard did during 1995 was to contact its customers to ask them for comments on actually running the cars. John Thompson says: 'You have to remember that when we handle cars in the factory they are cold. It is a different matter when they come into the pits after a few laps. With turbocharged engines and their plumbing, incredibly high temperatures are generated, and that can make a huge difference to the mechanics working on them. We asked for their comments and we listened to them.'

Bruce Ashmore comments: 'We used to do that when I was with Lola. The difference is that Reynard gets a much better response because our presence in America gives people more confidence that they will be listened to.

'I think that our '94 car wasn't bad, while the '95 car was good and we were helped by the fact that Penske did not advance because Nigel Bennett, the designer, takes the view that if you're winning, you don't change too much.'

Although Jacques Villeneuve was never headed in the points table after Indianapolis, it was a season which saw nine different drivers take a win, something which had not happened for a long time, and which was probably due in no small measure to the presence of Reynard in the series. We are not suggesting that it had to be Reynard in order to make a difference, but when you have two competitive makers, not just the one, in a customer car championship, it raises everybody's game.

Before, people had a choice between a Lola and the few previous year's Penskes which came up for sale; and if you went with Lola you knew that you were competing against Newman/Haas and you accepted that. Bring in a second constructor capable of winning and the picture changes, especially if you're competing against a company as experienced as Lola.

Experience means more than the ability to build a strong, quick car. It is the ability to place the cars, to know when to do a deal and when to ask for the full list price. It means concentrating your mind so that you can see off the invader and, in turn, that sets new standards for the invader.

After Indianapolis, Penske was able to make adjustments to its cars, which helped them handle their tyres better, and Penske once again moved into contention.

In the 17-races series Reynard took eight wins and 13 pole positions; Lola had four wins and four poles; Penske had five wins and no poles. By those figures, Reynard had a dominant season, but the margin of advantage over Lola was not great. Reynard won the newly-instituted Constructors' Championship with 286 points, but Lola was not far behind on 264 while, even having a disastrous year by their standards, Penske scored 197 points.

Wins are only the headlines. The guy who comes sixth because his car has given him an easy ride may be as equally delighted as the winner because, perhaps, before the race his best finish had been tenth. He naturally suspects that he isn't getting the best engines (every driver who isn't winning does), so obviously the car has helped his own blinding talent – just a little. Put it this way: on the odd occasion when Minardi has finished in the points in a Formula One race, it has been a victory of sorts.

Every engine builder will tell you, hand on heart, that all his engines are identical – but they are not. There will always be the odd one from a batch of 10 which, perhaps because of a quirk of casting or machining, is just that tiny fraction freer or more responsive than the other nine. The batch will all be made to a high minimum standard, but the odd one will always find its way to the driver who can make best use of it.

Still, it is the headlines we remember, and there was a party at the Reynard factory in Bicester to celebrate the Championship, and Moët et Chandon provided one bottle of champagne for each of Jacques' 172 points.

Further improvements were made on the car for 1996, when the equation was complicated not only by a choice of tyres, but by the fact that the Honda engine had come on song and was chosen by many teams in preference to the Ilmor (Mercedes-Benz) and Cosworth (Ford) units. The advantage swung back and forth as Cosworth and Ilmor responded and as Goodyear and Firestone produced compounds which suited some circuits more than others. There was little to choose between the various chassis, and much of the time it came down to the overall package of engine, tyre and chassis on a given circuit and, even, on a given day.

Bruce Ashmore said, in the middle of 1996: 'I would not say there is much between the chassis, but our 1997 car looks very good. There's not much to choose between Honda and Ilmor, and Cosworth seems to be catching up. In the days when Goodyear had a tyre monopoly, you basically had four different compounds: high or low speed road circuits and long or short ovals. Now the tyre companies are coming up with new compounds for every track.

'So far as chassis set-up is concerned, it has not been a problem for any team, but being able to tune one tyre and chassis to an optimum set-up has been hard since the compounds change from race to race.'

One small change to the regulations was that the front wing end-plates had to curve in slightly. During 1995, one driver had his end-plates filed so that a brush with another car's rear tyre could cut it. The spirit of Queen Boadicea lives!

As for the future, work was in progress in mid-1996 on a car with a transverse gearbox. Malcolm says: 'A change of rules governing the size of the rear diffusers will allow us to fit one without compromising the time it will take to change ratios. We are also looking at aerodynamics, of course, and at weight distribution, and we'll have a stiffer rear suspension layout.

'We have exclusive use, 250 days a year, of a wind tunnel at the Royal Military College of Science at Shrivenham. It was basically built for us, but we provided the measuring system.

'I'd say that our '96 car was OK, but Lola made a relatively bigger improvement over its '95 car and we were about even.'

In 1997 Reynard will face opposition from Swift and, possibly, from Ralt. Carl Haas terminated his relationship with Lola in the spring of 1996, and shortly afterwards announced that he was combining with Swift to make a new Indycar for 1997 which, initially at any rate, was to be for the exclusive use of Newman/Haas. By the end of 1996 there should be in existence Lola Cars Inc., a rough equivalent of Reynard North America. The reason for the split was not made public, but it was not amicable and lawyers were soon involved.

The Lola/Haas split was a move which people at Reynard took seriously because Swift has a fine factory, with its own wind tunnel, even if it hasn't turned out a racing car since the early 1990s. Its key personnel are held in the highest regard at Reynard – and at Lola – while Carl Haas has years of experience, and Newman/Haas has continuous Indycar data stretching back to 1984. Nobody was complacent about the move.

Adrian says: 'Following the domestic problem between Chip Ganassi and ourselves over the ordering of spares, Carl was interested in some sort of relationship with us, but we felt that our philosophies are too different. In fact we used his special relationship with Lola against him when we entered the market because, through Chip, we have always passed on development parts to other teams.

'Carl going with Swift is, oddly, good news for us because Swift has not made cars for some time, but has developed a wider engineering base. Lola, Penske and ourselves will be competing against a maker with a serious manufacturing facility and good people. It gives us a yardstick.

'If Carl is successful, then he will have demonstrated that Americans can make racing cars. We are now thinking on a global scale and would not rule out having cars made in, say, Korea if they can deliver the quality to the price demanded by some categories.'

For 1996, Tony George announced that 25 of the 33 places on the grid for the Indianapolis 500 would be reserved for IRL drivers who, for the most part, were unknowns driving obsolete cars, but who had competed in the first two events of a three-race series.

Gil de Ferran has driven a Reynard throughout his career, from Formula Vauxhall Lotus to Formula Three, Formula 3000 and now Indycar. Rick Gorne assisted him with his move to America in 1995 to drive for Hall Racing.

The CART teams were not having any of it and, on the same day, staged a rival race, the US 500 at Michigan, while drivers, who could not normally have dreamed of racing at Indianapolis, performed before packed grandstands. It makes you sorry for all those drivers who qualified 34th, one short of the cut, in those years when the cream of drivers were present.

Indianapolis went ahead, and the driver on pole even set a new qualifying record, which appeared to demonstrate that it was business as usual. In fact, the apexes on the corners had been relieved in order to boost speeds artificially. As it happens, a Reynard won both at Indianapolis and at Michigan – Buddy Lazier taking Indy with a Cosworth-powered car, Jimmy Vasser taking the US 500 with his Reynard-Honda.

With the introduction of the IRL, Reynard and Lola faced a dilemma which probably no racing car manufacturers have ever had to face before. Nobody had said that Reynard was disloyal to its Formula Three customers when it built cars for Formula Vauxhall/Opel. 'We make sports equipment,' is a phrase you often hear at the factory, and that carries with it the implication that if you are selling tennis racquets, you sell racquets, you do not lay down conditions about who can buy them.

In the case of IRL, however, the sellers of sports equipment had a conflict of loyalties because there were two opposing camps and they owed a degree of allegiance to one of them. No problem was seen in 1996 when IRL races were run to the CART formula – people who bought a new, or used, Reynard or Lola were buying sports equipment and they were entitled to use it as they wished. They were also entitled to the same back-up with spares as anyone else.

The crunch came when tenders were invited to supply cars for IRL. Lola did not bid because, as well as Indycar, it also had the contract to supply Indy Lights. Reynard was less tied, and Adrian says: 'We had our existing customers and we had loyalty towards them; they had been very good to us. On the other hand we make sports equipment, so we spoke to Tony George.

'We had a problem with IRL's pricing policy, however. We think we should be entitled to set our own prices in the market. If we cannot offer an attractive package, people will not buy from us.

'IRL wants manufacturers to sell complete cars for what we charge for just the monocoque of an Indycar. We would not want to put cars on oval circuits which are built down to a price. You cannot re-invent safety parameters and we are looking to improve the safety and integrity of our designs, which you cannot do by cutting corners.'

In motor racing, the lighter a car is, the more expensive it is likely to be. In mid-1996, both Reynard and Lola were keeping their options open for the future.

In the event, the contract to supply cars for the 1997 IRL series went to Dallara and G-Force. If you compete in IRL in 1997, you buy one or the other, you cannot turn up with a '96 Lola or Reynard with the appropriate engine and gearbox. Other tenders will be invited from makers for 1998 – you first have to surmount that obstacle, then you design your car and, moreover, you agree to make a minimum of 10.

If IRL is a success, then it must affect Reynard and Lola. If it is so successful that it forces an amalgamation with CART, then both companies will find themselves competing for the same market as G-Force, Dallara and whichever other firms win the right to make cars for 1998 (Riley & Scott, for one, has expressed interest), to say nothing of the threat already looming from Carl Haas and Swift.

The CART versus IRL conflict is yet another illustration of how precarious making production racing cars can be. There are rules which makers of tennis racquets have to comply with, but nobody lays down their price or restricts major tournaments to selected brands. You don't have to have someone's permission before you offer your racquets for sale.

Chapter Twenty-Two

The Story Continues . . .

Writing a book about a racing car manufacturer which is still active is like trying to solve a jigsaw puzzle on which the picture is constantly changing and the pieces are altering shape. That is true of any manufacturer, but Reynard is special because it has diversified into new areas, including consultancy. Even as recently as 1993, Adrian and Rick thought it well-nigh impossible for any company, but Reynard may have cracked the problem.

In John Piper, who heads RSVP, Reynard has a Reynard person. He has been through the mill. He took a degree in engineering, got bored with his job and, through helping out a friend on his racing car, was taken on as a mechanic by David Price Racing in 1978. He progressed through Dave's operation and was taken on by Williams as a designer. He was even Nigel Mansell's race engineer for a season.

He left to set up his own consultancy business and while, in the early days, much of his work was for Benetton, Reynard had been a client since 1986. He is both a newcomer and an old hand. He not only helped design the Metro 6R4, a Williams project, but worked on Prodrive's Subaru rally cars and also the Jaguar XJR-14 which won Le Mans. He's been a mechanic and he's been a Technical Director, and most other things in between. He has no illusions about the business he's in: 'It's war without the bullets,' he says, and he's a battle-scarred veteran.

On the other hand, he talks with pride about the flexibility, rapid response and the lateral thinking of the people he works with. People say 'There's no business like Show Business', but in the motor racing industry you're never stuck in the same part in a hit show for years on end. He has both a car for Le Mans and an airline seat to supervise, and that is just for starters.

We will see. Things change rapidly in motor racing. Had we finished this story at the beginning of 1993, we might have confidently predicted that Reynard would dominate British Formula Three. The early results from the season, together with the fact that Ralt and Dallara had only a nominal presence, would have made that a sensible forecast. It would also have been a blooper on an heroic scale, yet nobody at the time would have said that the prognosis was wrong even though they'd have had a laugh by the time this book was out. Hindsight is so wonderful that someone should consider marketing it.

Reynard had no plans to re-enter Formula Three at the time of writing but, of course, someone could right now be asking his secretary to put in a call to Bicester to discuss a deal.

In July 1996 Adrian said: 'I am uncomfortable with the fact that, so far as production racing cars are concerned, we are presently a one-product company until the Panoz Esperante comes on stream'.

In Indycar in 1996 there were so many variables at play – including teams, engines and tyres, let alone the drivers – that the true position of the various chassis builders was obscured. Jimmy Vasser, running for Chip Ganassi with a Reynard chassis, Honda

Jimmy Vasser, the 1996 Indycar World Series Champion. He is pictured during a pit stop in 1995 in his Chip Ganassi Reynard 95I. During 1996 both Jimmy and his team-mate, Alessandro Zanardi, were a dominant force in the Championship.

engine and Firestone tyres looked virtually unbeatable after the opening rounds. Then the equation became more complicated.

At the end of the season, Penske trailed a poor third in the Constructors' Championship, which does not reflect the fact that Al Unser Jr was in serious contention for the title until late in the season. Rather it reflects the fact that Penske had only three team cars in the series and they were tied to Mercedes-Benz engines and Goodyear tyres, whereas Lola and Reynard had a mix of tyres and engines. Then there was the fact that Emerson Fittipaldi crashed heavily and a rookie was drafted in to replace him.

The fact that Penske scored barely half the points of Reynard is not a true reflection of the competence of each outfit's cars. Paul Tracy put his car on pole a couple of times, and that is not possible if the car is hopeless. The fact remains, however, that Team Penske took 12 wins in 1994, and 1996 was the first year in its history when it failed to take a single victory.

New engines from Cosworth soon seemed to be on a par with the Honda units in terms of power and response, but they tended to be not as reliable – at first. Later in the season, the Cosworths came on strongly. The Ilmor (Mercedes-Benz) engines were probably a tad away in terms of power, but they were more consistent than the Cosworths.

Over the season there was little in it. It came down to getting the mix right more often than the opposition. In 1996, a Reynard plus Honda plus Firestone tended to the the right mix, on most tracks. The 1996 Indycar season was more diverse than it had been for a very long time, as first one combination was tuned to the track, then another, but who knows about 1997?

Alessandro Zanardi came on strong for the Ganassi team late in the season, and he might have been in contention for the title had he been more patient in the earlier races. He ended the year with three wins, the title of 'Rookie of the Year', and on equal points to Michael Andretti in a Newman/Haas Lola. With five wins to Zanardi's three, Andretti took the runner-up spot, but the fact that Zanardi set pole six times (to Vasser's four and Paul Tracy's two) says a lot.

In terms of the Constructors' Championship, Reynard beat Lola by 16 points, but nine of those were because Reynard drivers scored a point for pole on 11 occasions to the two points for pole scored by Lola drivers. The Reynard was clearly better at using its tyres during qualifying, but there was damn-all in it over a race distance.

Al Unser Jr chipped away at Vasser's lead with a string of consistent finishes in his Penske, and he moved into the frame just one point adrift in late summer. Then Michael Andretti in a Newman/Haas Lola came back with two wins from the last three races.

Starting the last race, the Toyota Grand Prix at Laguna Seca, Vasser had a 14-point lead over Andretti, which was comfortable but, given the scoring system, by no means unassailable. In the event, Zanardi won with Vasser fourth, which meant the race, the Championship and the 'Rookie of the Year' award went to the Ganassi team.

It was due return for the faith Chip had shown in Adrian's plans in the summer of 1993. It's easy to be wise after the event, but a lot of people had been approached by Reynard, and all but Chip had turned down the proposal.

As soon as the season was over, the elements for 1997 were being put into place. Jim Hall finally retired from motor racing after a distinguished career as a driver, engineer and team owner, which spanned more than 40 years. His driver, Gil de Ferran, moved to Walker Racing who also took on Hall's Honda engines and announced it would run Reynards in 1997.

Mike Blanchet sprung his surprise by announcing his departure from Lola after 20 years with the company. How this will affect Lola is anyone's guess.

Long before the end of the 1996 season Reynard was preparing for 1997 and, in mid-August, began track-testing its new transverse gearbox in conjunction with Derrick Walker's team. Like the clock on the wall, the calendar is an enemy of a racing car constructor.

When Reynard entered Indycar at the beginning of 1994, it became the third chassis supplier. In 1997 there will be at least five chassis, four engine suppliers and two tyre manufacturers. The competition is hotting up.

Lola built a Formula One car in 1996 and was hoping to enter the category in 1997. Formula One remains on Adrian's agenda and he will not be happy until he's cracked it. It matters to him whether or not he does, but it perhaps does not matter in the wider sense. If motor racing ended tomorrow he would still have a record of achievement to look back on that is more substantial than some Formula One teams who turn up to races and regard the odd points finish as a victory of sorts.

Adrian has designed and built cars – designing is one thing and building is another – which have won hundreds of races and dozens of championships from Formula Ford 1600 to Indycar. He achieved his own level as a driver – so fulfilled that ambition. He has given employment to hundreds of people and, indirectly, to thousands. He has helped drivers and engineers to progress in their careers, and has given the opportunity to craftsmen to be able to feel they are making something important and are not just a number on a production line.

If motor racing ended tomorrow, Adrian could be satisfied with his life.

Of course, if motor racing did end tomorrow – and motor racing was suspended during two world wars – he'd be on the phone first thing making appointments with companies to sell them the idea that they need carbon-fibre widgets – now. Rick Gorne would be preparing a world-wide widget marketing strategy. Malcolm Oastler and the rest of the crew would see the design of the perfect widget as their calling in life, and Paul Owens would be gearing up to make widgets on time and at a price.

Everyone at Reynard, and every guy in every other factory and team, is a racer. Motor racing is merely the way they express it. It is the acceptable face of total warfare.

Reynard Statistics

The following lists the cars built by Reynard and sold under the Reynard name. Cars which have been built by other concerns, but have run under the Reynard name appear in Appendix 2. Cars built by Reynard for other firms are listed in Appendix 3.

Reynard Production 1973

Type	Description	Number Made	Running Total
73FF	FF1600	1	1

Prototype car for Adrian Reynard, later owned by Jeremy Rossiter and Nick Foy.

Independent front suspension by trailing lower wishbones, upper link and radius arm; independent rear suspension by long reversed wishbone, top link and radius rods; outboard coil springs and dampers all round. Front-mounted radiator.

Reynard Production 1974

Nil. 1973 prototype used by Adrian Reynard, but entered as Reynard 74FF.

Reynard Production 1975

Type	Description	Number Made	Running Total
75FF	FF1600	1	2
75SF	FF2000	4	4
			6

First production cars. Similar chassis to prototype, but with full-width nose, side radiators and aluminium side-pods.

Reynard Production 1976

Type	Description	Number Made	Running Total
76FF	FF1600	5	7
76SF	FF2000	1	5
			12

A further up-date of the prototype; four of the five FF1600 cars were sold to the USA via an arrangement with Hawke for whom Adrian Reynard was designing Formula One and Formula Three cars.

Reynard Production 1977

Type	Description	Number Made	Running Total
77SF	FF2000	16	21
			28

A further up-date. Jeremy Rossiter was runner-up in Lord's Taverners Championship and British Air Ferries Championship, each time to Rad Dougall's Royale RP25.

Reynard Production 1978

Type	Description	Number Made	Running Total
78SF	FF2000	23	44
			51

A further up-date of the 1973 car. The most successful Reynard driver was Rick Gorne with nine wins (including non-Championship events). He finished fourth overall in one British series, fifth in the other.

Reynard Production 1979

Type	Description	Number Made	Running Total
79SF	FF2000	18	62
79SV	Super Vee	1	1
			70

David Leslie in a works-run car, with

sponsorship from Duke's Pallets, won the ShellSport Martini and Computacar Championships; Adrian Reynard won the European (EFDA) Championship.

Reynard Production 1980

Type	Description	Number Made	Running Total
80SF	FF2000	11	73
80SV	Super Vee	1	2
			82

Unsuccessful ground-effect bodywork on chassis developed from 1973 prototype. Dave Greenwood won the Volkspares Super Vee (British) Championship which had engines about 50 bhp more than FF2000.

Reynard Production 1981

Type	Description	Number Made	Running Total
81SF	FF2000	6	79
			88

Non-ground-effect car similar to 79SF and the last version of the original Reynard concept.

Reynard Production 1982

Type	Description	Number Made	Running Total
82FF	FF1600	44	51
82SF	FF2000	1	80
			133

First raced at the 1981 Formula Ford Festival, the 82FF was a new design with front suspension by top rocker arms and lower wishbones with inboard coil springs and shock absorbers; and rear suspension by top links, reversed lower wishbones, radius arms and inboard coil spring and damper units.

For the first time, Reynard made significant inroads into overseas markets – just 11 cars, including those used by the works, stayed in the UK – while the majority went to the USA, Canada, Germany, South Africa and the UAE.

Andrew Gilbert-Scott led the prestigious Townsend Thoresen FF1600 Championship until running out of money.

Reynard Production 1983

Type	Description	Number Made	Running Total
83FF	FF1600	39	90
83FF	FF2000	42	122
			204

Both cars were similar to the 1982 models but had revised aerodynamics and a more friendly rear suspension set-up.

Penistone Racing was virtually the Reynard works team in FF2000 and Tim Davies dominated the season. The first FF1600 car was delivered to Madgwick Motorsport in July, and its driver, Maurizio Sandro Sala, went on to win the Esso FF1600 series.

Championships won:
FF2000 – British, European, Dutch, Benelux, German, European 'Golden Lion', Canadian Walter Wolf, Canadian Chipwich, Radio Trent (Donington).

FF1600 – Esso, British Northern, Canadian, SCCA Pacific Division, SCCA North East Division, SCCA South East Division, Noram Pro-Ford, North East American, Irish Formula Ford Festival, British Formula Ford Festival.

Reynard Production 1984

Type	Description	Number Made	Running Total
84FF	FF1600	68	158
84SF	FF2000	60	182
84FTF	Formula Turbo Ford	1	1
			333

Figures include replacement chassis.

An additional 40 84FF chassis kits were supplied to Ford for the launch of FF1600 in France where they were assembled by Rondeau and raced under that name. Rondeau provided new bodywork and developed the Reynard chassis for the next three years.

The unique 84TFT was an 84SF fitted with larger wings and wheels and a turbocharged Ford engine as a prototype for a new formula proposed by Motor Circuit Developments (Brands Hatch) and Ford as a cheaper alternative to Formula Three. The formula was abandoned after the car was tested.

Championships won:
FF2000 – Austrian, British, Donington,

Dutch, European, Irish, Northern Irish, Benelux, Northern British, BRSCC Northern, Canadian Tire, German, European Golden Lion, Danish, Canadian National, First Edition World Cup.

FF1600 – Austrian, Belgian, BP Superfind, Esso, Dunlop Star of Tomorrow, Castle Combe, P&O Ferries, Motovox Irish, European, Ford of Ireland, Franco Benelux, SCCA South Eastern, SCCA South Western.

Reynard Production 1985

Type	Description	Number Made	Running Total
85FF	FF1600	66	224
85SF	FF2000	32	214
84SF	FF2000	10	224
853	Formula Three	24	24
			465

The Reynard 853 was the first production Formula Three car to feature a monocoque tub made from aluminium honeycomb and carbon composites. There was an aluminium floor panel; and inboard pushrod suspension was used all round which was designed to shear on impact in order to minimise damage to the hull. The 853 was designed to take a range of engines, but the VW unit (developed by John Judd of Engine Developments) was the most popular choice in Britain.

Andy Wallace, entered by Swallow Racing, won with an 853 on its debut with Russell Spence (entered by PMC) second. Wallace and Spence won the first six rounds of the British Championship.

The 85FF/SF was a new design by Weit Huidecoper which copied the successful Swift from America. It was fitted with pull-rod suspension all round and the radiator was mounted in front of the engine with air fed by ducts. It was a disaster and unsold cars, together with spares, jigs, moulds, etc. were sold to Hungary which was setting up a national race series prior to hosting its first World Championship Grand Prix.

The failure of the 85SF led to some teams converting 1984 FF1600 cars to FF2000 specification. During the season a further 10 84SFs were built by the factory. All Reynard's race and Championship wins were achieved with 1984 cars.

Championships won:
FF2000 – British, European, Benelux, German, Austrian, Donington, Golden Lion, Canadian, First Edition, BBC Grandstand.

FF1600 – Australian, Dutch, New Zealand, 750 Motor Club, Castle Combe, Mallory Park, Oulton Park.

Marlboro British Formula Three Championship

1	Mauricio Gugelmin Ralt RT30-VW	84 (86)
2	Andy Wallace Reynard 853-VW	76
3	Russell Spence Reynard 853-VW	64
4	Dave Scott Ralt RT30-VW	52
5	Gerrit van Kouwen Ralt RT30-VW	46
6	Tim Davies Reynard 853-VW	39

Thomas Danielsson in a Saab-powered Reynard 853 won the Swedish Championship, and Reynards won rounds in most other Formula 3 Championships. For the first time a Reynard was sold to Japan.

Reynard Production 1986

Type	Description	Number Made	Running Total
86FF	FF1600	16	240
86SF	FF2000	31	244
863	Formula Three	20	44
			532

The 863 followed the broad principles of the 853, but with revisions to the monocoque, suspension and aerodynamics. The production figure of 20 includes five up-rated 853s, two of which had new monocoques.

The 86SF was a reversion to the 84SF concept, developed by Malcolm Oastler, with squared-off lower aluminium side panels.

Reynard supplied 15 86FFs to Ford of Finland to start FF1600 there. Winner of the first championship was JJ Lehto.

Championships won:
FF2000 – Austrian, British, European, European World Cup, Scottish, Canadian,

Dutch, Benelux, Knockhill, Kirkiston, SCCA run-offs.

FF1600 – European, Finnish, Scandinavian, Knockhill, Dutch.

Lucas British Formula Three Championship

1	Andy Wallace Reynard 863-VW	121
2	Maurizio Sandro Sala Ralt RT30/86-VW	83
3	Martin Donnelly Ralt RT30/86-VW	59
4	Gerrit van Kouwen Ralt RT30/86-VW	24
5	Gary Brabham Ralt RT30/86-VW	22
6	Julian Bailey Ralt RT30/86-VW	21

Stephano Modena in an Alfa-Romeo-powered Reynard 863 won the FIA Formula 3 Nations Cup at Imola and Andy Wallace won the Macau GP and at Fuji. Niclas Schonström took the Swedish Championship.

Reynard Production 1987

Type	Description	Number Made	Running Total
87SF	FF2000	70	314
873	Formula Three	*59	103
			661

* One car was supplied to Michael Jourdain in Mexico fitted with a turbocharged Chrysler engine and modified bodywork. It was the prototype for a proposed new formula which progressed no further.

The basic design of the 853 was carried a stage further with a longer wheelbase, narrower track and improved aerodynamics which resulted in part from a narrower engine bay which was possible due to a multi-purpose gearbox and oil tank casing which carried the rear suspension links and anti-roll bar.

The Reynard 87SF was a new model designed by Malcolm Oastler which featured an integral gearbox oil tank, a cast alloy front bulkhead and a stepped chassis underside.

Reynard also built 10 FF1600 cars, based on the FF2000 car. The project, however, was taken over by Fulmar Competition Services in May 1987, and these cars appear in FCS-Reynard production figures in Appendix 2.

Championships won:

FF2000 – British, British Class 'B', European, European Class 'B', Canadian, Scottish, Irish, Knockhill, Swiss, Dutch, Northern Irish, SCCA South East, First Edition World Cup, BBC Grandstand.

FF1600 – Finnish, Swedish, Scandinavian, French – all with 1986 cars.

Lucas British Formula Three Championship

1	Johnny Herbert Reynard 873-VW	79
2	Betrand Gachot Ralt RT31-Alfa Romeo	64
3	Martin Donnelly Ralt RT31-Toyota	61
4	Thomas Danielsson Reynard 873-Alfa	56
5	Damon Hill Ralt RT31-Toyota	49
6	Gary Brabham Ralt RT31-VW	37

Gary Dunn won class B (for year-old cars) in the Lucas British Formula 3 Championship with a Reynard 863-VW.

EFDA Euroseries Championship

1	Dave Coyne Reynard 873-VW	67
2	Victor Rosso Ralt RT31-VW	41
3	Johnny Herbert Reynard 873-VW	40
4	Peter Zakowski Ralt RT31-VW	36
5	Roland Ratzenberger Ralt RT31-VW	35
6	Betrand Gachot Ralt RT31-Alfa Romeo	30

Reynard 873s also won the FIA European Cup, the French 'Class B' Championship, the Cellnet Superprix, the All-Japan Championship and the Japanese Formula Three Association Championship.

Reynard Production 1988

Type	Description	Number Made	Running Total
88SF	FF2000	70	384
883	Formula Three	54	157
88D	Formula 3000	22	22
			807

In addition to the above, Reynard built a Sports 2000 car to a commission from Fulmar Competition Services, which owns the rights to the design.

Towards the end of the year, production of all Reynard cars for the Ford Formulae was taken over by Fulmar Competition Services. Thereafter FCS built the chassis and bodies, while Reynard supplied about 40 per cent of the components. The arrangement continued until 1992.

In 1988 FCS-Reynard built a total of 27 cars (see Appendix 2).

As well as the above cars, Reynard built 95 chassis for Vauxhall/Opel-Lotus championships which, with the FCS-Reynard cars, established a new record for annual production of any racing car manufacturer at 268 cars.

The 883 had a new tub and some aerodynamic changes. On the whole, the year belonged to Ralt, as many teams in the British Championship switched chassis during the season. Pacific Racing ran a works development 883 (and won the Championship) which had its engine lower in the car, but it was not used for all races.

Reynard's first Formula 3000 car was a winner on its debut and was based on the Formula 3 monocoque with a similar suspension layout. The aerodynamic package, however, was different to take account of different tyre sizes and bodywork design parameters.

FIA International Formula 3000 Championship
Reynard Victories

Jerez	Johnny Herbert
Pau	Roberto Moreno
Silverstone	Roberto Moreno
Monza	Roberto Moreno
Brands Hatch	Martin Donnelly
Birmingham	Roberto Moreno
Dijon-Prenois	Martin Donnelly

Final Championship Standings

1	Roberto Moreno	
	Reynard 88D-Cosworth DFV	43
2	Olivier Grouillard	
	Lola T88/50-Cosworth DFV	34
3	Martin Donnelly	
	Reynard 88D-Cosworth DFV	30
4	Pierluigi Martini	
	March 88B-Judd	23
5	Bertrand Gachot	
	Reynard 88D-Cosworth DFV	21
6	Mark Blundell	
	Lola T88/50-Cosworth DFV	18

Reynard won seven of the 11 rounds of the championship.

Lucas British Formula Three Championship

1	JJ Lehto	
	Reynard 883-Toyota	113
2	Gary Brabham	
	Ralt RT32-VW	81
3	Damon Hill	
	Ralt RT32-Toyota	57
4	Martin Donnelly	
	Ralt RT31-Toyota	54
5	Eddie Irvine	
	Ralt RT32-Afa Romeo	53
6	Ross Hockenhull	
	Ralt RT32-VW	22

Alistair Lyall won the Class B section of the Championship with a Reynard 873-VW.

Jo Winklehock won the German Formula 3 Championship and the FIA Europa Cup with a Reynard 883-VW.

Reynard Production 1989

Type	Description	Number Made	Running Total
893	Formula Three	64	221
89H	F Atlantic	10	10
89D	Formula 3000	36	58
			917

In conjunction with Reynard, FCS produced the 89FREN for Formula Renault.

The 893 was a revision of the 883, mainly in the area of aerodynamics. It had a new gearbox and the power train was 22mm lower than previously, which caused problems with the starter motor gear.

Although the 893 sold more strongly than any previous Reynard Formula Three car, most of its sales were outside Britain with a significant proportion going to South America and Japan.

The 89H ('H' for Haas) was based on the Formula Three car but had a full ground-effect aerodynamic package.

A new monocoque formed the basis of the 89D, which retained its predecessor's suspension layout, but it had a slightly longer wheelbase, revised nose, different side-pods and a high, ducted, engine cover.

FIA International Formula 3000 Championship
Reynard Victories

Silverstone	Thomas Danielsson
Pau	Jean Alesi
Pergusa	Andrea Chiesa
Brands Hatch	Martin Donnelly
Birmingham	Jean Alesi
Spa	Jean Alesi

Final Championship Standings

1	Jean Alesi		
	Reynard 89D-Mugen		39
2	Erik Comas		
	Lola T89/50-Mugen		39
3	Eric Bernard		
	Lola T89/50-Mugen		25
4	Marco Apicella		
	Reynard 89D-Judd		23
5	Eric van de Poele		
	Lola T89/50-Cosworth DFV		19
6	Andrea Chiesa		
	Reynard 89D-Cosworth DFV		15

Reynard won six of the 10 rounds. Martin Donnelly driving for Eddie Jordan Racing won in Vallelunga but was disqualified because, in common with some other teams, EJR used a development nose section which had not then passed the mandatory crash test. The nose section passed the test after the race and before Donnelly was disqualified.

Gary Brabham won the British Formula 3000 Championship for year-old cars with a Reynard 88D-Cosworth DFV. Reynards won every round, and the top six drivers in the series used Reynards.

Lucas British Formula Three Championship

1	David Brabham	
	Ralt RT33-VW	80
2	Allan McNish	
	Ralt RT33-Mugen	70
3	Derek Higgins	
	Ralt RT33-Mugen	46
4	Rickard Rydell	
	Reynard 893-VW	35

5	Steve Robertson	
	Ralt RT33-VW	27
6	Philippe Adams	
	Ralt RT33-VW	23

Jean-Marc Gounon won the French Formula 3 Championship in a Reynard 893-Alfa Romeo and Thomas Nilsson won the Swedish series with a VW-powered 893. Antonio Tamburini won the Monaco GP support race in a Reynard 893-Alfa Romeo and was runner-up in the Italian Championship, and Heinz-Harald Frentzen was runner-up in the German series.

Reynard Production 1990

Type	Description	Number Made	Running Total
903	Formula Three	102	323
90H	Formula Atlantic	11	21
90D	Formula 3000	29	87
			1,059

Forty Reynard 903s were supplied to Mexico for a one-chassis (but free engine) national Formula Three Championship. It was the first time in history that an FIA International Championship was run with a 'control' chassis.

The 90D had a new gearbox which suffered from lack of development when the designer left Reynard – it caused a great deal of trouble for much of the season. The departure of key personnel had an adverse effect on the car's development, and Lola won its first, and only, European Formula 3000 Championship.

FIA International Formula 3000 Championship
Reynard Victories

Pau	Eric van de Poele
Hockenheim	Eddie Irvine
Birmingham	Eric van de Poele
Nogaro	Eric van de Poele

Final Championship Standings

1	Erik Comas	
	Lola T90/50-Mugen	51
2	Eric van de Poele	
	Reynard 90D-Cosworth	30
3	Eddie Irvine	
	Reynard 90D-Mugen	27
4	Allan McNish	
	Lola T90/50-Mugen	26

5= Marco Apicella
   Reynard 90D-Mugen   20
5= Gianni Morbidelli
   Lola T90/50-Cosworth   20

Reynards won every round of the British Formula 3000 Championship, the overall winner being Pedro Chaves in a Reynard 90D-Cosworth.

British Formula Three Championship

1 Mika Hakkinen
   Ralt RT34-Mugen   121 (126)
2 Miko Salo
   Ralt RT34-Mugen   98 (99)
3 Steve Robertson
   Ralt RT33-VW   49
4 Christian Fittipaldi
   Ralt RT34-Mugen   36
5 Peter Kox
   Ralt RT33-VW   28
6 Phillipe Adams
   Ralt RT33-VW   25

The German Formula Three Championship was won by Michael Schumacher in a Reynard 903-VW, and Schumacher also won the prestigious races at Macau and Fuji.

Roberto Colciago won the Italian Formula 3 Championship in a Reynard 903-Alfa Romeo. The French title was won by Eric Hélary, and Niclas Jonson won the Swedish Championship.

Reynard Production 1991

Type	Description	Number Made	Running Total
913	Formula Three	36	359
91D	Formula 3000	30	117
			1,125

No Formula Atlantic cars were built, but an up-date kit was supplied. At the end of the season Reynard introduced a new Formula Atlantic car, the 92H, which won the (New Zealand) Pacific Championship.

FIA International Formula 3000 Championship
Reynard Victories

Vallelunga   Alessandro Zanardi
Jerez   Christian Fittipaldi
Mugello   Alessandro Zanardi
Enna   Emanuele Naspetti
Hockenheim   Emanuele Naspetti
Brands Hatch   Emanuele Naspetti
Spa   Emanuele Naspetti
Le Mans-Bugatti Antonio Tamburini
Nogaro   Christian Fittipaldi

Final Championship Standings

1 Christian Fittipaldi
   Reynard 91D-Mugen   47
2 Alessandro Zanardi
   Reynard 91D-Mugen   42
3 Emanuele Naspetti
   Reynard 91D-Cosworth   37
4 Antonio Tamburini
   Reynard 91D-Mugen   22
5 Marco Apicella
   Lola T91/50-Mugen   18
6 Jean-Marc Gounon
   Ralt RT23-Cosworth   13

Reynards won nine of the 10 rounds. Jean-Marc Gounon won Pau for Ralt and crossed the line first at Enna, but was penalised for a 'jumped start' which many observers felt was an unfair decision. Paul Owens engineered Christian Fittipaldi's car which was run by Pacific Racing.

Paul Warwick (Reynard 90D-Cosworth) won the first five rounds of the British Formula 3000 Championship for Madgwick Motorsport and then was killed in an accident at Oulton Park. His performances, however, secured him a posthumous title.

British Formula Three Championship

1 Rubens Barrichello
   Ralt RT35-Mugen   74
2 David Coulthard
   Ralt RT35-Mugen   66
3 Gil de Ferran
   Reynard 913-Mugen   54
4 Jordi Gene
   Ralt RT35-Mugen   50
5 Marcel Albers
   Ralt RT35-Mugen   43
6 Rickard Rydell
   TOM'S 031F-TOM'S Toyota   41

Reynard Production 1992

Type	Description	Number Made	Running Total
92H	F. Atlantic	10	31
923	Formula Three	26	375
92D	Formula 3000	38	155
			1,199

A works Formula Atlantic team was established in North America in conjunction with 3001 International, and Adrian Reynard engineered one of the cars.

FIA International Formula 3000 Championship
Reynard Victories

Silverstone	Jordi Gene
Pau	Emanuele Naspetti
Montmelò	Andrea Montermini
Enna	Luca Badoer
Hockenheim	Luca Badoer
Nürburgring	Luca Badoer
Spa	Andrea Montermini
Albacete	Andrea Montermini
Nogaro	Luca Badoer

Final Championship Standings

1	Luca Badoer	
	Reynard 92D-Cosworth	46
2	Andrea Montermini	
	Reynard 92D-Cosworth	34
3	Rubens Barrichello	
	Reynard 92D-Judd	27
4	Michael Bartels	
	Reynard 92D-Cosworth	25
5	Jordi Gene	
	Reynard 92D-Mugen	21
6=	Jean-Marc Gounon	
	Lola T92/50-Cosworth	19
6=	Emanuele Naspetti	
	Reynard 92D-Cosworth	19

Reynards won nine of the 10 rounds.

Reynards won every round of the British Formula Two Championship for year-old Formula 3000 cars. Winner of the series was Yvan Muller in a Reynard 91D-Cosworth.

British Formula Three Championship

1	Gil de Ferran	
	Reynard 923-Mugen	102 (109)
2	Philippe Adams	
	Ralt RT36-Mugen	56
3	Kelvin Burt	
	Reynard 923-Mugen	55
4	Oswaldi Negri	
	Reynard 923-Mugen	43
5	Mikke van Hool	
	Reynard 923-Mugen	29
6	Marc Goossens	
	Reynard 923-Mugen	28

Pedro Lamy won the German Formula 3 Championship in a Reynard 923-Opel.

Reynard Production 1993

Type	Description	Number Made	Running Total
93H	F. Atlantic	3	34
933	Formula Three	31	406
93D	Formula 3000	28	183
			1,261

FIA International Formula 3000 Championship
Reynard Victories

Donington Park	Olivier Beretta
Silverstone	Gil de Ferran
Pau	Pedro Lamy
Enna	David Coulthard
Hockenheim	Olivier Panis
Nürburgring	Olivier Panis
Spa	Olivier Panis
Magny-Cours	Franck Lagorce
Nogaro	Franck Lagorce

Final Championship Standings

1	Olivier Panis	
	Reynard 93D-Cosworth AC	32
2	Pedro Lamy	
	Reynard 93D-Cosworth DFV	31
3	David Coulthard	
	Reynard 93D-Cosworth AC	24
4=	Gil de Ferran	
	Reynard 93D-Cosworth AC	21
4=	Franck Lagorce	
	Reynard 93D-Cosworth AC	21
6	Olivier Beretta	
	Reynard 93D-Cosworth DFV	20

Every competitor in the European Championship used a Reynard chassis.

Reynard chassis won each of the 10 rounds of the British F2 Championship, with Phillipe Adams taking the title.

Ross Cheever, driving a Reynard 93D-Mugen,

was a close third in the Japanese Formula 3000 Championship.

British Formula Three Championship

1	Kelvin Burt	102 (113)	
	Reynard 933/Dallara 393-Mugen		
2	Oliver Gavin		
	Dallara 393-Vauxhall		77
3	Marc Goossens		
	Reynard 933/Dallara 393-Mugen		51
4	Warren Hughes		
	Dallara 393-Fiat		45
5	André Ribiero		
	Dallara 393-Mugen		19
6=	Pedro Martinez de la Rosa		
	Reynard 933/Dallara 393-Mugen		18
6=	Ricardo Rosset		
	Ralt RT37/Dallara 393-Mugen		18

Reynard won the first five rounds of the 15-round championship, but most front-runners switched to Dallara during the season – it was the first time that Dallaras had run on a regular basis in Britain.

Reynard Production 1994

Type	Description	Number Made	Running Total
94D	Formula 3000	*18	201
94I	Indycar	13	13
	Patriot	3	3
			1,295

* Formula 3000 production also included eight up-date kits for 1993 cars.

For the first time since 1985 Reynard made no Formula Three cars. Some progress was made on a new design intended to be exclusive to Renault to run in the British and German Championships, but the deal fizzled out.

CART PPG Indycar World Series
Reynard Victories

Surfers Paradise	Michael Andretti
Toronto	Michael Andretti
Elkhart Lake	Jacques Villeneuve

Final Championship Standings

1	Al Unser Jr	
	Penske PC23-Ilmor	225
2	Emerson Fittipaldi	
	Penske PC23-Ilmor	178
3	Paul Tracy	
	Penske PC23-Ilmor	152
4	Michael Andretti	
	Reynard 94I-Cosworth	118
5	Robbie Gordon	
	Lola T94/00-Cosworth	104
6	Jacques Villeneuve	
	Reynard 94I-Cosworth	94

FIA International Formula 3000 Championship
Reynard Victories

Silverstone	Franck Lagorce
Pau	Gil de Ferran
Barcelona	Massimiliano Papis
Pergusa	Gil de Ferran
Hockenheim	Frank Lagorce
Spa	'Jules' Boullion
Estoril	'Jules' Boullion
Magny-Cours	'Jules' Boullion

Final Championship Standings

1	'Jules' Boullion	
	Reynard 94D-Cosworth AC	36
2	Franck Lagorce	
	Reynard 94D-Cosworth AC	34
3	Gil de Ferran	
	Reynard 94D-Zytek Judd KV	28
4	Vicenzo Sospiri	
	Reynard 94D-Cosworth AC	24
5=	Didier Cottaz	
	Reynard 94D-Zytek Judd KV	13
5=	Massimiliano Papis	
	Reynard 94D-Zytek Judd KV	13

Reynard Production 1995

Type	Description	Number Made	Running Total
95D	Formula 3000	*11	212
95I	Indycar	27	40
			1,333

* Formula 3000 production included an additional 12 up-date kits for 1994 cars.

CART PPG Indycar World Series
Reynard Victories

Miami	Jacques Villeneuve
Phoenix	Robby Gordon
Indianapolis	Jacques Villeneuve
Detroit	Robby Gordon
Elkhart Lake	Jacques Villeneuve
Cleveland	Jacques Villeneuve

New Hampshire   Andre Ribeiro
Monterey   Gil de Ferran

Final Championship Standings

1	Jacques Villeneuve	
	Reynard 95I-Cosworth	172
2	Al Unser Jr	
	Penske PC24-Ilmor	161
3	Bobby Rahal	
	Lola T95/00-Ilmor	128
4	Michael Andretti	
	Lola T95/00-Cosworth	123
5	Robby Gordon	
	Reynard 95I-Cosworth	121
6	Paul Tracy	
	Lola T95/00-Cosworth	115

Manufacturers' Championship

1 Ford (Cosworth)	310
2 Mercedes-Benz (Ilmor)	272
3 Honda	40
4 Menard Buick	36

Constructors' Championship

1 Reynard	286
2 Lola	264
3 Penske	197

FIA International Formula 3000 Championship
Reynard Victories

Silverstone	Ricardo Rosset
Barcelona	Vicenzo Sospiri
Pau	Vicenzo Sospiri
Pergusa	Ricardo Rosset
Spa	Vicenzo Sospiri
Estoril	Tarso Marques
Magny-Cours	Kenny Bräck

Final Championship Standings

1	Vicenzo Sospiri	
	Reynard 95D-Cosworth AC	42
2	Ricardo Rosset	
	Reynard 95D-Cosworth AC	29
3=	Marc Goossens	
	Lola T95/50-Cosworth AC	24
3=	Kenny Bräck	
	Reynard 95D-Zytek Judd KV	24
5=	Tarso Marques	
	Reynard 95D-Cosworth AC	15
5=	Emmanuel Clérico	
	Reynard 95D-Cosworth AC	15

Reynard Production 1996

Type	Description	Number Made	Running Total
96D	Formula 3000	*8	220
96I	Indycar	33	73
			1,374

* In 1996, European Formula 3000 was a one-make formula serviced by Lola. The eight 96Ds all went to Japan for the Formula Nippon series along with some up-date kits for existing cars.

Reynard has also made:
40 chassis kits to launch FF1600 in France
204 Vauxhall/Opel-Lotus cars
30 cars for 'Formula Sigma' in Japan (using a derivative of the 'Lotus' car) and 16 for 'Formula Reynard' in Mexico using the same chassis.

A further 138 Reynards were built by Fulmar Competition Services (see Appendix 2). This brings the total of production racing cars built by mid-1996 to 1,802.

CART PPG Indycar World Series
Reynard Victories

Homestead	Jimmy Vasser
Surfers Paradise	Jimmy Vasser
Long Beach	Jimmy Vasser
US 500 (Michigan)	Jimmy Vasser
Portland	Alessandro Zanardi
Cleveland	Gil de Ferran
Mid-Ohio	Alessandro Zanardi
Laguna Seca	Alessandro Zanardi

Final Championship Standings

1	Jimmy Vasser	
	Reynard 96I-Honda	154
2	Michael Andretti	
	Lola T96/00-Cosworth	132
3	Alessandro Zanardi	
	Reynard 96I-Honda	*132
4	Al Unser Jr	
	Penske PC96-Ilmor	125
5	Christian Fittipaldi	
	Lola T96/00-Cosworth	110
6	Gil de Ferran	
	Reynard 96I-Honda	104

* Rookie of the year. Andretti took second place in the series by winning four races to Zanardi's three.

Constructors' Championship

1 Reynard	276
2 Lola	260
3 Penske	139
4 Eagle	9

Manufacturers' Championship

1 Honda	271
2 Cosworth (Ford)	234
3 Ilmor (Mercedes-Benz)	218
4 Toyota	9

In addition, Buddy Lazier (Reynard 95I-Cosworth) won the Indianapolis 500, held on the same day as the US 500, but run by the USAC for the rival Indy Racing League.

Japanese Formula Nippon
Reynard Victories

Mine	Ralf Schumacher
Takachi	Ralf Schumacher
Suzuka	Toranosuke Takagi
Sugo	Toranosuke Takagi
Fuji	Naoki Hattori
Mine	Ralf Schumacher
Suzuka	Naoki Hattori
Fuji	Katsutomo Kaneishi

Final Championship Standings

1	Ralf Schumacher Reynard 96D-Mugen	40
2	Naoki Hattori Reynard 96D-Mugen	38
3	Kazuyoshi Hoshino Lola T96/52-Mugen	31
4	Toranosuke Takagi Reynard 96D-Mugen	25
5	Norberto Fontana Lola T96/51-Mugen	22
6	Shinju Nakona Dome F104i-Mugen	20

Reynard won eight of the ten Championship rounds.

Fulmar Competition Services

Fulmar competition Services was founded by Mike Taylor, a long-time and successful driver of Reynard FF2000 cars, and Alan Cornock, who had been a competitor of Reynard in FF2000 when he ran Royale, which was one of the most successful makers of Ford Formulae cars for many years. In 1987 FCS took over the manufacture and marketing of Reynards for FF1600, which were based on the SF87 Formula Ford 2000 car. FCS built the chassis and bodies and Reynard supplied about 40 per cent of the components. A design consultancy agreement continued between Reynard and FCS, but all cars derived from Malcolm Oastler's 1987 designs.

FCS-Reynard Production 1987

Type	Description	Number Made	Running Total
87FF	FF1600	10	210

These cars were actually assembled by Reynard, but sold by FCS who took over the project in 1987.

Championships won:
FF2000 – British FF2000 (FCS works car). Reynards also won: British Class B, European, European Class B, Canadian, Scottish, Irish, Knockhill, Swiss, Dutch, Northern Irish, SCCA South East, First Edition World Cup, BBC Grandstand.

FCS-Reynard Production 1988

Type	Description	Number Made	Running Total
88FF	FF1600	25	235
88S	Sports 2000	2	2

The Sports 2000 car was commissioned from Reynard by FCS, which still owns all rights to it, and Reynard built the first two.

Championships won:
FF1600 – Ford of Ireland, Irish Formula Ford Festival, Mallory Park, Swedish, French.

FF2000 – British.

FCS-Reynard Production 1989

Type	Description	Number Made	Running Total
89FF	FF1600	29	264
89SF	FF2000	3	317
89REN	Formula Renault	5	5
89S	Sports 2000	2	4

The Formula Renault was an adaptation of the Formula Ford design. One finished second in the 1989 British Championship.

Championships won:
FF1600 – RAC British, Ford of Ireland, Budweiser Northern Irish, Finnish, Swedish, German.

FF2000 – British, Irish, Northern Irish, Danish, Road Atlanta Run-offs.

FCS-Reynard Production 1990

Type	Description	Number Made	Running Total
90FF	FF1600	25	289
90SF	FF2000	12	329
90FREN	Formula Renault	6	11
90S	Sports 2000	2	2

The comparatively small sales of the Sports 2000 car are explained by the decline of the category in Europe. The North American market was effectively closed since Reynard's agent, Carl Haas, also imported the Lola

S2000 car, and since he also imported Lola Indycars, when it came to a potential conflict of interest he naturally chose Lola. Despite there being so few cars, the only Reynard sports car (so far) did well, and one finished second in the 1989 British Championship.

FF2000 was also in steady decline and faded away at the end of the year.

Championships won:
FF1600 – Motorcraft (Britain), Swedish Junior, Danish, Scandinavian, Southern Irish, Southern Irish Junior, Oulton Park, Finnish, Scottish, French, SCCA Finals, Irish Formula Ford Festival, South West (Britain).

FF2000 – Canadian Pro-series.

FCS-Reynard Production 1991

Type	Description	Number Made	Running Total
91FF	FF1600	11	300
91FREN	Formula Renault	3	14

Production of Reynard cars ceased at the end of 1991, although subsequently some cars were assembled from existing spares and others were up-dated to the latest spec.

Championships won:
FF1600 – Motorcraft Dunlop Autosport (Britain), Northern Irish, Southern Irish, Scottish, South West (Britain), Oulton Park, Cadwell Park, Scandinavian, South African, New South Wales.

FCS-Reynard Production 1992

Type	Description	Number Made	Running Total
91FF	FF1600	3	303

These cars were assembled from existing spares, and a further 10 older cars were up-dated to the latest spec.

To the total of 303 FF1600 cars must be added an unknown number of 'Hungaro-Reynards' built in Hungary after Reynard sold the entire 85FF project there.

In all, FCS built (or had built for it by Reynard) a total of 138 cars plus 10 up-date kits.

Championships won:
FF1600 – Finnish, Scandinavian, South West (Britain), Oulton Park, Scottish Junior.

In addition, a Reynard 91FF won the Kent-engine (FF1600) section of the Formula Ford Festival.

Fulmar Competition Services is an agent for Vauxhall/Opel-Lotus cars (a Reynard design), supplies spares for cars it produced and deals in used Reynards.

Fulmar Competition Services is at Unit 9, Roman Way Industrial Estate, Godmanchester, Huntingdon, Cambs PE16 8LN. Phone/Fax: 01480-433280. Contact: Alan Cornock.

Appendix Three

The Reynard Group's Outside Projects

In 1983/84 Reynard supplied 40 84FF chassis kits to Ford for the launch of FF1600 in France. They were assembled by Rondeau, who fitted a new body, and raced as Rondeau 845s. Rondeau developed the concept for the next two years, and produced a stiffer chassis for 1985. Development continued until the firm folded following the death of its founder, Jean Rondeau.

In 1984 Reynard designed and built a space-frame chassis to accept Jaguar running gear for the kit-car maker, RAM. Most cars had 'Cobra' bodies, but some had 'Jaguar D-type' bodies. Reynard made the early chassis, then contracted out the work. RAM replicas were still being made in 1996.

The entire 85FF (Formula Ford 1600) project was sold to Hungary to form the basis for a one-make championship. Reynard provided some cars and spares, but other cars were built locally – the exact number is not known. They were raced as 'Hungaro-Reynards'.

For 1988 Reynard designed a single-seater for General Motors which was used for Formula Vauxhall-Lotus in Britain and Formula Opel-Lotus on the Continent – at the time, General Motors owned Lotus while its independent offshoot, Team Lotus, carried the name in Formula One.

Between 1988 and 1991 204 cars were made, and then production was taken over by Schubel Engineering in Germany.

Formula Mirage in Japan, a one-make formula using Mitsubishi engines, uses Reynard chassis which are a development of the Vauxhall/Opel-Lotus concept. Thirty cars were made for this formula in 1990, and a further 16 cars made to the 'World Car' concept were supplied to Mexico in the same year for Formula Reynard.

In 1992/93 Reynard Composites built five carbon-fibre monocoques for a road-going version of the Porsche 962 Group C car for Vern Schuppen's company.

Other work has included the design and construction of the Pacific PR01 Formula One car, a Formula One car for DAMS which did not get beyond initial testing, the Chrysler Patriot hybrid-engined sports racer, the body for a Mazda test vehicle, and 30 carbon-fibre bodies for competition versions of the Dodge Viper.

Reynard has also undertaken some consultancy work for road car manufacturers, mainly on suspension systems, much of which is covered by confidentiality agreements.

On an informal basis, Adrian Reynard helped Jackie Stewart sort out a problem he could perceive in the steering behaviour of the Ford Mondeo.

Reynard was responsible for the mechanical design on the Ford Indigo concept car.

In 1995 Reynard joined with Chrysler to prepare the Stratus road car for Touring Car racing, initially in North America.

At the beginning of 1996 a new division, Reynard Special Vehicle Projects, was established to undertake outside work which did not bear the Reynard name. Among its first work was an evaluation vehicle for a major manufacturer, the development of the Panoz Esperante and the design of Ford Mondeos for Touring Car racing.

Index